Competition Policy and Regional Integration in Developing Countries

UMOA	Union Monétaire Ouest Africaine (Monetary Union of West Africa)
UNCTAD	United Nations Conference on Trade and Development
WAEMU	West African Economic and Monetary Union
WIPO	World Intellectual Property Organization
WTO	World Trade Organization

OMVG	Organisation pour la mise en valeur du Fleuve Gambie
OMVS	Organisation pour la mise en valeur du Fleuve Sénégal
PTA	Preferential Trade Areas
RBP	restrictive business practices
RBTT	Royal Bank of Trinidad and Tobago
RCA	Regional Competition Agreement
RIDE	Revue Internationale de Droit Economique
RJCA	Regional Joint Competition Law Authority
RTA	Regional Trade Agreements
RTC	Revised Treaty of Chaguaramas
SACU	Southern African Customs Union
SADC	Southern African Development Community
SADCC	Southern African Development Coordination Conference
SEACF	Southern and Eastern Africa Competition Forum
SME	small and medium-sized firms
TC	Tariff Commission
TFEU	Treaty on the Functioning of the European Union
TNC	Transnational Corporations
Treaty of Rome	Treaty establishing the European Economic Community
TRIPS	Agreement on Trade-Related Aspects of Intellectual Property Rights
U.S.C.	United States Code
UEMOA	Union Economique et Monétaire Ouest Africaine

Competition Policy and Regional Integration in Developing Countries

Edited by

Josef Drexl

Director, Max Planck Institute for Intellectual Property and Competition Law, Munich, Germany

Mor Bakhoum

Senior Research Fellow, Max Planck Institute for Intellectual Property and Competition Law, Munich, Germany

Eleanor M. Fox

Walter J. Derenberg Professor of Trade Regulation, New York University School of Law, USA

Michal S. Gal

Professor of Law, University of Haifa School of Law, Israel

David J. Gerber

Distinguished Professor of Law, Chicago-Kent College of Law, Illinois Institute of Technology, USA

Edward Elgar

Cheltenham, UK • Northampton, MA, USA

Published by
Edward Elgar Publishing Limited
The Lypiatts
15 Lansdown Road
Cheltenham
Glos GL50 2JA
UK

Edward Elgar Publishing, Inc.
William Pratt House
9 Dewey Court
Northampton
Massachusetts 01060
USA

A catalogue record for this book
is available from the British Library

Library of Congress Control Number: 2012935326

MIX
Paper from responsible sources
FSC® C018575

ISBN 978 1 78100 430 2

Typeset by Columns Design XML Ltd, Reading
Printed and bound by MPG Books Group, UK

Contents

Contributors

Anthony Amunategui Abad, JD (Ateneo), MPA (Harvard), CEO and Managing Director of TA Trade Advisory Group and Professor of International Economic Law, Center for International Economic Law, Ateneo Law School, Philippines

Mor Bakhoum, PhD (Lausanne), LLM (Lausanne/Chicago-Kent), Senior Research Fellow, Max Planck Institute for Intellectual Property and Competition Law, Munich, Germany

Delroy S. Beckford, PhD (Rutgers University), LLM (Columbia University), Senior Legal Counsel, Fair Trading Commission, Jamaica; Lecturer on International Trade Law, Faculty of Law, University of the West Indies, Mona, Jamaica

Javier Cortázar, Colombian lawyer practicing in competition law and a lecturer in various Colombian Universities

Josef Drexl, Dr. iur. (Munich), LLM (UC Berkeley), Director of the Max Planck Institute for Intellectual Property and Competition Law, Munich; Honorary Professor of Law at the University of Munich, Germany

Eleanor M. Fox, Walter J. Derenberg Professor of Trade Regulation, New York University School of Law, USA

Michal S. Gal, Professor of Law and Director of the Forum for Law and Markets, University of Haifa School of Law, Israel

David J. Gerber, Distinguished Professor of Law, Chicago-Kent College of Law, Chicago, USA

George K. Lipimile, Director and Chief Executive Officer of the Common Market for Eastern and Southern Africa (COMESA) Competition Commission

Gladmore Mamhare, Programme Officer in Competition Policy, SADC Secretariat

Julia Molestina, PhD candidate at the Max Planck Institute for Intellectual Property and Competition Law, Munich, Germany

Kasturi Moodaliyar, Senior Lecturer in Competition Law, University of Witwatersrand, South Africa

Mbissane Ngom, Professor of Law, University Gaston Berger of Saint-Louis, Senegal

Taimoon Stewart, Associate Senior Fellow, Sir Arthur Lewis Institute of Social and Economic Studies, The University of the West Indies; Senior Advisor at the University of the West Indies Business Development Office; consultant in the areas of international trade, competition law and policy

Lawan Thanadsillapakul, PhD (Lancaster University); Professor of Law at Kyushu University, Japan, and Sukhothai Thammathirat Open University, School of Law, Thailand

Inbal Faibish Wassmer, LLM, EMLE, Lawyer, Rosenberg, Keren-Polak & Co., Advocates

Abbreviations

AEC	ASEAN Economic Community
AEGC	ASEAN Experts Group on Competition
AFAS	ASEAN Framework Agreement for Liberalisation on Trade in Services
AFTA	ASEAN Free Trade Area
AIA	ASEAN Investment Area
AICO	ASEAN Industrial Co-operation Scheme
AMSs	ASEAN member states
APEC	Asia-Pacific Economic Cooperation
ARTP	Agence de Régulation des Télécommunications et des Postes (Sénégal)
ASEAN	Association of Southeast Asian Nations
BCEAO	Banque Centrale des Etats de l'Afrique de l'Ouest
BCI	Blue Circle Industries
BOP	balance of payment
CAC	Competition Appeal Court (South Africa)
CAFTA	Central American Free Trade Agreement
CAIPIR	Centro Andino para la Implementación de Políticas de Integración Regional (Andean Centre for the Implementation of Policies of Regional Integration)
CARICOM	Caribbean Community (and Common Market)
CARIFORUM	Caribbean Forum
CARIFTA	Caribbean Free Trade Area
CCC	CARICOM Competition Commission

CCC	Consultative Committee on Competition (UEMOA)
CCJ	Caribbean Court of Justice
CCS	Competition Commission of Singapore
CDC	Commonwealth Development Corporation
CEDEAO	Communauté Economique des Etats de l'Afrique de l'Ouest
CEMAC	Communauté Economique et Monétaire de l'Afrique Centrale
CEPMLP	Centre for Energy, Petroleum and Mineral Law and Policy
CER Agreement	Australian New Zealand Closer Economic Relations Agreement
CFA franc	Franc de la Communauté Financière de l'Afrique
CHG	Conference of Heads of Government
CILSS	Comité permanent Inter-Etats de lutte contre la Sécheresse dans le Sahel
CIMA	Conférence Interafricaine des Marches d'Assurance
CIPRES	Conférence Interafricaine de la Prévoyance Sociale
CIRAC	Centre d'Information et de Recherche sur l'Allemagne contemporaine
COMESA	Common Market for Eastern and Southern Africa
CONATEL	Comisión Nacional de las Telecomunicaciones
COTED	Council for Trade and Economic Development
CRS	computerized reservation system
CSM	CARICOM Single Market
CSME	CARICOM Single Market and Economy
CU	customs union
DCI	Direction du Commerce Intérieur

DG	Directorate General
Div Ct.	Divisional Court
DTI	Department of Trade and Industry
EA	Europe Agreement
EAC	East African Community
EC	European Community
ECJ	European Court of Justice
ECOWAS	Economic Community of West African States
ECR	European Court Reports
ECT	EC Treaty
EEC	European Economic Community
EPA	Economic Partnership Agreements
EU	European Union
EU-CARIFORUM EPA	Economic Partnership Agreement with the CARIFORUM States
FCA	Fair Competition Act
FDI	Foreign Direct Investments
FTA	Free Trade Area
FTC	Fair Trading Commission
GATS	General Agreement on Trade in Services
GATT	General Agreement on Tariffs and Trade
GDP	Gross Domestic Product
GNI	Gross National Income
GNP	Gross National Product
IADB	Inter-American Development Bank
ICN	International Competition Network
IDC	Industrial Development Corporation

IMF	International Monetary Fund
INCSOC	International Network of Civil Society Organizations on Competition
INDECOPI	National Institute for the Defense of Competition and Protection of Intellectual Property
INEADEC	Institut Euro-Africain de Droit Economique
INTERCAN I project	Proyecto INTERCAN I de apoyo a la integración económica de la Comunidad Andina
IP	Intellectual Property
ISI	Import Substitution Industrialization
IT	Information Technology
KPPU	Commission for the Supervision of Business Competition
LDC	less developed country
MCR	Merger Control Regulation
MDC	more developed state
MERCOSUR	Mercado Común del Sur (Common Southern Market)
MMDS	Multichannel Multipoint Distribution Service
NAFTA	North American Free Trade Agreement
NGO	non-governmental organization
OAPI	Organisation Africaine de la Propriété Intellectuelle
OECD	Organisation for Economic Co-operation and Development
OECS	Organization of Eastern Caribbean States
OHADA	Organisation pour l'Harmonisation en Afrique du Droit des Affaires (Organization for the Harmonization of Business Law in Africa)

Introduction

Mor Bakhoum

The last decade has witnessed an increasing number of developing countries enacting competition laws and policies either on the national or on the regional level in the framework of regional trade agreements (RTAs). This development seems to stem from a mainstream view that regionalizing competition policies is a pertinent policy for developing countries. Regional competition policies, it is thought, would help developing countries not only overcome their lack of efficient institutional settings and enforcement challenges, but also ensure better control over free competition in their newly created common free trade areas.

As a consequence, competition-related provisions in RTAs are becoming 'commonplace'. This trend has even been referred to by Michal Gal as the 'new wave of regionalism'.[1] Not surprisingly, competition-related provisions in RTAs have attracted a lot of attention in the international arena recently and developing countries are keen to enact regional competition policies given the promise of such an approach. Although a broad consensus seems to exist on the benefits of regionalizing competition policies for development, *the issue of the design of a regional competition law and policy adapted to the economic, political and cultural situation of developing countries remains an unsettled question.*

The literature[2] exploring this new trend in developing countries is very optimistic on the potential benefits of regional integration and regional competition policies in achieving their development objectives. The current scholarship has the merits of providing valuable insights on the experiences in different regional integration systems. However, studies are rare that

---

1 See, Gal, M. (2011), 'International Antitrust Solutions: Discrete Steps or Causally Linked?' in J. Drexl, W.S. Grimes, C.A. Jones, R.J.R. Peritz and E.T. Swaine (eds), *More Common Ground For International Competition Law?* Cheltenham, UK and Northampton, MA, USA: Edward Elgar, p. 239.

2 See Gal, M. (2010), 'Regional Competition Law Agreements: An Important Step for Antitrust Enforcement', **60**, *U. Toronto L.J.*, 239 et seq.

address the interface between *regional integration* and *competition policy* while taking into account the specific issues faced by the developing jurisdictions. The often-heard argument is that a regional competition law is a must in the process of creating a regional market. However, the issues are more complex.

This book considers a new approach in dealing with regional competition policies. Rather than merely analysing and discussing the regional competition experience *stricto sensu*, as is commonly done in the literature, it addresses fundamental questions relating to *regional competition policy integration*; its incentives, goals, driving forces and its potential to help developing countries achieve their development goals. It is only when the issue of regional integration is analysed that the role of competition law and policy in the process can meaningfully be discussed.

Why do developing countries enter into RTAs in the first place? How does competition law help to achieve the goals set up in a regional integration group? If adopting a regional competition policy makes sense in an economic integration endeavour, what kind of competition policy would be suitable? From an 'integrationist' perspective, and against the backdrop of the experience in the European Union, it is often assumed that RTAs would help developing countries promote trade with neighbouring countries and that a regional competition policy would be needed to fight cross-border anti-competitive practices that arise from the setting up of a regional market. This general assumption is, as highlighted in this book, at least less convincing, sometimes even questionable in the context of developing countries.

Designing and implementing a regional competition law should not be done in the abstract. It has to fit the local context. Hence the historical context, the political situation, the economic features of the member states, the size of the member states, the degree of intensity of trade within a common market, the legal traditions (civil law or common law), the language differences, and the institutional settings of the member states, should all be fully taken account of when crafting and implementing competition rules within RTAs.

What kind of competition-related issues do developing countries face in the framework of RTAs? Should a regional competition policy be more centralized or decentralized? What effects does the intensity of intra-community trade have on the policy choice between centralization and decentralization? Does the fact that countries share the same language or belong to the same currency zone have an effect on intra-community trade? Should national competition authorities be given decision-making power in the enforcement of the community law? Should the member states' different experiences be taken into account in the delimitation of competences between the regional level and the national level? Is a regional competition law even desirable in certain regional economic organizations? How should the relative smallness of the participating states influence the design of regional competition law? Does the trend of regionalizing competition policies in developing countries make the adoption of an international competition policy more likely or less likely?

These questions will most likely have to be answered differently according to the specificities of each regional organization. Of course, issues such as enforcement, lack of efficient institutional settings, and lack of resources, pose similar challenges in the developing countries. However, they should not lead to a generalization of the approach to regional competition laws in the developing world.

At a more fundamental level, in its concluding part, the book discusses the issues of the integration process itself and the role of competition law in this endeavour. The kinds of competition law countries need from a development and from a political perspective are also discussed.

The overall approach of the book has two components: reporting and discussing the regional integration experiences in different developing jurisdictions on the one hand, and taking a more transversal approach, drawing conclusions and lessons and providing guidance on how to approach regional integration of competition policies in the context of developing countries, on the other hand. This is done in the different contributions dealing with regional competition law experiences in ASEAN, WAEMU, COMESA, CARICOM, the Andean Community and the SADC. The conclusions in the last part of the book are devoted to the common and shared features of the different regional integration groups.

This book brings together 14 contributions by leading competition experts, scholars and practitioners from Europe, Africa, Latin America, Asia and the United States. It is the fruit of a workshop held at Frauenchiemsee in Bavaria in the summer of 2010. This workshop and the present book are part of a larger project on 'Competition Law in Developing Countries' initiated by Josef Drexl, Michal Gal, Eleanor Fox and David Gerber.

The book is divided into four parts, each dealing with a specific aspect relevant to the process of creating regional integration groups and enacting regional competition laws.

In Part I, 'Promises and Challenges in Implementing Regional Competition Policy Regimes', the obstacles some regional integration groups face in the process of creating a regional competition policy framework are discussed. In her opening contribution, Lawan Thanadsillapakul argues for a regional competition regime in the context of ASEAN as a tool to complement and enhance the economic integration process in the region. Hence, according to her, as ASEAN is in the process of developing its integrated regional market, a regional competition law would facilitate intra-ASEAN trade and investment, by protecting, at the regional level, against anti-competitive practices. A regional competition regime, which does not exist yet, would complement and reinforce the ASEAN investment regime and regulations. But which approach is most suitable in designing a regional competition law for ASEAN? Building on the discussions at international level pertaining to an international competition framework and taking into account the specific challenges facing the ASEAN countries and what she terms the ASEAN 'open regionalism', and more specifically the ASEAN way, Thanadsillapakul proposes at the initial stage a synchronized model combining harmonized laws in member states and enforcement networks. With this approach, the regional law would set some standards that would take particular features and shapes in the specific national competition laws. At the regional level, she argues, a regional competition committee may be needed to oversee and enforce competition law in cross-border cases.

In his contribution, Anthony Abad points out the considerable diversity amongst the ASEAN member countries in terms of their respective economic and policy heritage, political governance systems, legal and economic institutions and policy frameworks. He describes the state of play in competition law in ASEAN member states. His analysis demonstrates that marked differences also exist in their level of implementation and enforcement of their national competition laws. He argues at the outset that those differences should be taken into account when designing and implementing national competition regimes. This approach, consisting of relying on national competition enforcement, is in line with the ASEAN Economic Community Blueprint whereby ASEAN member states are committed to introducing national competition policies and laws by 2015.

Regarding the South African Development Community (SADC), Gladmore Mamhare and Kasturi Moodaliyar discuss issues resulting from the differing levels of development and different competition law regimes in their respective chapters. Furthermore, they discuss the consequent issues that are raised at the regional level. Gladmore Mamhare provides us with an account of the different national experiences in SADC member states and the current status of the discussion on a regional competition law. So far, only a Declaration on Regional Cooperation in Competition Law and Consumer Policy regulates the regional framework. There is no regional competition law as such. This creates issues at the regional level regarding the fact that South Africa, which has a well-functioning national competition law, is able to protect its own market, whereas other SADC members confronted with outbound restrictions of competition initiated by powerful South African firms are not. Hence, the issue of abuse of dominant position and anti-competitive practices by dominant South African firms in countries that do not have an effective competition law and policy, or whose competition laws are not advanced enough to address those issues, is a serious concern in the region. As the leading competition authority in the region, the integration of South Africa in a regional competition policy would help offset those regional competition concerns. Kasturi Moodaliyar is aware of the issue. However, in a very realistic assessment, she supports a step-by-step approach in building a regional competition law. She argues that SADC member states should first strive to develop their own national competition regimes. This bottom-up approach could constitute a stepping stone in the process of creating a sound regional competition regime. At this stage, she argues, it is doubtful that advanced competition jurisdictions such as South Africa and Zambia would be willing to surrender their jurisdiction in favour of a regional agency. Fostering national competition regimes, according to her, should be the first step towards harmonization at the regional level.

Part II of the book deals with 'Institutional Coherence, Regional Integration and Competition Policy' and discusses the respective experiences of the West African Economic and Monetary Union (WAEMU), the Economic Community of West African States (ECOWAS) and the Andean Community. Mor Bakhoum and Julia Molestina in their contribution highlight the enforcement issues resulting from the centralized approach of WAEMU competition policy. Against the backdrop of eight years of enforcement experience and the practical limits of the centralized decision-making power in WAEMU, they call for a reform of the regional institutional design. Relying on the analysis of what they term 'competition constraints', they provide guidelines for the redefinition of the competences between the Commission and the national competition authorities. This contribution and its conclusions are very timely, since the WAEMU Commission has recently mandated a study on the revision of the institutional framework for the enforcement of the regional competition law.[3] The conclusions of the

[3] This study, conducted by the Max Planck Institute, has three components: (1) assessment of the regional institutional enforcement framework; (2) assessment of the national institutional framework; and (3) reform proposals on how best to design the enforcement orientation with a focus on the distribution of competences between the national level and the regional level. The study puts forward important

report, which are in line with Bakhoum's and Molestina's proposal, were discussed and approved by the WAEMU Consultative Committee on Competition (CCC) in its seventh session held in Dakar in November 2011. WAEMU is heading towards recognizing more decision-making power in its national competition authorities.

ECOWAS is in an advanced stage of creating a regional competition law. The regulations are adopted and a regional competition authority is in the process of being created. The new regional competition law would likely create enforcement and coordination issues with the already existing WAEMU competition law, because WAEMU is a sub-region within ECOWAS. Therefore, theoretically, ECOWAS' regional law is also directly applicable to all WAEMU member states. This issue, which so far has not been resolved, is a major highlight of Mbissane Ngom's contribution. The author discusses ways of breaking the deadlock. However the issue is still pending and no solution has yet been identified as to the mechanisms of collaboration between the ECOWAS regional authority and the WAEMU Commission.

The regional competition framework in the Andean Community is regulated by Decision 608 of 2005. One of the innovative features of Decision 608 is the way it aims at correcting the lack of competition laws in some of its member states. Namely, Decision 608 empowered Bolivia and Ecuador to directly apply the provisions of Decision 608 in their domestic setting. This mechanism has been referred to as the 'downloading' option. This transitory device is discussed by Javier Cortázar in his contribution. As now Ecuador and Bolivia have enacted domestic competition laws, the 'downloading' option is no longer applicable. However, this innovative approach seems to constitute a convincing mechanism to introduce a competition culture in countries that do not have national competition laws. In its current reform project of its institutional design, WAEMU is considering applying the same mechanism by allowing member states that so far do not have

---

reform proposals for the regional institutional framework. Three main recommendations need to be highlighted here: (1) to foster the enforcement tools of the regional competition authority; (2) to decentralize the decision-making power by recognizing national competition authorities' competence to apply the community competition law to national cases; and (3) to establish collaboration channels between the regional authority and the national competition authorities. The findings of the study were presented before the WAEMU regional Consultative Committee on Competition (CCC) in its 7th session held in Dakar in November 2011. The study will be published after the validation of the findings by the WAEMU Commission.

national competition laws to directly apply the community competition law in domestic cases. This would be the case with Guinea-Bissau.

In Part III of the book, 'Economic Structure, Regional Integration and Competition Law Enforcement', the competition-related issues in regional integration groups with specific economic structures are discussed. In a very informative chapter that interfaces economic structure with the historical, political, legal and social dimension, Taimoon Stewart discusses the case of the Caribbean Community (CARICOM). The importance of a regional competition law in the context of CARICOM cannot be overstated, according to her. She makes it clear: 'Integration is not an option for these territories; it is a necessity for survival in the world economy.' As pointed out, the small size of the economies and the need of firms to achieve economies of scale to be viable have led to the emergence of oligopolies, and the concentration of capital has already largely been inherited from colonial times. Furthermore, most consumer goods are imported to CARICOM which predominantly consists of small island states. Regional competition law is therefore crucial in order to discipline large capital holders and prevent them from engaging in cross-border anti-competitive practices. This is especially true for regional trade and investment, which is dominated by a few firms, mainly from Trinidad and Tobago. Stewart concludes that 'introducing and enforcing competition law is vital to preserving market access and to preventing abuse of dominance and high concentration in markets'.

From an institutional perspective, Delroy Beckford addresses the issue of the governance arrangements within CARICOM and the enforcement of the regional competition law. The institutional arrangements give competence to the regional authority to deal with conduct having cross-border effects, while national competition practices are dealt with by national competition authorities. When dealing with cross-border practices, the Community Commission can request that national competition agencies conduct a preliminary examination of the conduct. In jurisdictions such as Jamaica this would require amending the national law. In other member states, the regional authority does not have national competition authorities to rely on. So far, the only two fully functioning competition authorities in the region are to be found in Jamaica and Barbados. Delroy Beckford points out those issues that pose specific challenges to effective enforcement of competition policy in CARICOM.

The Common Market for Eastern and Southern Africa (COMESA) is the largest economic integration group in Africa. It comprises countries with different political backgrounds and levels of economic development. Advocating a sound regional competition regime, George Lipimile stresses the role of the COMESA Competition Regulations as a means to establish the foundation stones of the economic integration process. This is most urgent in a context where the dismantling of public monopolies has led to a concentration of economic power in the hands of a few regional and national business operators. Various cross-border cases affecting two or more member states exemplify the need to have an effective regional competition policy. The Coca-Cola Company/Cadbury-Schweppes merger, the global Rothmans of Pall Mall/British American Tobacco merger and the takeover by Pretoria Portland Cement of South Africa and Lafarge of France of various cement companies in the region, although they affect the structure of the regional market, have been reviewed separately by different national competition authorities. As Lipimile rightly points out, 'a regional competition law with merger-control provisions would … ensure that the beneficial effects of merger-control provisions will accrue to all COMESA countries'.

Concluding, Part IV of the book is devoted to 'The Development Dimension of Regional Integration and Competition Policy'. It builds on the different experiences of regional integration and competition policies discussed throughout the book and makes a transversal analysis of the issues and challenges that developing countries face in their integration process. In an analytical approach, this part draws conclusions and provides insights and recommendations on the factors to take into account when creating a regional economic area and crafting a regional competition law. Detangling the issue of 'economic integration' and the role of a regional competition law in the process, Josef Drexl discusses the very objective of economic integration in developing countries. From the outset, he questions the role of economic integration in the framework of developing countries. This question is very often overlooked in the current literature. Whereas in the case of the EU, economic integration was justified by political and economic considerations, in the case of developing countries, he argues, 'the role of economic integration may well have to be redefined in times of globalization'. In this vein, he observes that 'the role of regional integration in *integrating developing countries in the world economy*, and the benefits accruing from it, are much more important than what can be gained from integration of the individual economies'. In line with the proposed redefinition, he concludes that the goals of regional competition law should also be defined in the light of 'international economic integration'. In addition to this new approach of regional competition policies, Josef Drexl points out the benefits of fostering competition culture in the participating member states and empowering individuals to participate in the economy. The latter he refers to as 'social integration'. Practical guidelines on how to organize the allocation of competences when designing the institutional approach are also discussed in his contribution.

Every regional integration endeavour is initiated, shaped and driven by political considerations. The political dimension has played and is still playing a crucial role in the integration process in the EU. After acknowledging the central role of the political dimension in the regionalization process, David Gerber puts forward some conceptual tools in order to discuss it meaningfully. Exploring the political dimension of regionalization, development and competition law, the author discusses the different incentives and decisional influences that come into play in the process of locating a competition law and policy at the regional level. In the political dimension, he considers regionalization as a process in which 'decisions' are taken every step of the way. Influences on the decisions have three dimensions: national, regional or 'supranational'. Gerber applies those analytical tools to two important aspects of the process of regionalizing competition policies: one relates to the decision to regionalize competition law in the first place; the other relates to the actual implementation of competition on a regional level. Applying the national, regional and supranational influences respectively to the process of locating a competition law at a regional level and to effectively implementing it, David Gerber draws several conclusions. On the one hand 'decisional influences relating to political authority tend to support formal regionalization'; however, 'political factors provide far less support for implementation of competition law at the regional level'. Put in other terms, the political decision to formally create a regional framework is not supported at the implementation stage. As a consequence, Gerber stresses the importance of having a long-term perspective when it comes to enforcement.

In her contribution, Eleanor Fox discusses the development dimension of competition law and policy. After stressing the specific challenges developing countries face and their development objectives, she questions the suitability of the developed countries' competition-law models for developing countries. She argues that 'developing countries must develop their own brand of competition law, resisting pressures to copy "international standards" without regard to fit'. Developing countries' need for sustained and inclusive growth and development commands a different kind of competition law, she argues. This new approach runs counter to the trend of forcing 'international standards' into developing countries' legal landscapes, a temptation developing countries should resist. She stresses the urgency for developing countries to choose their own brand of competition law and to develop their own 'perspective or center of gravity' around which their substantive competition principles are framed. 'What is good for America is not necessarily good for (for example) sub-Saharan Africa', she contends. In this vein, she sketches different options that developing countries could choose from when developing their competition law. These guidelines are by no means complete models; they only constitute leads for developing countries to follow when crafting their competition policies. Returning to the regional dimension, she argues that regional antitrust for developing countries is a potential showcase for 'Spence antitrust', or antitrust fit for inclusive growth.

Concluding the book, Michal Gal and Inbal Faibish Wassmer, after addressing the potential benefits and the possible obstacles to the successful realization of regional competition agreements, discuss in length the preconditions for the adoption of an RCA. Those preconditions are inter alia related to the Pareto-optimality for each member state, the equal distribution of benefits, the pre-existence of a competition culture, and sufficient resources. Most importantly, the authors submit ten recommendations in order to unleash the potential of regional agreements of developing jurisdictions. Those recommendations relate to: the clarity of the objectives, acknowledging and resolving the difficulties of collective action, the issue of membership in the RCA, the mode of cooperation among agencies, the case-selection aspect, sequencing, monitoring and enforcing compliance, the conflict-resolution mechanisms, the institutional-design issues, and the mechanisms to change the rules.

This publication is a result of teamwork. The editors are grateful to many people whose support and collaboration were crucial to the birth of this book. In addition to agreeing to attend the workshop in Frauenchiemsee in the summer of 2010 the authors have demonstrated close cooperation during the editing process. The editors express their heartfelt thanks to all of them. Olivia Raitt and Delia Zirilli were instrumental in the organization of the workshop. Julia Molestina not only worked closely with the editors from the very beginning of the editing process but also translated into English the contribution on ECOWAS. Anna Mattes was also helpful in the process of editing the contributions. Allison Felmy, the English editor of the Max Planck Institute, had the challenging task of reviewing all the contributions.

The editors also thank the Max Planck Society and the German-Israeli Foundation for financially supporting this publication and the project on 'Competition Law in Developing Countries' of which this publication is an integral part.

On behalf of the editors, Mor Bakhoum
Munich, November 2011

PART I

Promises and challenges in implementing regional competition policy regimes

1. The harmonization of ASEAN: competition laws and policy from an economic integration perspective

Lawan Thanadsillapakul

1. INTRODUCTION

The Association of Southeast Asian Nations (ASEAN)[1] is an economic group comprised of the countries of Southeast Asia.[2] The Asia Pacific

[1] The Association of Southeast Asian Nations, or ASEAN, was established in Bangkok on 8 August 1967 by the five original member countries: Indonesia, Malaysia, Philippines, Singapore and Thailand. Brunei Darussalam joined on 8 January 1984, Vietnam on 28 July 1995, Laos and Myanmar on 23 July 1997 and Cambodia on 30 April 1999. The ASEAN region has a population of about 500 million, a total area of 4.5 million square kilometres, a combined gross domestic product of US$ 737 billion and a total trade volume of US$ 720 billion. Recently, ASEAN launched several new economic co-operation schemes: the ASEAN Free Trade Area (AFTA), the ASEAN Framework Agreement for Liberalisation on Trade in Services (AFAS), the ASEAN Investment Area (AIA) and the ASEAN Industrial Co-operation Scheme (AICO) for implementing open regionalism aimed at enhancing economic integration and creating an open regional economic group. See Thanadsillapakul, L. (2000), 'Open Regionalism and Deeper Integration: the Implementation of AFTA, AIA, and AFAS', available at: http://www.dundee.ac.uk/cepmlp/journal/html/vol6/vol6–16.html (the CEPMLP Internet Journal).

[2] The new approach to ASEAN economic integration based on 'open regionalism', which balances intra and extra-regional liberalization of trade and investment and is aimed at creating a natural, *de facto*, integrated regional market, was launched by ASEAN in its new integration schemes: AIA, AFAS and (new) AFTA. This model (new paradigm) is legally based on the 'negative regional economic integration theory', unlike the conservative pattern of the European Union, which need not necessarily be followed by other regions; in fact, the EU is a model implemented by the European countries to accommodate the different strands of historical, political, social and economic backgrounds in the region. ASEAN is fundamentally different from the EU as it has its own development. See Pinder, J.

region has been the most dynamic and fastest growing region in the world,[3] but the 1997 Asian crisis sent the 'Asian Tigers' into turmoil. The rise and fall of Asia clearly reflects both the interdependence of the East Asian countries and the world economy, on the one hand, and the impact of the changing global legal and economic environment on these countries, on the other hand.

The ASEAN countries have gone through a volatile period, and in response have embarked on a process of deeper integration to strengthen their regional economic self-reliance while committing themselves to an open-market orientation. A new direction for ASEAN, dubbed 'open regionalism', will balance regional integration and global liberalization. The ASEAN countries need to develop their sustainable regional market to replace the current separate national ASEAN markets, and to do so they need to regionalize ASEAN laws and regulations, especially those relating to trade and investment, in order to facilitate the free flow of goods, capital, services and labour. A more liberalized trade and investment regime in ASEAN will enhance its members' free economies and create a more favourable trade and investment climate in the region.

Consequently, the ASEAN countries need to develop effective legal systems to encourage and oversee the increasingly competitive business activities in the region. The need to eliminate barriers to trade and investment in turn generates a need to provide, at regional level, effective

---

(1972), 'Positive Integration and Negative Integration: Some Problems of Economic Union in the EEC', in Hodges, M. (ed.), *European Integration*, Middlesex, UK: Penguin Books. See also Garnaut, R. (1996), *Open Regionalism and Trade Liberalisation: An Asia Pacific Contribution to the World Trade System*, Institute of Southeast Asian Studies (Singapore) and Allen and Unwin (Sydney). See also Eliassen, K.A. and C.B. Monsen (1997), 'Institutions and Networks: A Comparison of European and South East Asian Integration', paper presented in Panel F1.3 Regional Institutions and Globalisation at the Conference on 'Non-State Actors and Authority in the Global System', University of Warwick, 31 October–1 November, and Garnaut, R.P. and J.K. Drysdale (eds) (1994), *Asia Pacific Regionalism: Readings in International Economic Relations*, Australia: Harper Educational Publishers.

[3] See World Bank (1993), 'The East Asian Miracle: Economic Growth and Public Policy', *A World Bank Policy Research Report*, New York: World Bank; see also Petri, P.A. (1993), 'The Lessons of East Asia: Common Foundations of East Asian Success', The World Bank (Washington, DC); and UNCTAD (1992), *Transnational Corporations as Engines of Growth*, New York and Geneva: United Nations.

protection against restrictive business practices,[4] to govern the economic activities and transactions of the transnational corporations (TNCs) located in the ASEAN region. As more liberal trade and investment regimes are established in the ASEAN countries, competition rules will be called for to regulate competition among business players and to supervise their conduct.[5] Korah has stated that there would be very little point in removing the various internal barriers and national boundaries imposed by governments if these governmental restraints were replaced by concentrations, other restrictive business practices and concerted practices among private firms.[6] Since the rationale for a regional competition law is to strengthen economic integration in the ASEAN region, it is important that any agreements restricting competition as well as abuse of dominant market positions be controlled[7] by effective competition laws. Control of restrictive business practices in the process of liberalization is a key element in the new approach to positive integration.[8] This approach is different from neo-liberalism, which tends to assert that the free market needs no control, regulation or restriction, either by government or public bodies.

This article analyses the rationale, scope and basis for a comprehensive competition law in ASEAN to enhance the implementation of economic integration in the region. This includes a discussion of the complementarity between competition law and policy, liberalization of trade and investment within and outside the ASEAN region and regional economic integration, as

---

4 As stated by UNCTAD, the main objective of competition laws is 'to preserve and promote competition as a means to ensure the efficient allocation of resources in an economy, resulting in the best possible choice of quality, the lowest prices and adequate supplies for consumers', UNCTAD (1996), 'Competition Policy and Legislation: Information Note 21', Note by the UNCTAD Secretariat to the Intergovernmental Group of Experts on Competition Law and Policy, UNCTAD Document TD/B/RBP/INF.37, mimeo.

5 The liberalization of FDI policies can lead to an increase in competition in national or regional markets. See UNCTAD (1997), 'World Investment Report 1997: Transnational Corporations, Market Structure and Competition Policy', UNCTAD/ITE/IIT/5, New York and Geneva: United Nations.

6 Korah, V. (1997), *An Introductory Guide to EC Competition Law and Practice*, Oxford: Hart Publishing (6th edn), 1.

7 To 'control' here means to 'check', 'verify' and 'vet' substantive rules of competition laws. It means to exercise restraint or direction on the free action of another, to command market participants to comply with the rules in order to keep the market open and to refrain from abuse of dominant market power.

8 Picciotto, S. (1998), 'Linkages in International Investment Regulations: The Antinomies of the Draft Multilateral Agreement on Investment', **19** (3) *University of Pennsylvania Journal of International Economic Law* 731, 735–8.

well as the interaction between industrial/investment policy and competition law and policy, especially the way in which competition law and policy reinforces the liberalized investment regime in the region. Also, this chapter attempts to provide various models of regional competition law and policy in ASEAN.

Following a brief introduction, Section 2 focuses on competition law and policy as a tool to reinforce the ASEAN investment regime and regulations. Since ASEAN is committed to developing its integrated regional market, it requires a regulatory regime that can facilitate the free movement of intra-ASEAN trade and investment. Competition law is compatible with open regionalism[9] because it is basically neutral and non-discriminatory. Moreover, the development of a regional competition law and policy that enhances fair competition among firms doing business in the region may also provide a basis for evaluating the economic benefit to ASEAN of entry by a foreign investor on competitive grounds rather than by means of the discriminatory criteria used in screening procedures. In this way, ASEAN regional competition laws and policies would play a multifunctional role, that is, they would encourage the free flow of trade and investment, monitor the conduct of firms, and evaluate the economic role or potential dominance of extra-ASEAN TNCs in the region. Unlike the assumptions of neo-liberalism,[10] competition law and policy accept the important role of states and good governance institutions in regulating firms' behaviour. This perspective is also more compatible with the new approach of positive integration ideology.[11] Moreover, competition law generally takes a pro-consumer policy perspective that takes into account the public good and social welfare, thereby ensuring that the advantages of liberalization within ASEAN resulting from economic integration contribute directly to the general public wealth through consumers. The harmonization/unification of ASEAN competition law, rather than shaping separate, and probably diverse, competition laws in each ASEAN country, would ensure that

---

[9] Thanadsillapakul, *supra* n. 1.

[10] Neo-liberalism regards regulation as an unnecessary burden; as Picciotto states, the perspective of neo-liberal ideologues toward economic integration is that 'international integration means the creation of open markets, which requires only strong provision for the protection of property rights, the maintenance of public order, and not much else'. See Picciotto, *supra* n. 8, at 738.

[11] Picciotto (*supra* n. 8) argues that the current phase of restructuring of the global political economy needs the creation of positive linkages across regulatory regimes, to facilitate a shift from negative to positive integration. This is also applicable to economic integration at a regional level.

competition be evaluated on a regional basis, thus maintaining the principle of open regionalism in ASEAN. However, the central issue to be considered is to what extent and at what level ASEAN substantive competition law and policy can be harmonized among its members.

Section 3 focuses on the rationale for a regional ASEAN competition law. Section 4 provides model options of such law and policy and Section 5 looks at the interaction between it and open regionalism. Section 6 sums up the argument.

2. COMPETITION LAW AND THE ASEAN INVESTMENT REGIME

2.1 Why Does ASEAN Require a Competition Law?

First, since ASEAN aims to strengthen economic integration in the region, it needs laws and institutions to support the implementation and elaboration of trade and investment liberalization within the ASEAN market. The interaction between government, consumers and producers has generated a concern that the rules-based system needs to be strengthened. How the competitive process actually works and to what extent governments should regulate relationships between producers and consumers is significant. In this sense, competition law is essential as an instrument to regulate fair competition, since, as mentioned above, it is compatible with liberalization in that it is basically neutral and non-discriminatory.

Second, in the emerging ASEAN free market economy, monopolies and restrictive business practices are viewed as undesirable, being likely to distort prices and inhibit the efficient allocation of resources. Thus, there is a call for contestability to ensure that free entry and the pressure of new competitors can function properly and balance the market powers and structures within the ASEAN market. Ultimately, the goal of market contestability and undistorted competition is to benefit consumers and enable a wide variety of product ranges at the lowest prices.[12] Competition law generally takes a pro-consumer policy perspective that fundamentally consolidates social wealth and the well-being of consumers.

In addition, competition law and policy enables small and medium-sized enterprises to enter the market; as such, it may form an alternative to an industrial-strategy-based policy, which has been regarded as a non-neutral

---

12 UNCTAD (1997), *supra* n. 5.

form of government intervention. Hence, competition law enhances consumer interests and helps small and medium-sized firms to compete on equal terms with other businesses in the regional economy, while complying with the principles of liberalization on a non-discriminatory basis. In addition, states continue to play an important role in preventing market failure, so that the ASEAN countries may feel confident in their role of monitoring conduct in the private sector, preferring, as they do, to take part in overseeing economic transactions and not leaving private-sector enterprises a free hand to interact with each other as in the neo-liberal ideology. It would be advantageous for the ASEAN countries to launch an effective, comprehensive competition law in the region, in parallel with the implementation of trade and investment liberalization.

As regards foreign investment, the implementation of competition law in the ASEAN countries would yield further advantages, apart from liberalizing the entry, establishment and operation of foreign investors. It would regulate and control mergers and acquisitions as well as abuse of dominant market positions in the ASEAN economy. This would probably be a better way of dealing with the fear of economic conquest by powerful foreign TNCs than the investment screening process that is the current trend in all ASEAN countries. The implementation of competition law and policy in the ASEAN region could be a key factor in phasing out the currently somewhat restrictive investment laws and regulations, though admittedly some investment restrictions tend to be applied in almost all, if not all, countries,[13] not only in ASEAN. The implementation of competition law in ASEAN countries in the same direction as those laws implemented elsewhere may pave the way for possible future general agreement on the regulation of foreign direct investment (FDI).[14]

---

[13] Geist, M.A. (1995), 'Towards a General Agreement on the Regulation of Foreign Direct Investment', **26** (3) *Law and Policy in International Business* 673. Geist surveyed national investment laws in 11 countries from every region of the world and found that every country, including the US and the UK, which are the most liberal, employs common restrictions on entry of foreign investors in specific areas that affect the economy or security of the country (restricted industries). Geist further found that the convergence of FDI policy has led to significant similarities in the standards and procedures applied to the admission of FDI internationally. The countries surveyed have adopted general policies of permitting FDI subject to certain exceptions. The almost uniform means of notification and/or prior approval procedure are widely used.

[14] Geist (*supra* n. 13), Part III, framework for a General Agreement on the regulation of FDI.

2.2 Interaction Between Competition Laws and Investment Laws in the ASEAN Countries

Currently, all ASEAN countries use a screening process and apply pre-entry requirements to all foreign investors. There are also some regulations to prevent foreign investors and firms from becoming a dominant force in the economy – for instance, limitations on foreign equity or ownership and divestment requirements. These laws and regulations can be used to prevent foreign investors from merging with or acquiring local firms, since these investors are not permitted to own shares exceeding a specified limit.[15] Likewise, foreign firms cannot merge with or acquire other foreign firms if their equity in the new company exceeds the equity ratio set by the law. Obviously, under these circumstances, the ASEAN countries need a competition law to control mergers and acquisitions. While they have been relaxing some of the regulations relating to foreign investors' equity ratio, this has been on a case-by-case basis and under specific conditions only. At the same time, these regulations do not control local firms or prevent them from merging with or acquiring other local or foreign firms. Indeed, local companies have been known to establish an oligopoly position in specific sectors. In the Thai market, for instance, in the telecommunications sector, Shinnawat Co. Ltd have a dominant position for mobile phones and related products; Telecom Asia, TOT and TT&T are dominant telephone network providers and Samart Telecom Co. Ltd are the sole providers of satellite dishes. The oligopolistic market can hardly be regarded as espousing fair competition, and could, in fact, easily distort prices and restrict consumers' choices.

The ASEAN countries also reserve some business sectors by barring them from foreign investment. It is now time for all these laws and regulations to be phased out. The countries have agreed to open up all industrial sectors to ASEAN investors by 2010 and to all investors by 2020, with some exceptions.[16] In thus liberalizing their investment regimes, the ASEAN countries may feel some concern at this sweeping move from a system of screening all foreign take-overs of national firms to screening none. They may fear that foreign firms will acquire dominant positions. Yet replacing these investment laws with competition laws may not only prove

---

[15] Generally, in all ASEAN countries except Singapore, foreign ownership or share equity may exceed 49 per cent of the total share, except when the company is granted promoted status under a promotion scheme.

[16] See Thanadsillapakul, *supra* n. 1.

more effective than the screening process, it may also be a more efficient way of assessing the competitive impact of foreign firms both at the time of entry and thereafter.

Competition laws and policies thus have a major role to play in the process of ASEAN liberalization, not least in ensuring that the ASEAN market is kept as open as possible to new entrants and that firms do not frustrate this goal by engaging in anti-competitive practices. In this manner, the vigorous enforcement of ASEAN competition law may provide reassurance that investment liberalization will not leave the government powerless against anti-competitive transactions or subsequent problems.

Competition laws may replace the current restrictive investment laws and regulations, incorporating principles based on non-discrimination in the control of restrictive business practices among firms regardless of their origin or nationality. Competition laws normally apply to all firms operating in given national or regional territories, whether in the field of domestic sales, imports, affiliates, or non-equity types of FDI. They do not, in principle, discriminate between national and foreign firms, or between firms of different national origins. In this way, competition law monitors the competitive behaviour of TNCs in the ASEAN host countries. It ensures that firms do not abuse dominant market positions and prevents inefficiencies stemming from market-allocation agreements, which might curb trade and investment. Therefore, competition law strengthens the principle of national treatment and enhances investment liberalization in compliance with the objectives of the ASEAN investment area and economic integration in ASEAN.

3. RATIONALE FOR A REGIONAL ASEAN COMPETITION LAW

The removal of internal barriers among the ASEAN countries to promote regional economic integration should not be allowed to result in companies creating territorial protection through cartels or the abuse of a dominant position. While investment liberalization within ASEAN can encourage the free entry of firms and enhance the contestability of the ASEAN market, this is not enough. Competition laws are needed to ensure that the former statutory obstacles to contestability are not replaced by anti-competitive business practices, thereby wiping out the benefits that might arise from liberalization.

The reduction of barriers to FDI in ASEAN and the establishment of positive standards of treatment for TNCs must go hand in hand with the adoption of measures aimed at ensuring the proper functioning of the market and at controlling anti-competitive business practices. The 1997 World Investment Report suggested that '[t]he culture of FDI liberalization that has grown world-wide and has become pervasive needs to be complemented by an equally world-wide and pervasive culture of competition, which needs to recognise competing objectives'.[17]

This statement has great relevance for ASEAN regulatory practice. Anti-competitive business practices that are common among international firms, and are likely to spread to the ASEAN countries, include the following:[18]

(a) *Horizontal restraints* or hard-core cartels among firms in an oligopolistic market, engaging, for example, in price fixing, output restrictions, market division, customer allocation, collusive tendering and other types of anti-competitive co-operation between firms selling competing products. All these business practices distort prices and the allocation of resources and result in a dysfunctional market to the disadvantage of consumers.[19] Fair competition would exist if no single supplier or consumer were able to influence market prices. Competition laws and policy may play an important role not only in prohibiting the formation of cartels but also in balancing the competitive effects of each firm's activity on the market.
(b) *Vertical restraints* or distribution strategies between manufacturers, suppliers or distributors, such as: tying the sale of one product to the purchase of another; exclusive dealing (the seller requires the buyer to purchase products only from the same seller); territorial restraints (the

---

17 UNCTAD (1997), *supra* n. 5.

18 Compiled from various sources: UNCTAD (1997), *supra* n. 5; Petersmann, E.U. (1993), 'International Competition Rules for the GATT-WTO World Trade and Legal System', **27** (6) *Journal of World Trade* 35; *idem* (1996), 'International Competition Rules for Government and Private Business', **30** (3) *Journal of World Trade* 5; Schoenbaum, T. (1996), 'The Theory of Contestable Markets in International Trade: A Rationale for "Justifiable" Unilateralism to Combat Restrictive Business Practices?', **30** (3) *Journal of World Trade* 161.

19 If market prices are distorted through either cartels or monopolies, they are likely to distort the allocation, co-ordination and distribution functions of market competition as well, so that consumer welfare will be reduced by higher prices, fewer products and less freedom of choice.

seller requires the buyer/distributor to resell the product within a limited geographical area); and resale price maintenance (the seller requires the buyer to resell the product only at a specified price). Resale price-fixing also tends to be generally prohibited. The pro- and anti-competitive effects of such restraints need to be evaluated and, where necessary, controlled.

(c) *Abuse of intellectual property rights* (IPRs), for example where technology-licensing arrangements abuse the monopoly position of IPR holders, for example through non-competition clauses and the so-called grant back. This means the licensee is required to assign inventions made in the course of working with the transferred technology back to the licensor. Another type of IPR abuse is that of 'non-contestation clauses', by which the licensee is prevented from contesting the validity of the IPR or other right of the licensor. IPR abuse may be subject to general competition rules on horizontal and vertical restraints.

(d) *Abuse of market dominance*: dominant firms accounting for a significant market share may attempt to monopolize a market, for instance through price discrimination, predatory low pricing, refusal to deal or vertical restraints. Rules against the abuse of a dominant position may be conduct-oriented, in other words, a general prohibition against monopolizing and foreclosure of competition. Another approach is result-oriented, with a prohibition, for example, on predatory pricing only if the losses can be recouped.

(e) *Mergers and acquisition policies*, where horizontal, vertical or conglomerate mergers are apt to reduce competition or decrease efficiency. Merger policies may be designed to ensure market contestability by preventing a monopoly or price-setting by a single seller and price-taking by a single buyer, as well as oligopolistic or monopolized market power. On the other hand, acquisition policies also overlap with industrial policy instruments.

(f) *Public undertakings and enterprises with special privileges*, which are not required to behave according to market principles (GATT Article XVII and Article 106 TFEU [ex Article 86 EC Treaty; ex Article 90 Treaty of Rome]) in view of their market power or financial independence. This includes firms with exclusive trading rights and monopolies.

In the new era, the ASEAN countries will need to regulate these anti-competitive business practices so as to achieve fair competitive conditions.

However, they will have to be wary of balance-of-market failure and government failure. If governments intervene to correct market failure or supply public goods, the risk of market failure has to be weighed against that of the alternative, government failure, since government intervention may lead to additional distortions. Therefore, fair competitive conditions rely on the rational behaviour of market participants or firms, perfect information, perfect market mobility and the need to reflect all costs in the prices of goods and services.[20] All these conditions require a comprehensive set of competition laws and regulations in the ASEAN countries.

Currently, laws and policies dealing with restrictive business practices differ from one ASEAN country to another and focus on different aspects such as anti-monopoly, anti-dumping, protection against state competition, and so on. There are no systematic competition laws in the ASEAN countries except in Indonesia, Singapore and Thailand. Now, however, all ASEAN countries are called upon to introduce such comprehensive competition laws and policies and to enforce them effectively. In fact, the general infrastructure and other comparative economic advantages of the ASEAN countries appear good; the only important drawback is that these countries lack good governance and a rule-based system. Therefore, a combination of sound ASEAN legal and economic systems may be viewed as favourably created factor endowments[21] capable of producing a positive effect on ASEAN's competitiveness in international trade and investment.

4. THE BASES OF AN ASEAN REGIONAL COMPETITION LAW AND MODELS OF A REGIONAL COMPETITION REGIME

In the modern, globally integrated world economy, both private enterprise and governments engage in competition.[22] In the ASEAN countries in particular, governments have widely implemented strategic policies in the

---

[20] Petersmann (1993), *supra* n. 18.

[21] International competition among firms is influenced not only by 'natural' production factor endowments, but also by government-determined conditions of competition; see Dunning, J.H. (1992), 'The Global Economy, Domestic Governance, Strategies and Transnational Corporations: Interactions and Policy Implications', **1** (3) *Transnational Corporations* 7. Dunning discusses in detail 'created' and 'natural' endowments.

[22] Porter, M. (ed.) (1990), *The Competitive Advantage of Nations*, New York: The Free Press.

trade and investment sphere. In this respect, government plays an important role, as Petersmann[23] has pointed out: 'By means of industrial policies aimed at enhancing economies of scale and positive externalities of national industries, strategic trade policies aimed at shifting rents away from foreign to domestic industries, or by means of investment policies designed to attract scarce foreign capital through tax incentives and favourable investment conditions.'

Markets, then, are imperfect in many ways. In effect, two kinds of competition law are required: the first, to deal with private restraints of competition and market failures (abuses of market power, externalities and asymmetries in information); the second, aimed at government competition to limit government failures, which may affect the supply of public goods and created endowments/comparative advantages.

On the one hand, fair competition should aim to protect less highly organized firms, such as small and medium-sized enterprises, upon entry into the market while protecting the public interest and consumers in a liberal economy. On the other hand, competition rules may need to be assessed so as to determine to what extent they should regulate the behaviour of firms. For instance, in an example given by Korah,[24] in some business areas, merged lines of business or operators may result in more adequate and effective operation, greater product variety and more readily available services – including advanced research and technological development – than those that individual, separate smaller firms or operators are able to provide. For instance, if a single plant or a merged enterprise can process all the spent nuclear fuel in a region at substantially lower cost than could smaller plants separately, it would be unprofitable for a second firm to establish such a smaller plant. Therefore, there is a concern that competition rules may be applied to protect smaller firms at the expense of larger enterprises irrespective of efficiency. Whether collaboration or competition in a particular market leads to better use of resources is always a difficult question to answer. While competition is desirable in lessening economic power, businessmen believe that in some industries resources are put to better use if competition is limited. Therefore, collaboration or natural monopolies may sometimes occur in response to the need for economies of scale. For instance, if a firm has merely expanded its plant in good time to

---

[23] Petersmann, E.U. (1993), 'International Competition Rules for the GATT-MTO World Trade and Legal System', **27** (6) *Journal of World Trade*, 35–86, at 35.

[24] Korah, V. (1968), *Monopolies and Restrictive Practices*, Middlesex, UK: Penguin Books, 64.

meet an expected increase in demand such that it is unprofitable for other firms to enter the industry, there is no objection to its exercising a monopoly.[25] Many markets can be supplied only after considerable capital investment has been made or appropriate technology developed.

Korah has further explained that, if capital requirements are a hindrance to the entry of small and medium-sized firms into the market and if one goal of competition is to enable small firms to compete in the market, then entry barriers exist on the ground of financial constraint. Hence, in this case, while there are no barriers to the entry of an equally efficient firm where a huge investment is required, small and medium-sized firms are obviously unable to compete with these larger firms. Should this be regarded as unfair competition? The evaluation of whether there is unfair competition requires consideration of the public good: an enhanced distribution system, provision of goods and services, reduced cost of operation, a technological lead or reduced capital requirements in the fields of business under consideration. It should be noted that a small firm protected for such reasons alone cannot hold its customers or suppliers to ransom except in the short term.[26] Therefore, to control the conduct of firms by such flimsy protection of small firms may discourage larger firms from making investments to enable them to compete aggressively. This implies that the regulation of restrictive business practices is intended to both ensure fair competition and maximize the public good and sound resource management. The ASEAN countries should give careful thought to this particular issue when they establish and enforce their competition law. They need to have a clear perspective in mind that balances the imperatives of collaboration, competition, the public good, and efficient resource allocation.

A dichotomy between market function and the role of government lies at the heart of competition law. On the one hand, a liberal law of the market implies that the market needs no barriers, no intervention and no control, but should be left to function based solely on the rule of supply and demand. On the other hand, fair competition implies that there should be no dominant enterprise, no restrictive business practices, no predatory pricing and no mergers and acquisitions that impede competition. All such conduct

---

[25] Ibid. Korah concludes that 'it is so much cheaper to produce a product in a large plant that can be continuously used than in many smaller ones, where one or two plants of the minimum efficient size can supply the expected demand and there is room for only one or two suppliers' (p. 64).

[26] Korah, V. (ed.) (1997), *An Introductory Guide to EC Competition Law and Practice*, Oxford, UK: Hart Publishing.

may need control through competition laws. However, if there is absolute freedom from constraints or, in other words, if there is no regulation at all to ensure fair competition, dominant firms could easily conquer the market, preventing anyone else from competing. Hence, the proposed criteria for regulating the behaviour of firms may need to consider type, size, competitive position, range or category of business so that the same level of undertaking may be treated fairly subject to the same conditions, rules and laws, as well as the economic environment itself.

4.1 Development of an International Competition Regime

There have previously been various attempts to develop international competition laws for the private sector, such as part of the *1948 Havana Charter for an International Trade Organization*, the *UN Codes of Conduct* and the *OECD Decisions and Guidelines*,[27] the *Set of Multilaterally Agreed Equitable Principles and Rules for the Control of Restrictive Business Practices*[28] and the Resolution adopted by the same UN Conference to strengthen implementation of the *Set of Rules*.[29] However, these were 'soft-law rules' rather than international/multilateral treaty law, aimed

---

27 Petersmann, E.U. (1992), 'Codes of Conduct', in Bernhardt, R. (ed.), *Encyclopaedia of Public International Law*, Vol. I, Amsterdam: North-Holland Publishing Company, 627.

28 Source: UNCTAD (1981), *The Set of Multilaterally Agreed Equitable Principles and Rules for the Control of Restrictive Business Practices*, United Nations Document TD/RBP/CONF/10/Rev.1, New York: United Nations. This was adopted by the United Nations General Assembly at its 35th session on 5 December 1980 (Resolution 35/36). 'The Second United Nations Conference to Review all Aspects of the Multilaterally Agreed Equitable Principles and Rules for the Control of Restrictive Business Practices' was held in Geneva from 26 November to 7 December 1990. That conference adopted a resolution on 'Strengthening the Implementation of the Set' at its sixth meeting on 7 December 1990. A third Review Conference took place on 13–21 November 1995 and adopted a resolution calling for a number of concrete actions to give effect to the implementation of the Set of Rules. *The Set of Principles and Rules* was also adopted by the United Nations Conference on Restrictive Business Practices as an annex to its resolution of 22 April 1980.

29 Source: UNCTAD (1991), 'Resolution Adopted by the Conference Strengthening the Implementation of the Set', *Report of the Second United Nations Conference to Review all Aspects of the Multilaterally Agreed Equitable Principles and Rules for the Control of Restrictive Business Practice*, United Nations Document TD/RBP/CONF.3/9, Geneva: United Nations, Annex, 48–51.

generally at avoiding mutually harmful competition policy conflicts[30] and overcoming the policy divergences and jurisdictional gaps between national competition laws.[31] Regulatory differences in competition laws and the decentralized administration of competition policies are mainly due to specific national conditions. For instance, the final decision as to whether the costs of restraint of competition may be outweighed by economies of scale and positive externalities will require case-by-case analysis with due regard to the particular conditions prevailing in a given national market. Conflicts between national regulations can also result in barriers to market access, market distortions and harmful international externalities.

4.2 The New Search for an International Competition Regime[32]

Recently the issue of competition law and policy in the global trading system has been looked into by various international organizations, including GATT/WTO, OECD and the World Bank. The approach to a common international competition law and the various routes to achieve it have been studied in order to shape and elaborate a comprehensive multilateral regime. The WTO has sought a consensus on the issue of internationalization of antitrust law focusing either on the extent to which antitrust rules should be harmonized or on the content of such rules.[33] The World Bank and OECD have jointly developed a framework for the design and implementation of a competition law and policy that could be used as a model by

---

30 Since the more than two hundred international sovereign states have different resources, preferences, comparative advantages and political and regulatory systems, the national competition laws also differ in many respects, such as: exclusion of regulated sectors, exemption of exporters, rule-of-reason exceptions, focus on corporate conduct or market structures, support of 'crisis cartels' and small businesses, actual enforcement, and judicial review of the 'law on the books'.

31 Petersmann (1993), *supra* n. 18, at 37.

32 See Graham, E.M. and D.J. Richardson (eds) (1997), *Global Competition Policy*, Washington, DC: Institute for International Economics; also see Zäch, R. (ed.) (1999), *Towards WTO Competition Rules: Key Issues and Comments on the WTO Report* (1998) on Trade and Competition, The Hague/London/Boston: Kluwer Law International; Yang-Ching, C., S. Gee, L. Changfa and H. Jiming (eds) (2001), *International and Comparative Competition Laws and Policies*, The Hague/London/New York: Kluwer Law International; and Drexl, J. (ed.) (2003), *The Future of Transnational Antitrust – From Comparative to Common Competition Law*, Max Planck Institute for Intellectual Property, Competition and Tax Law, Munich Series, The Hague/London/New York: Kluwer Law International.

33 Zäch, *supra* n. 32.

developing countries and transitional economies. Several options of models for creating a common international law of competition have been proposed by various experts. Nonetheless, no consensus exists among countries on any single model. A variety of ideologies, methodologies and competition regimes, especially regarding the issue of effective enforcement of competition law in cross-border transactions, have stood in the way of such consensus.[34]

On the one hand, the proposed models[35] for an international competition/antitrust law are, essentially: (1) the *WTO model*, which is one of international agreement. It would include an international enforcement system and there would be an international agency or commission responsible for ensuring respect of the international antitrust rules or competition law; (2) the *sovereignty model*, which applies purely national law to all antitrust disputes within the jurisdiction of the nation-state involved but which would apply the extraterritorial principle where the disputes related to cross-border transactions; and (3) The *network model*, which relies on the adoption of agreements of mutual assistance and co-operation or formal protocols, enforcement networks, information-sharing and networking among the entities involved in substantive competition law.

On the other hand, the proposed routes to an international competition law are:[36]

---

[34] At the OECD Conference on Trade and Competition held at Paris on 29–30 June 1999, the US and the EU, the two leaders in the competition regime stakes, defended diametrically opposing views. The EU suggested that negotiations on multilateral or international competition law should begin immediately, while the US insisted that 'it was far too early to move in that direction'. However, according to Frédéric Jenny, 'the divergence of opinions was really a question of methodology: one believes in negotiating before agreeing on the solutions to be found, and the other believes in exploring alternative solutions before agreeing to negotiate', Jenny, F. (2001), 'Globalization, Competition and Trade Policy: Convergence, Divergence and Cooperation', in Yang-Ching et al., *supra* n. 32, at 56-–67 (discussing the pros and cons of establishing a multilateral framework for competition consistent with WTO principles of transparency and non-discrimination). Also see Jenny, F. (2001) 'Globalization, Competition and Trade Policy: Convergence, Divergence and Cooperation', in *EC Law Facing the New Millennium Challenges*, XIV Congress of the European Lawyer's Union, Brussels: Bruylant. See Wilson, J. (2003), *Globalization and the Limits of National Merger Control Laws*, The Hague/London/New York: Kluwer Law International, 241.

[35] First, H. (1999), 'Towards an International Common Law of Competition' in Zäch, *supra* n. 32.

[36] Fikentscher, W. (1999), 'Antitrust, Market Conceptualization and the World Trade Organization – the Convention Approach', in Zäch, *supra* n. 32.

(a) *uniform law*, the most complete but least frequently achieved approach;
(b) *harmonized law*, which is less than uniform and narrows the distinctions between national laws while leaving variations in details to national legislatures;
(c) *convention law*, which has less harmonizing effect (convention law permits national laws to be implemented in solving cross-border cases while avoiding heavy inroads by claims to national sovereignty); and
(d) *the conflicts-of-law approach* or 'choice-of-law approach'.

All these approaches and models have their strong and weak points that suit the particular legal and economic structure of each economy or group of countries. For instance, uniform law or harmonized law may be more effectively implemented and better suited to more closely integrated regional economies. Convention law may be more flexible for countries engaged in bilateral or multilateral economic co-operation. The WTO model, which would be more comprehensive to implement, may be efficient in a global trading system. Co-operation between WTO and WIPO, which has long experience in setting international competition rules, is regarded as helpful in drafting an international competition code. International attempts at drafting international competition law have influenced the ASEAN move towards a regional competition regime, especially in the Asia-Pacific Economic Cooperation (APEC) grouping as a whole. APEC strongly encourages the development and enhancement of regional competition law and policy.[37]

4.3 ASEAN Regional Competition Law: Harmonization and the Networking Approach

There is no single agreed set of international competition laws that suits all and no consensus has been reached so far on any of the proposed models or approaches towards a multilateral competition regime. Therefore, ASEAN countries need to develop their own consensus on what will suit them for a regional competition regime. Now, in fact, would be the time for ASEAN to implement a regional competition law and policy, since all ASEAN countries have now embarked on their own national competition law, and it

---

[37] Washington University (2002), 'Symposium on APEC Competition Policy and Economic Development', **1** (1–2) *Washington University Global Studies Law Review*. See also Yang-Ching et al., *supra* n. 32.

would be easier to agree on the design of a regional competition regime by harmonizing the substantive national competition rules to achieve the effective enforcement of competition law at the regional level.

Adapted from the above-described models for, and approaches to, international competition or multilateral competition law, there are two main avenues to regional harmonization of competition law. The first rests on trade policy measures, which have indeed been implemented in ASEAN through its trade and investment liberalization. Under this approach, governments can rely on trade liberalization and favour FDI to promote competition. In this case, existing trade rules can be used or else some competition principles may be incorporated into trade policy measures. This approach is consistent with the WTO system.[38] The alternative approach is based on competition rules, which opens up three options.[39] First, under the coordinated, or sovereignty, model, governments can rely on the coordinated application of national competition laws based on positive agreements. Second, using the harmonized law model, countries can harmonize their national competition laws in accordance with international guidelines. Finally, the highest degree of collaboration would be an agreement on international competition laws, implicating a notion of supranationality. Of these three options the harmonized law model (the second), is the most suitable for an ASEAN regional competition law. Why is this?

ASEAN must bear in mind the diversity of its economic structures, economic history, legal systems, societal goals and culture, as well as the differences in national socio-economic infrastructure. As Jenny puts it, 'any solution to the general problem of promoting the complementarity of trade

---

[38] See Bacchetta, M., H. Horn and P.C. Mavroidis (1997), 'Does Negative Spill-Over from Nationally Pursued Competition Policies Provide a Case for Multilateral Competition Rules?', mimeo, 4 June; Hoekman, B.M. and P.C. Mavroidis (1994), 'Competition, Competition Policy and the GATT', **17** *World Economy* 121; Messerlin, P.A. (1996), *Development in European Competition Policy*, European Institute of Public Administration, Maastricht; Petersmann, E.U. (1996), 'The Need for Integrating Trade and Competition Rules in the WTO World Trade and Legal System', *PSIO Occasional Paper, WTO Series No. 3*, The Graduate Institute for International Studies, Geneva.

[39] See Mattoo, A. and A. Subramanian (1997), 'Multilateral Rules on Competition Policy: A Possible Way forward', **31** (5) *Journal of World Trade* 95.

liberalization, regulatory reform (regional economic integration) and competition policy must be flexible enough to allow such national differences to continue to exist',[40] and:

> the existing international commitments at the multilateral level in the trade area are not designed to prevent countries from pursuing the domestic policies they see fit to pursue. Multilateral agreements allow differences in national legislation as long as these differences are not contradictory with the underlying principles of the WTO.[41]

Even within the European Union, national competition laws are still in effect. With this in mind, this author agrees with Jenny's statement, especially where it applies to ASEAN. Currently, a single, unified or unique regional competition law is too ambitious a goal for ASEAN for several reasons. First, ASEAN is not a supranational organization, and thus there is no regional institution or court to implement or enforce supranational law. Under these circumstances, it would be difficult to create a supranational competition law at this stage unless ASEAN were to develop a regional legal and institutional framework for the purpose. Second, even though ASEAN has embarked upon *de facto* regional economic integration, there is not yet the political will to develop such a supranational organization. Third, the ASEAN countries enjoy widely diverse levels of economic development: Singapore is regarded as a more highly developed economy, Indonesia, Malaysia and Thailand are placed somewhere in the middle, Cambodia and Laos are less highly developed economies and Vietnam and Myanmar are transitional economies. Fourth, the ASEAN countries' economic structures are different. For example, Brunei is a small, rich oil country and Thailand, Indonesia and the Philippines are mixed agricultural/industrial/commercial economies, while Malaysia is an industrial/commercial economy endowed with oil resources, and Singapore is a commercial economy. This variety of economic structures within ASEAN affects the competition regime in each member state. Economic theory and policy in each ASEAN country are geared towards that country's own brand of economic development, and so, perforce, are their national competition laws and policies. Consequently, in harmonizing its national competition laws, ASEAN may need to tolerate the persistence of some national differences until the individual economies are more evenly developed.

---

40 See Jenny, F. (2001), 'Globalization, Competition and Trade Policy: Convergence, Divergence and Cooperation' in Yang-Ching et al., *supra* n. 32, at 68.

41 Ibid.

A combination of these factors, the structure of ASEAN's 'open regionalism' – and more especially the 'ASEAN way' – and concerted action in terms of economic co-operation have forced ASEAN to consider the synchronized model[42] of harmonized law and enforcement networks. For substantive competition law enforceable at the regional level, ASEAN can refer to the general basic rules of conduct in the various codes and guidelines that have common features, while leaving the national authorities to deal with particular features of their specific competition laws. At the regional level, ASEAN may need the Regional Competition Committee to oversee and enforce competition law in cross-border cases, as well as to coordinate with the national authorities. This may be regarded as an initial step towards further development of common regional institutions designed to lead ASEAN to a higher degree of integration.[43] As Bilal and Olarreaga have argued, '[i]ndeed, successful [regional trade agreements] inevitably entail the existence of common rules, the creation of common institutions, the delegation of authority to supranational instances, and more generally the development of a co-operative framework among member countries. Of course, a crucial aspect here is the degree of regional integration.'[44]

---

[42] See Thanadsillapakul, *supra* n. 1.

[43] Winters has identified five forms of economic integration, ranked in increasing order of integration:

1. Preferential Trade Areas (PTAs), in which member countries agree to levy reduced, or preferential, tariffs on partner countries;
2. Free Trade Area (FTAs), in which trade barriers between partner countries are abolished, but each member country determines its own external barriers;
3. Custom Unions (CUs), in which intra-union free trade prevails and a common external trade policy is adopted by member countries;
4. Common Markets, which are CUs with further provisions to facilitate the free movement of goods, services and factors of production, and the harmonization of trading and technical standards;
5. Political Unions, which are the ultimate form of economic integration.

Winters, L. Alan (1997), 'What Can European Experience Teach Developing Countries About Integration?', *The World Economy*, **20** (7), 889–912. While PTAs and FTAs do not require inter-governmental institutions, since each member country remains in complete charge of its own policy, CUs and higher forms of economic integration do involve a delegation of sovereignty, and thus an element of supranationality, as at least external trade policy is the result of a common decision by member countries.

[44] Bilal, S. and M. Olarreaga (1998), *Regionalism, Competition Policy and Abuse of Dominant Position*, Working Paper, European Institute of Public Administration, The Netherlands, p. 9.

4.4 Some Concerns in Designing Substantive Competition Law

4.4.1 Determination of 'market power'

In principle, competition policy does not seek to prohibit market power *per se*, but rather *abuse* of a dominant position. The basic idea is that competition law should not penalize efficient firms that have established a dominant position in the market by performing better than their competitors. The objective is rather to ensure potential access to the relevant market and to guarantee 'fair' competition.[45]

The contentious issues are how to determine what behaviour constitutes 'abuse' of market power and how to promote competition without penalizing successful enterprises that are possibly in a dominant position. Generally, competition law specifies that if an enterprise gains a market share exceeding the specified ratio, it must be carefully monitored for possible abuse of its dominant market position.

However, market share is not a correct indicator of market power for at least three reasons, as argued by Wood.[46] First, the definition of the relevant market is not clear when there is high substitutability in consumption. This is illustrated in *United States v. E. I. du Pont de Nemours & Co. (Cellophane)*.[47] If the relevant product market was 'all flexible packaging material', then du Pont's share was only 20 per cent. But if, instead, it was only 'cellophane', du Pont had cornered 75 per cent of the market.

Second, small market shares may be consistent with market power. Indeed, this would be the case if several small firms colluded to control a market. For example, ten firms, each with 10 per cent of the market, may collude to charge monopolistic prices. Obviously, there is a limit to this, given the free-rider problem when the number of firms increases in a collusive agreement, as in any other co-operative agreement.[48]

---

[45] See Wood, D.P. (1995), 'Competition and the Single Firm: Monopolization and Abuse of Dominant Positions', paper presented at the Symposium on Competition Policy in a Global Economy, Pacific Economic Co-operation Council, Taipei, Taiwan; and see citation in Bilal and Olarreaga, *supra* n. 44.

[46] Wood, *supra* n. 45.

[47] *United States v. du Pont & Co.*, 351 U.S. 377 (1956); *United States v. E. I. du Pont de Nemours & Co.* Appeal from the United States District Court for the District of Delaware. No. 5. Argued October 11, 1955. Decided June 11, 1956.

[48] See Olson, M. (ed.) (1965), *The Logic of Collective Action: Public Goods and the Theory of Groups*, Cambridge, MA: Harvard University Press.

Third, large market shares may be consistent with low market power. Indeed, potential entry may significantly reduce incumbent firms' market share, as underlined by the 'contestability theory'. For firms with a large market share, the presence and nature of barriers to entry is a much more useful guide to policy than are the market shares themselves.[49]

A thorough analysis of entry barriers is clearly crucial to the proper implementation of competition law, in particular when it comes to assessing levels of dominance, since a firm may not exercise significant market power over time in the absence of barriers to new entries in the relevant market. Barriers to entry can be of three types: *artificial* (introduced by government regulation or trade associations), *natural* (linked to the production technology, scale and scope economies) and *strategic* (created by firms to deter entrants, for example through over-investment or loyalty bonuses). Common practice in US and EU competition law suggests that while most effort has been put into determining the relevant market and assessing market power – usually in terms of market share – little (or at least not enough) attention has been paid to entry barriers.[50] In applying Article 102 of the TFEU (ex Article 82; ex Article 86 ECT) on the abuse of dominant position, 'the primary indicator' of dominance is market shares, while the level of entry (and exit) barriers is only a 'secondary indicator'. Another proxy for market power sometimes used is the level of profits. The idea is that firms with high profit levels abuse their dominant position.

Any legislation implicitly or explicitly forbidding high profit levels may have unexpected effects. If the competition authority regulates the abuse of a dominant position by imposing profit ceilings, firms will have a serious incentive to artificially inflate costs. This, in turn, provokes misallocation of resources. Competition authorities, when regulating, should bear in mind that firms react strategically to competition rules. More importantly, as already mentioned, high profits may simply reflect the greater efficiency of the firm with a competitive edge.[51]

---

[49] See Kuhn, K.U., P. Seabright and A. Smith (1992), 'Competition Policy Research: Where Do We Stand?', *CEPR Occasional Paper No. 8*, London: Centre for Economic Policy Research.

[50] See Harbord, D. and T. Hoehn (1994), 'Barriers to Entry and Exit in European Competition Policy', **14** (4) *International Review of Law and Economics* 411.

[51] See Demsetz, H. (1974), 'Two Systems of Belief about Monopoly', in Goldschmid, H. et al. (eds), *Industrial Concentration: The New Learning*, Boston: Little Brown.

To summarize, competition policy, as any other government policy, should include efficiency considerations. If, in dealing with abuse of a dominant position, competition policy tends to focus on firms' market shares rather than on strategic barriers against entry into the market, then efficient firms may be penalized. This will give the wrong signals to firms, which will concentrate on controlling their market shares, rather than on becoming more efficient. This is particularly important in developing countries where market failures are due to market distortions. Clearly, if a firm has a dominant position owing to credit constraints in the domestic market, the best policy must surely be not to prevent 'abuse' of a dominant position by the incumbent firm, but rather to correct the credit shortage and so allow for entry of new firms.

4.4.2 Monitoring horizontal agreements, vertical restraints and unfair competitive practices

Bollard and Vautier have suggested seven criteria to assess the competitive environment under competition law and policy in developing economies: (1) merger regimes; (2) abuse of dominant power; (3) horizontal agreements; (4) vertical restraints; (5) jurisdiction exemption; (6) unfair trade practices; and (7) enforcement and powers.[52]

In many developing countries, mergers and abuse of dominant power are monitored while horizontal agreements, vertical restraints and unfair competitive practices are not. In addition to this shortcoming of their competition laws, the existing rules appear to be poorly enforced in these countries. Among the ASEAN member states, only Indonesia and Thailand regulate competition. The other members, while legislating on competition law, regulate non-competitive behaviour by alternative means. Singapore promotes competition by inducing foreign competition under liberalized trade and FDI regimes, and now Singapore stipulates competition law to further enhance trade and investment liberalization. The ASEAN countries differ considerably as to the type of rules they impose and the basic design and type of enforcement arrangements. Last but not least, competition law in Indonesia and Thailand and the draft competition laws in other ASEAN members are predominantly structure-based, not outcome-based, and

---

[52] See Bollard, A. and K.M. Vautier (1998), 'The Convergence of Competition Law within APEC and the CER Agreement', in Wu, Rong-I and Yub-Peng Chu (eds), *The Asia-Pacific: Competition Policy, Convergence and Pluralism*, London and New York: Routledge, p. 126.

enforcement is administration-based, not judicially based.[53] This entails difficulties in effectively enforcing competition law and monitoring horizontal agreements, vertical restraints and unfair competitive practices.

4.4.3 The interaction of competition law and other government measures, laws and regulations

A competition regime encompasses any government measure that affects private-sector activity. State-owned enterprises constitute a typical form of regulated activity, though they are by no means the only one. Regulations generally fall into one of two categories: first, *economic*, including agricultural price restrictions and restrictions on entry into certain sectors – such as telecommunications; second, *social*, including environmental and sanitary requirements for certain products. Generally, economic regulations induce cost efficiency, while social regulations are considered beneficial from a public welfare point of view. However, social regulations can be created for and used to provide industrial protection. The ASEAN governments therefore need to balance economic and social regulations and carefully analyse the impact of all their laws and regulations on the competitive economy. It is very important to re-assess all relevant government legislations and regulations to ascertain to what extent they distort or enhance competition by minimizing the risk of anti-competitive conduct through appropriate disciplining of business conduct. Competition policy that comes along with the national competition law also emphasizes the importance of international co-operation between both competition agencies and authorities to deal with ever-increasing cross-border issues and capacity building in the ASEAN members. National competition policy should serve an important role in formulating and implementing an environment of fair competition in the ASEAN member countries' economies.

5. THE INTERACTION BETWEEN REGIONAL COMPETITION LAW AND POLICY AND OPEN REGIONALISM[54]

The functions of a feasible ASEAN regional system of competition law and policy (discussed in the introduction to this chapter) should include the promotion of:

---

[53] Ibid.

[54] See Garnaut; Eliassen and Monsen; and Garnaut and Drysdale, *supra* n. 2.

(a) liberalization of trade and investment in ASEAN;
(b) free and fair competition among firms in ASEAN by monitoring the behaviour of firms doing business in the region; and
(c) a proper competitive balance between intra- and extra-ASEAN business enterprises.

These three functions will play an important part in facilitating ASEAN open regionalism. They will ensure that ASEAN keeps its regional market open for both intra- and extra-regional trade and investment (the first two functions). The third function is fundamental to open regionalism, which ensures a proper competitive balance between intra- and extra-ASEAN firms.

Competition law and policy should help to promote the growth of small and medium-sized enterprises, which form the majority in local ASEAN economies, and allow them to compete with their stronger rivals.[55] The liberalization of trade and investment based on fair competition will enable local small and medium-sized firms to develop their economic strengths, upgrade their technological production processes and improve managerial systems and commercial skills in order to compete with foreign firms. Competition law will ensure that both local and foreign firms are prevented from engaging in restrictive business practices, abusing a dominant position, forming a cartel or engaging in any other type of unfair practice that might damage other firms. Under such fair competition circumstances, every firm, be it small or large, will be able to compete in its respective market, size and field of business. Furthermore, competition law would permit the ASEAN countries to assess the economic benefit deriving from the influx of foreign firms on the basis of whether or not they are likely to damage local small and medium-sized firms, and thus enable them to use competition policy to protect these local firms. This may be achieved through, for example, merger control regulations preventing TNCs from merging with or acquiring another company to create or strengthen their commercial dominance in the market. This would encourage foreign investment to be made on a 'green field' basis that could contribute to the regional economy, ensuring that it could compete with other (local or foreign) firms on the same fair basic grounds and conditions.

Since there are many small and medium-sized firms in the ASEAN countries, and since these firms fear that an ASEAN regional market open to

---

[55] See Whish, R. and B. Sulfrin (1993), *Competition Law*, London and Edinburgh: Butterworths.

powerful TNCs might significantly affect smaller local businesses, efforts to protect the competitive position of these local companies and to ensure fair competition will help to increase these firms' confidence in doing business in the single ASEAN open market.[56] A regional competition law and policy could be instrumental in ensuring this.

Competition law could also allow each single country to protect its indigenous enterprises or national/cultural industries to preserve country-specific values or safeguard the country's international renown for a given speciality.[57] In the Czech beer case, an American firm, Anheuser-Busch, brewer of the American Budweiser lager beer, made a fruitless bid for a stake in Czech Budvar, famous for its Budweiser Budvar lager beer. Both companies produce beer with the brand name 'Budweiser', but neither has an exclusive right to use the name internationally. They settled the matter of the name by allocating its use in different markets.[58] However, a dispute arose when they both entered the European market, since the agreement did not clearly define the territory assigned to each party in using the brand name. Anheuser-Busch wished to merge the two companies so that they could produce and sell the product world-wide without any constraint. However, Czech Budvar is traditionally regarded as the producer of the true Czech Budweiser lager beer, and consumers both in the Czech Republic and elsewhere favour the typical, unique flavour of the original beer it produces. Consumer campaigns were mounted to preserve Czech Budvar as a national, indigenous industry and to block its acquisition by the American firm.

---

[56] In fact, the ASEAN countries are aware of this sensitive issue and have already canvassed the small and medium-sized firms in the region, preparing them to compete with extra-ASEAN firms. See *Joint Statement on East Asia Co-operation*, 28 November 1999, Manila, The Philippines. Also, each individual ASEAN country has set up Small and Medium Firm Networks to promote and strengthen small and medium-sized enterprises: for example, the Small and Medium Industry Development Office in Malaysia and the Bureau of Small and Medium Business Development in the Philippines.

[57] See Muchlinski, P.T. (1996), 'A Case of Czech Beer: Competition and Competitiveness in the Transitional Economies', **59** (5) *The Modern Law Review* 658.

[58] The dispute was settled by agreement of 4 September 1911, whereby the US brewer was granted exclusive use of the 'Budweiser' brand name in North America, while the Czech brewer was granted the name for the rest of the world. But it did not confer any rights or impose any restrictions with regard to use of the name in Europe, nor did it prevent any party from establishing an exclusive right to the Budweiser trade name as part of its trading style in any European country.

In relation to this case, Muchlinski has argued that, since the Czech Republic, alone among the transitional economies, has abolished specialized foreign investment laws and has actively liberalized investment, only privatization and competition law could act as vehicles for the close screening of foreign investment. EU law as a source of principles for the regulation of foreign investment would also be justified, since the Czech Republic and the EU have an agreement[59] to bring the Czechs' commercial and economic laws into line with EU law as a prelude to possible future EU membership. As a result, EU competition law, which concerns anti-competitive and concerted practices, abuse of a dominant position, and preferential state aids that distort competition, must be taken into account as regards any business practices in the Czech Republic. Competition law could provide an alternative screening procedure to examine any threat of damage to national industry by means of merger or acquisition by foreign investors. From this point of view, the protection of indigenous industries could be based on concerns for consumer interests and the availability of product choice, which are in keeping with cultural diversity.

The ASEAN countries follow an 'open door' policy in their investment-liberalization efforts so as to allow regional competition law, which is consistent with liberalization, to play an important role in protecting domestic firms from harm (such as in the Czech beer case). In this way, ASEAN can reconcile a positive approach to foreign investment, exemplified by a lack of regulatory control, with controls over any undesirable effects, both in the market and in social terms, of FDI, by means of laws that apply to foreign and domestic firms alike, notably competition law, merger and acquisition control regulation, and anti-monopoly control.[60]

In other words, ASEAN indigenous industries could be protected under the ASEAN regional competition law and policy and by regional merger control regulation. Moreover, the views of consumer and local interest

---

59 The Czech Republic has become party to an EU Europe Agreement (EA), which entered into force on 1 February 1995 to ensure greater convergence between EU economic laws and the national law of the non-EU Contracting States, as a precondition for any future application for membership.

60 Muchlinski argues that 'maximum foreign shareholding limits in national laws have tended to be relaxed. The most promising avenue for regulation should be competition law, in that a level of foreign ownership that may create an anti-competitive concentration can be legitimately challenged without upsetting the logic of free market policies' (Muchlinski, *supra* n. 56, at 659).

groups on particular businesses or industries can be taken into account by the authority concerned.[61]

6. CONCLUSION

In conclusion, the function of regional competition law and policy and regional merger control regulation would be to ensure the review of mergers and anti-competitive practices in the ASEAN countries, which currently lack both effective domestic controls and experience in dealing with mergers, acquisitions and anti-competitive practices. Therefore, in this way, member countries could enlist the support of the Regional Merger Committee in the event of concentrations with significant actual or potential anti-competitive impact. As regards the shaping of an ASEAN regional competition law, this may be developed and adapted from the models for international competition law and the approach towards a multilateral competition regime proposed at international level. Harmonization of substantive national competition law combined with the network model, especially the regional enforcement network, may be suitable for ASEAN's open regionalism infrastructure and its 'ASEAN way' and for concerted actions. ASEAN regional competition law and policy could enhance regional economic strengths and ensure that the regional market, open to non-ASEAN trade and investment, would prevent powerful transnational corporations from dominating the regional economy. This is consistent with the main concept of open regionalism, which enhances both intra- and extra-ASEAN trade and investment, so that regional competition law and policy would be suitable instruments to achieve this goal.

---

[61] For instance, the issue can be brought to the Regional Merger Committee, within the spirit of the Regional Merger Regulation; consumer groups can request that the Committee review a concentration in which FDI creates or strengthens a dominant position or merges with or acquires such domestic firms.

2. Competition law and policy in the framework of ASEAN

Anthony Amunategui Abad

1. INTRODUCTION

It is widely acknowledged that a strong and well-crafted framework of competition law and policy, with effective enforcement capacity and competition-based economic reform, promotes increased efficiency, economic growth and development. These benefits are of particular interest to developing countries and countries in transition, such as a number of the economies in the Association of Southeast Asian Nations (ASEAN). During the last decade, a majority of ASEAN member states have adopted or begun the process of enacting competition laws. As globalization proceeds, countries are becoming substantially more open and market oriented, aware of the adverse effects of anti-competitive practices and of the potential benefits that derive from competition law enforcement.

The rationale for competition law and policy is compelling. A well-designed and effective competition law and policy framework is good for efficiency, as it promotes competitiveness; for economic growth, through productivity gains and greater innovation; for price stability, as competition tends to keep prices low; and for trade and investment, as it tends to make liberalization more effective and meaningful. Consumers are the biggest beneficiaries, as competition policy and law not only protect consumers against monopolistic and restrictive practices but also enable them to enjoy the fruits of competition in the form of lower prices and/or better products. The experiences of developed and developing countries show that having competition policy and law reinforces macroeconomic stabilization policies and contributes to industry development. One major outcome is the avoidance of abuse of dominance.

This chapter discusses the current state of competition laws in ASEAN and aims to identify the emerging issues in setting up an ASEAN competition law and policy regime. Only four out of the ten countries in ASEAN have competition laws – namely, Indonesia, Singapore, Thailand and Vietnam. For the countries without competition law and policy, the primary policy questions are whether to introduce competition policies and, if so, in what form. For the countries with existing competition policies, the key issues are whether, and how, they should integrate their competition policies with one another. A uniform system of competition law and policy is only equitable when nations enjoy similar or compatible levels of economic development, research and development capability, infrastructure and technological prowess.

2. ASEAN COMPETITION POLICY

2.1 Introduction and Background

At the outset, it needs to be acknowledged that there is considerable diversity among the ASEAN member countries in terms of their respective economic and policy heritage, political and governance systems, legal and economic institutions and policy frameworks, stages of economic development, and exposure to and reliance on international trade and investments. The immediate implication of this regional diversity is that there is no such thing as 'one size fits all'. While the core principles of competition policy and law may be similar, their design, implementation, capacity-building requirements and institutions will need to take account of member country differences. Some member countries such as Cambodia and the Lao People's Democratic Republic (Laos) are in advanced stages of drafting competition laws. In Malaysia, the legislature has only recently passed a competition law, which will come into effect 18 months after its enactment. Brunei, Myanmar and the Philippines do not have a framework of competition policy and law but rely on sector-specific policies. The range and depth of experience of countries with competition laws such as Indonesia, Singapore, Thailand and Vietnam vary considerably. These differences will need to be reflected not only in the context of the challenges faced by and the needs of individual member countries, but also at the ASEAN regional level.

2.2 Competition Law and Policy in the ASEAN Economic Community

The ASEAN was created in 1967, not for economic integration but for political and security reasons. Initial efforts towards economic cooperation began only after almost ten years. In 1976, a preferential trading scheme was developed, followed by industrial cooperation schemes. Serious economic integration efforts through the ASEAN Free Trade Area (AFTA) started only in 1992 in reaction to globalization, the emergence of the North American Free Trade Area (NAFTA) and the EU Single Market, and the rise of the People's Republic of China. AFTA covered only trade in goods, and had to be complemented by the ASEAN Framework Agreement on Services (AFAS) in 1995 and by the ASEAN Investment Area (AIA) in 1998. In 1997, ASEAN produced the ASEAN Vision 2020, with the aim of forging closer economic integration and narrowing the development gap between older and newer members.

The ASEAN leaders have agreed to establish an ASEAN Economic Community (AEC) by 2015 and to transform ASEAN into a region with free movement of goods, services, investment and skilled labor and freer flow of capital. In their Declaration on the AEC Blueprint in Singapore in November 2007, the ASEAN Leaders adopted

> the AEC Blueprint which each ASEAN Member Country shall abide by and implement the AEC by 2015. The AEC Blueprint will transform ASEAN into a single market and production base, a highly competitive economic region, a region of equitable economic development, and a region fully integrated into the global economy.[1]

ASEAN member states (AMSs) committed themselves in the AEC Blueprint to introducing nationwide competition policy and law by 2015. This is to ensure a level playing field and incubate a culture of fair business competition for enhanced regional economic performance in the long run.

In August 2007, the ASEAN economic ministers endorsed the establishment of the ASEAN Experts Group on Competition (AEGC) as a regional forum to discuss and cooperate in competition policy and law. There had previously been no official working body on competition policy in ASEAN, since not all AMSs have established competition regulatory bodies in their countries.

The AEGC first met in 2008 and agreed to focus, for the next three to five years, on building up competition-related policy capabilities and best practices in the AMSs, developing the ASEAN Regional Guidelines on

---

[1] ASEAN Economic Community Blueprint, Jakarta: ASEAN Secretariat, January 2008, p. 2.

Competition Policy and compiling a Handbook on Competition Policies and Laws in ASEAN for Businesses.[2]

At present, only Indonesia, Singapore, Thailand and Vietnam have established national competition policy and law as well as competition regulatory bodies. Laos, Cambodia and Malaysia plan to initiate and introduce national competition policy and law soon. The remaining countries – Brunei Darussalam, Myanmar and the Philippines – have relied on sector-level policies and regulations to achieve competition policy objectives in various domestic markets for productive factors and final or intermediate goods and services. As observed by the Malaysian Institute of Economic Research (2008), competition policy in the ASEAN countries is, in many cases, industry specific, ad hoc and incoherent. Table 2.1 summarizes the current state of competition policy and law in the ASEAN countries.

2.2.1 Competition policy in the Philippines

To date, the Philippines do not have a comprehensive and developed legislation relating to antitrust and monopoly activities. There have been several antitrust bills that were long pending before the Philippine Congress and efforts have been made in the past to enact a comprehensive competition law, but currently the country's competition laws are widely fragmented. The Philippine Constitution prohibits and regulates monopolies, combinations in restraint of trade and other unfair competition practices. The Revised Penal Code defines and penalizes anti-competitive behavior that is criminal in nature. The Civil Code of the Philippines allows for the collection of damages arising from unfair competition or from abuse of dominant position by a monopolist. There is also an Act to Prohibit Monopolies in Restraint of Trade.

There is no central government agency that monitors the implementation of competition policy and law, with various government agencies being tasked with both the regulation and the promotion of competition in different economic sectors, such as the National Telecommunications Commission for telecommunications, the Energy Regulatory Board for power, the Maritime Industry Authority for the shipping industry, the Philippine Ports Authority for ports and arrastre services and the Civil Aeronautics Board for air commerce.

---

[2] Available at: http://www.asean.org/publications/HandbookonCompetition.zip.

Table 2.1 Current state of competition laws in ASEAN countries

Philippines	Competition clauses in: • Philippine Constitution (1987) • Revised Penal Code of the Philippines (1930) • Civil Code (1949) • Act to Prohibit Monopolies and Combinations in Restraint of Trade (1961) • Corporation Code (1980) • Price Act (1992) • Consumer Act (1992) Competition clauses in specific sectors: • Securities Act (1982) • General Banking Act (1948) • Retail Trade Liberalization Act (2000) • Executive orders for maritime industry, civil aviation, port services, telecoms, energy, water
Malaysia	Laws that regulate enterprise activities and protect consumer interests: • Control of Supplies Act (1961) • Companies Act (1965) • Hire Purchase Act (1967) • Trade Descriptions Act (1972) • Food Act (1983) • Direct Sales Act (1993) Competition clauses in specific sectors: • Electric Supply Act (1990) • Communication and Multimedia Act (1998)
Thailand	Trade Competition Act (1999) Price of Goods and Services Act (1999) Telecoms Business Act (2001)
Singapore	Competition Act (2004) Competition clauses in specific sectors: • Telecoms Act (1999) • Electricity Act (2001) • Gas Act (2001)
Indonesia	Law on the Prohibition of Monopolistic Practices and Unfair Business Competition (1999)
Vietnam	Competition Law (2004)
Laos	Prime Minister's Decree on Trade Competition (2004)
Cambodia	Criminal Law and Procedure Act (1992) Law of Procedure Act (1993)
Brunei Darussalam	Telecommunications Order (2001)
Myanmar	Special Investigation Administrative Board and the Bureau of Special Investigation Act (1951)

The Corporation Code of the Philippines covers the rules on mergers, consolidations and acquisitions, but does not address competition issues such as the possible abuse of dominant position arising from mergers and acquisitions.

These laws have been ineffective in addressing anti-competitive behavior mainly due to lack of enforcement. The laws have been hardly used or implemented, as may be seen in the lack of cases litigated in court against anti-competitive behavior. Since the laws are penal in nature, guilt must be proven beyond reasonable doubt, and hence the amount of evidence required so that the case may prosper is tremendous. The fines are also insufficient to deter would-be criminals.

Due to a lack of appreciation and political will to pass a comprehensive law, previous administrations never prioritized the legislation of proposed competition bills. As a result, the government has not been able to deal effectively with industries that are allegedly engaged in anti-competitive practices.

Case study: alleged cartel in the Philippine cement industry The Philippine cement industry was at one time highly regulated and protected through high tariff and non-tariff barriers. After liberalization and deregulation, industry concentration and price cost margins have remained high.

Shortly following the Asian crisis, a wave of mergers among foreign investors ensued. Soon afterwards, price increases were observed in the midst of excess supply and depressed demand in the industry.

Amidst accusations of cartel activities in the industry, the House of Representatives' Committee on Trade and Industry and the Department of Trade and Industry (DTI) immediately conducted investigations but no resolution of the issue was reached.

The industry was able to divert the government's attention from the cartel issue by filing an anti-dumping case against imports. The Tariff Commission (TC) failed to find sufficient evidence to prove that the industry suffered serious injury from imports. The DTI reversed the decision of the TC by granting safeguarding measures to protect the industry against imports. Thereafter, the Supreme Court voided the safeguard duty on imported cement.

2.2.2 Competition policy in Indonesia

In 1997 Indonesia agreed to enact an anti-monopoly law as part of the conditions imposed by the International Monetary Fund (IMF). The law, known as the Prohibition of Monopoly and Anti-Competitive Practice, was legislated in 1999 and has been in force since March 2000.

Indonesia's Anti-Monopoly Law is generally a standard anti-monopoly law covering basic elements such as monopolization, abuse of dominant position, integration, collusion, cartel and anti-competitive pricing strategy.

The government created the KPPU (Commission for the Supervision of Business Competition) as an independent institution with the authority to conduct supervision of business competition and impose sanctions in the form of administrative measures. The KPPU reports directly to the president and the parliament. So far, its tasks have focused not only on law enforcement but also on competition advocacy through its role in providing advice and recommendations to the government.

Indonesia is still in its adjustment phase in implementing its competition law. Some of the important issues it has continued to face include a weak competition culture in the country, resistance from lobby groups, a weak regulatory environment and legal infrastructure, lack of readiness by the court system to effectively implement the law, lack of competition expertise, and an inadequate academic infrastructure to conduct research and education on competition.

Indonesia's anti-monopoly law provides exemptions for cooperatives and small businesses as well as monopolies that are licensed by law through parliament. These exemptions have been controversial issues.

2.2.3 Competition policy in Thailand

Thailand introduced its fully-fledged competition law in 1999. Unlike in Indonesia, which passed its competition law under IMF conditionality, the decision to legislate the Trade Competition Act was made independently by the Thailand Parliament.

The Trade Competition Act of 1999 created the Trade Competition Commission as the agency responsible for the implementation of the law and the Office of Trade Competition Commission as the secretariat body. The Office resides within the Ministry of Commerce.

The Competition Act covers all the major substantive provisions on abuse of dominance, merger control, collusive practices and unfair trade practices. Besides a few horizontal restrictions, such as price fixing, quantity fixing and bid rigging, other restrictive practices are governed by a rule of reason.

The Act also provides exemptions for state enterprises, cooperatives and agricultural cooperatives, central and regional government agencies and other businesses stipulated by ministerial regulations.

The performance of the Thai Competition Commission has been described as dismal. Its poor track record can be attributed to factors including political intervention, lobbying by interest groups, legal loopholes, lack of human resources, inadequate funding and lack of transparency in administration.

Thailand's experience indicates that simply having a competition law is not sufficient to address competition problems. Political intervention, opposition from big business and institutional limitations have been major constraints to law enforcement and have paralyzed the competition agency. At the same time, state rules and regulations continue to serve as significant barriers to competition, especially in the services sector.

2.2.4 Competition policy in Singapore

Singapore's comprehensive law, known as the Competition Act, was legislated in October 2004 and its competition authority, the Competition Commission of Singapore (CCS), was established in January 2005.

The law prohibits anti-competitive agreements, abuse of dominant position, of one or more undertakings, and mergers and acquisitions that considerably lessen competition.

On 3 November 2009 the CCS announced its second infringement decision since the establishment of the Competition Act. This decision found that 16 express tour bus operators/agents and the Express Bus Agencies Association had contravened the Competition Act's provision on anti-competitive arrangements. The CCS imposed fines totaling nearly S$1.7 million (approximately US$1.23 million), a noticeable increase in financial penalties compared to those handed down to six pest-control companies in 2008 (the only other infringement finding in Singapore to date), where fines totaled little more than S$260 000 (approximately US$187 576).

On 12 January 2009, in order to eradicate cartel activities, the CCS introduced two procedural changes to its leniency program in an attempt to increase the ease of use and effectiveness of the system. With respect to mergers, five applications were made in the second half of 2007, seven applications were made in 2008 and three merger filings were made in 2009. It is expected that there will be an increase in competition law activity by the CCS this year, especially in relation to merger clearances. The CCS has yet to issue its first infringement notice for an abusive practice.

2.2.5 Competition policy in Malaysia

Malaysia has a new draft national competition law which is expected to be in force by January 2012. There is some similarity between the Singapore Competition Act and Malaysia's Fair Trade Practices Act. Both regimes will cover anti-competitive agreements and abuses of dominant position. The Malaysian regime, while not yet covering mergers, is also intended to prohibit unfair trade practices, which in Singapore are covered by legislation such as the Consumer Protection Fair Trading Act.

2.2.6 Competition policy in Vietnam

Vietnam is gradually being transformed from a socialist economy to a capitalist economy. Beginning in 1987, the government has introduced new foreign investment regulation to encourage the inflow of foreign direct investment. Vietnam's competition law has been effective since July 2005.

2.2.7 Competition policy in Laos

Laos has been declared a least developed country, where three-quarters of the population live in absolute poverty and are dependent on subsistence agriculture. The private sector is underdeveloped and foreign direct investment is relatively miniscule. However, recently there has been some attempt to introduce competitive bidding for hydroelectric projects. The telecommunications sector has also been liberalized. Although Laos is in an advanced stage of drafting a national competition law, it has not yet set up its competition agency.

2.2.8 Competition policy in Cambodia

Cambodia is also one of the least developed countries of the world, where more than 80 percent of the population live in rural areas and more than one-third live in absolute poverty. The economy is dominated by public monopolies, and growth has been dependent on foreign direct investment and textile exports. The services sector is large but underdeveloped and is best characterized as an informal sector. Growth is dependent on bilateral and multilateral aid and investment and trade. Similar to Laos, Cambodia is in an advanced stage of drafting a competition law.

2.2.9 Competition policy in Myanmar

Myanmar has been relatively isolated because of international economic sanctions applied against the military regime. It is a poor agrarian economy with very high levels of government intervention. Public monopolies are held by the military, which restricts entry into several sectors of the economy. The introduction of competition policy and law is premature given the political and economic problems that Myanmar currently faces.

2.2.10 Competition policy in Brunei

Brunei is an oil-rich economy that until the 1997 East Asian financial crisis did not see a reason to encourage foreign direct investment or enlarge its private sector. The government is dominant in the economy and operates several public monopolies. Recently there has been an effort to privatize non-strategic state-owned enterprises. The banking sector has been liberalized and is dominated by foreign banks. There has been an implicit recognition of the need for a competition policy but its implementation is not urgent as long as the economy can maintain its present standard of living with oil revenues.

Table 2.2 illustrates the discussion above and depicts the current status of competition laws in the ASEAN region.

3. CONCLUSION

Given that they are in the early stages of implementing their competition law, the ASEAN countries have faced some enforcement difficulties that demonstrate the complexities of designing and implementing effective competition law and competition policy. Some of the emerging issues in the development of competition policy in the ASEAN region include:

- lack of a culture of competition;
- resistance from various interest and lobby groups;
- inadequate regulatory and legal infrastructure, widespread corruption, poor corporate governance and lack of transparency;
- differences in competition policy objectives: consumer welfare versus efficiency;
- conflicts with other national policies such as selective protection; and
- differences in scope and coverage of competition laws with some countries having exemptions in certain activities.

Taking into account the wide differences in the ASEAN members' economic development and institutional capacity, an effective anti-monopoly system cannot be built overnight. It takes time for any country to develop a comprehensive competition regime and the regime will also need to be improved upon over time. But this should not discourage countries that are

Table 2.2 Competition laws in ASEAN

Country	Comprehensive competition law			Sectoral regulation	Unfair competition
	Anti-competitive agreements	Abuses of dominance	Merger control		
Brunei	No	No	No	Yes (e.g. telecoms)	No
Cambodia	No	No	No	No	No
Indonesia	Yes	Yes	Yes	No	Yes
Laos	No	No	No	No	No
Malaysia	Pending (targeted 2011)	Pending (targeted 2011)	No	Yes (e.g. media, energy, telecoms)	Pending (targeted 2011)
Myanmar	No	No	No	No	No
Philippines	No	No	No	Yes (e.g. telecoms, electricity, oil)	Yes
Singapore	Yes	Yes	Yes	Yes (e.g. telecoms, media, electricity, gas, post, airport)	Yes
Thailand	Yes	Yes	Yes	Yes (e.g. telecoms)	Yes
Vietnam	Yes	Yes	Yes	Yes (e.g. telecoms, electricity)	Yes

contemplating the legislation of a competition law. There already exists a wide understanding of the issue and its attendant problems, along with international best practices on competition policy and its implementation, and countries can draw from this in designing their own competition laws. The key challenge is finding the correct measures for the effective and judicious implementation of competition law.

Country experiences show the importance of administrative, legal, political and economic factors in the design and implementation of competition law and policy. Competition policy needs to be country specific, taking into consideration the current stage of a country's economic and industrial development as well as its institutional and governance capacity. Competition policy cannot be a uniform, one-size-fits-all policy that seeks to be appropriate for all developing countries.

It is recommended in the AEC Blueprint that the following pointers serve as ASEAN guidelines that member countries can take into account in crafting their competition policy, or fine-tuning what is already in place:

- Enact competition laws, as they can make positive contributions to economic growth, price stability, industry development, efforts at macroeconomic stabilization and consumer welfare.
- Pay special attention to the needs of small and medium enterprises, which may include technical assistance to domestic companies in preparing licensing arrangements with much larger international corporations.
- Adopt a relaxed or flexible approach to restraints on vertical arrangements, so as not to thwart innovations in establishing new distribution systems.
- Include misleading advertising, misrepresentation and fraud in competition laws to enhance consumer protection.
- Develop provisions directed explicitly at the abuse of intellectual property rights, as firms tend to hide behind them.
- Incorporate explicit provisions to ensure that all government business activities are adequately covered.
- Craft specific laws to address the special circumstances of industries undergoing regulatory reforms.
- Put in place explicit provisions that would empower competition agencies to handle the negative effects of local regulations on competition, for example inter-state trade barriers.
- Apply competition rules in regional trade agreements, instead of anti-dumping rules or subsidy-countervailing measures, which serve to restrict entry and lessen competition.
- Create provisions to address trans-border restrictive business practices (RBP) where the RBP activity takes place abroad with injury to consumers and industry in the home country through local counterparts.
- Work towards convergence in competition laws and cooperative efforts in the enforcement of such laws with member countries.
- Ensure that the legitimacy of the competition laws cannot be challenged under the existing laws in ASEAN.

- Publish guidelines and other information products that explain the main purposes of the key provisions.
- Develop a detailed program of work for the manpower of the competition agency to ensure smooth administration and effective enforcement.

Augmenting the role of competition law and the mechanisms for coordinating and handling competition matters between ASEAN member countries will require development. Among the issues that will need to be addressed are: (a) the nature and form of the relationship between member countries (on a bilateral and regional multilateral basis), such as memoranda of understanding and possibly treaties, especially between countries with significant trade and investment relations; and (b) the role that the ASEAN Secretariat could play as a regional body in terms of facilitating exchange of information to promote voluntary resolution of cases between two or more countries.

Differing levels of commitment to fostering competition through effective policy implementation may create an unlevel field and distort trade and investment between ASEAN member countries. Peer reviews have in other jurisdictions been found not only to identify areas where competition policy and law could be strengthened but also to buttress the mandate and role of competition authorities in the process of reforming economic policy regulations within countries. The peer review also provides a basis for sharing experiences and lessons among the ASEAN member countries.

BIBLIOGRAPHY

APEC (1999), *Study on Competition Laws for Developing Countries*, Singapore: APEC.

ASEAN Focus Group (1999), *Asian Analysis – Indonesia: An Uncertain Business Environment*, Canberra: ANU.

Association of Southeast Asian Nations (ASEAN) (1999), *Hanoi Plan of Action*, Jakarta: ASEAN Secretariat.

Budzinski, O. (2003), *Pluralism and Competition Policy Paradigms and the Call for Regulatory Diversity*, New York: New York University.

Choudry, A. (2003), 'Proposed WTO Competition Policy Agreement', ZNET, 24 August.

Choudry, A. (2003), 'WTO Competition Policy: Another Corporate Steal?', available at: http://www.scoop.co.nz/stories/HL0308/S00117.htm.

Christopher, W. (2003), *Statement by His Excellency Mr. Warren Christopher, Secretary of State of the United States of America*, Jakarta: ASEAN Secretariat.

Coase, R.H. (1991), *The Institutional Structure of Production*, Lecture to the Memory of Alfred Nobel, 9 December.

Cobb, C. (1999), 'Review of: *From Posner to Post-Modernism* by Mercero and Medema', *The School of Cooperative Individualism*, January.

Cook, P. (2002), *Competition Policy, Market Power and Collusion in Developing Countries*, Center on Regulation and Competition, Working Paper Series, Paper Number 33, University of Manchester.

Demsetz, H. (1979), *Industrial Concentration and the Market System*, Washington, DC: American Bar Association Press.

Devuyst, Y. (2000), 'Toward a Multilateral Competition Policy Regime', *Global Governance*, **6** (3), 319–339.

Dixit, A. (1982), 'Recent Developments in Oligopoly Theory', *The American Economic Review*, **72**, 12–17.

Gifford, D.J. and M. Matsushita (1996), 'Antitrust for Competition Laws Viewed in a Trading Context: Harmony or Dissonance', in J. Bhagwati and R.E. Hudec, *Fair Trade and Harmonization*, Volume 2, Cambridge, MA: The MIT Press.

'Government Draft Rules on Unfair Trade Practices', *The Nation*, 22 April 1999.

Hylleberg, S. and P.B. Overgaard (1998), *Competition Policy with a Coasian Prior?* Department of Economics, University of Aarhus, Denmark.

International Monetary Fund (IMF) (1997), *Letter of Intent, Indonesia*, 31 October, Washington, DC: International Monetary Fund.

Kerr, I.A. and M. Wood (2000), 'Globalization and Competition Policy: Policies for the Developing and Transitional Economies of Asia', paper presented at the EAMSA Conference on Globalization and the Uniqueness of Asia, INSEAD Campus, Singapore, 23–25 November.

Khemani, R.S. and M. Dutz (1995), 'The Instruments of Competition Policy and their Relevance for Economic Development', in C. Frischtak (ed.), *Regulatory Policies and Reform: A Comparative Analysis*, Washington, DC: The World Bank.

Lea, G. (1999), 'Who the Heck Is ... Judge Richard Posner', *The Register*, 22 November.

Lee, M. and C. Morand (2003), 'Competition Policy in the WTO and FTAA: A Trojan Horse for International Trade Negotiations', available at: http://www.ic.gc.ca/app/oca/crd/dcmnt.do?id=745&lang=eng.

Lipczynski, J. and J.O.S. Wilson (2001), *Industrial Organization: An Analysis of Competitive Markets*, London: Financial Times, Pearson.

Lloyd, P.J. and Associates (2001), 'Harmonizing Competition and Investment Policies in the East Asian Region', paper presented at the Third Asia Development Forum on Regional Economic Cooperation in Asia and the Pacific, organized by the Asian Development Bank, 11–14 June, Bangkok.

Maddock, R. (1995), 'Australian Lessons in Implementing Competition Reform', *Economic Papers*, **14** (3), 31–40.

Malaysian Institute of Economic Research (MIER) (2008), *Competition Policy in ASEAN: Thematic Studies*, ERIA Joint Research Series No. 5, Chiba: IDE-JETRO.

New Internationalist (2002), 'The Facts', Issue 347 (July), available at: http://www.newint.org/features/2002/07/05/facts/.

Noland, M. (1999), *Competition Policy and FDI: A Solution in Search of a Problem?* Institute for International Economics, Working Paper, 99–3.

OECD (2002), *The Relationship between Regional Trade Agreements and the Multilateral Trading System: Competition*, Paris: OECD.

Oh, Celia (n.d.) 'Trade and Competition Policy in the WTO', available at: http://www.twnside.org.sg/title/cancun5.doc.

Schleifer, A. and R.W. Vishny (1998), *The Grabbing Hand, Government Pathologies and their Cures*, Cambridge, MA: Harvard University Press.

Schumpeter, J. (1954), *Capitalism, Socialism and Democracy*, London: Unwin.

Singleton, R.C. (1997), 'Competition Policy for Developing Countries: A Long-Run Entry-Based Approach', *Contemporary Economic Policy*, **15** (2), 1–11.

Smith, A. (1776), *An Inquiry into the Nature and Causes of the Wealth of Nations*, London: Methuen.

Stigler, G. (1966), *The Theory of Price*, New York: Macmillan.

Stigler, G. (1989), *Memoirs of an Unregulated Economist*, New York: Basic Books.

Stigler, J.G. (1989), 'Two Notes on the Coase Theorem', *Yale Law Journal*, **99** (3), 631–633.

The Bank of Sweden Prize in Economic Sciences in Memory of Alfred Nobel (1991), available at: http://www.nobelprize.org/nobel_prizes/economics/laureates/1991/.

Third World Network, *The Singapore Issues – Rhetoric and Reality* (reference in G. Sivalingam, *Competition Policy in ASEAN*, available at: http://www.incsoc.net/asean-rep.doc.

Williamson, J. (2002), *Did the Washington Consensus Fail?*, Washington, DC: Institute for International Affairs.

Williamson, J. (2004), 'The Washington Consensus as a Policy Prescription for Development', lecture in the series 'Practitioners for Development', delivered at the World Bank on 13 January, Institute for International Economics.

World Bank (1993), *The East Asian Miracle*, New York: Oxford University Press.

World Bank (2001), *World Development Report, 2001*, Washington, DC: World Bank.

World Trade Organization (WTO) (2004), *Trade and Competition Policy*, Geneva: WTO.

Yasuda, N. (2000), 'ASEAN Competition Laws: Current Status and Future Perspectives', Graduate School of International Development, Nagoya University. Paper presented at ASEAN Workshop: Making Markets Work, hosted by the Australian Competition and Consumer Commission, 6 March, Bangkok.

3. Southern African Development Community (SADC) regional competition policy

Gladmore Mamhare

1. BACKGROUND

The Southern African Development Community (SADC) has been in existence since 1980, when it was formed as a loose alliance of nine[1] states in Southern Africa known as the Southern African Development Coordination Conference (SADCC), with the aim of coordinating development projects. It was transformed into a Development Community in 1992, when the Declaration and Treaty was signed, thereby giving the organization a legal character. The SADC now consists of 15 member states.[2]

The total population of the SADC was 277 million people in 2010 and its total gross domestic product (GDP) was US$577 billion.[3] South Africa is the biggest economy in the Community, with a GDP of over US$282 billion, representing about 65 percent of the total SADC market. The largest country in terms of population is the Democratic Republic of Congo, with a population of about 61 million. In contrast, Botswana, Seychelles, Mauritius, Namibia and Swaziland each have populations of two million or less. The per capita GDP also varies widely, ranging from as high as US$7690 to as low as US$160. The average per capita GDP for the SADC region in 2010 was US$2074. The average growth in 2008 was 4.5 percent and declined to 2.7 percent in 2009, most likely due to the global financial crisis.

---

[1] Angola, Botswana, Lesotho, Malawi, Mozambique, Swaziland, United Republic of Tanzania, Zambia and Zimbabwe.

[2] Angola, Botswana, Democratic Republic of Congo, Lesotho, Madagascar, Malawi, Mauritius, Mozambique, Namibia, Seychelles, South Africa, Swaziland, United Republic of Tanzania, Zambia and Zimbabwe.

[3] All statistics in this section are from internal documents of the SADC Secretariat.

The SADC common agenda is based on various principles, such as development orientation, market integration and development, facilitation and promotion of trade and investment, and variable geometry. In pursuit of its development agenda, the SADC adopted milestones to facilitate the establishment of the SADC Free Trade Area (FTA) by 2008, the Customs Union by 2010, the Common Market by 2015, Monetary Union by 2016 and the single currency by 2018. The SADC Free Trade Area was launched in 2008. Whilst work towards the attainment of the Customs Union has progressed, the 2010 deadline for establishing an SADC Customs Union turned out to be unattainable; consultations were still in progress as of late 2011. A landmark development was the decision by the Tripartite Summit of Heads of State and Government of the members of the Common Market for Eastern and Southern Africa (COMESA), the East African Community (EAC) and the SADC in 2008 to establish a Free Trade Area encompassing the three regional economic communities. Studies to inform the tripartite arrangement have been undertaken and the recommendations are being considered.

2. STATUS OF COMPETITION LAW AND POLICY IN SADC MEMBER COUNTRIES

The 15 SADC member states are at different levels of development and implementation of competition laws and policies. They broadly fall into four categories as follows:

(i) *Category I*: countries with operational competition regimes; Mauritius, Namibia, Seychelles, Swaziland, Malawi, South Africa, Tanzania, Zambia and Zimbabwe. The focus now in these countries is on strengthening enforcement capacity.
(ii) *Category II*: countries that have passed laws that have not yet gone into effect; Madagascar and Botswana. Current activities include technical assistance to operationalize the competition agencies.
(iii) *Category III*: countries actively preparing competition laws; Lesotho and Mozambique. Draft Bills are now in place.
(iv) *Category IV*: countries in early stages of preparation; DR Congo and Angola. Current activities include advocacy programs to raise awareness and highlight the importance of formulating competition laws and policies.

The policy context and background to the development of national competition laws in SADC countries are wider and more diverse. In some countries competition law was developed as part of the government's program of liberalization and economic reform, to some extent under pressure from donors; in other cases it was a direct result of studies that had identified restrictive practices of private businesses.

In the category of operational competition regimes, the enforcement experience varies widely, with countries such as South Africa, Zambia and Zimbabwe boasting well over ten years' experience. In the same category, one also finds countries such as the Seychelles, which recently established its competition agency and commenced operations in 2010. South Africa's competition regime is by far the most developed among the SADC member states.

In addition to the varying levels of development and implementation of competition laws in the region, there is also the complex dimension of the different national competition law models adopted. They differ sharply in terms of both structure and substantive provisions as elaborated in the following paragraphs.

South Africa is believed to have the best structure, comprising three separate and independent institutions – namely, the Competition Commission, the Competition Tribunal and the specialized Competition Appeal Court. Most of the other countries have a unitary competition authority with a division of investigative and adjudicative functions between a board of commissioners and a secretariat. The competition laws of some countries, notably Zambia, Tanzania, Zimbabwe and Malawi, also include provisions on consumer protection, with one institution responsible for the administration of both.

The degree of autonomy and independence enjoyed by competition institutions in terms of funding and decision making varies across countries. In some legislations, there is a larger role for ministers than is now usual. The appointment processes, procedures and tenure of office for senior officers and board members also differ from country to country.

Though the substantive provisions may differ in terms of specific issues, such as objectives, scope of application, definitions, clear distinction between 'rule of reason' and 'per se' prohibitions, sanctions, remedies and appeal mechanisms, all the competition laws have core provisions to deal with anti-competitive agreements, abuse of dominance and merger control.

One common feature of most competition laws in the region is the inclusion of provisions on 'public interest considerations'. This means that substantive assessment of the competitive effects of a merger or conduct is weighed against likely benefits or gains (social benefits), such as employment or other strategic factors. This is not surprising given that competition policy is regarded as a development tool and is often used to achieve a wide range of objectives, including social goals.

There has been a fair amount of interaction and voluntary cooperation among the agencies, and, as a result of this, one finds some resemblances in the laws of some countries. For example, the Malawian competition law is closely modeled on the current Zambian law, while the Namibian law is closely modeled on the South African law. Cooperation between competition authorities in the review of mergers that fall within their respective jurisdictions has been common. For example, during the examination of the global mergers of Coca-Cola/Cadbury Schweppes and British American Tobacco/Rothmans of Pall Mall, the competition authorities of Zimbabwe and Zambia worked together.

Competition agencies have played an increasingly influential[4] role in recent years, particularly in countries with a long history of enforcement. In South Africa, conglomerates were restructured to focus on their core functions and more firms entered the banking, steel and other sectors. Cartels were exposed in the bread, milling, steel and milk industries largely due to the successful implementation of the leniency program.

Zambia witnessed more competitive markets, stable prices and wider consumer choice, though the challenge has been dealing with international mergers with subsidiaries in more than one country. Zimbabwe, before its economic challenges, witnessed increased employment, export earnings, more foreign direct investment and dismantling of monopolies and collusive activities in several sectors.

An analysis of 2008/2009 annual reports for most countries shows that merger cases top the list of competition offenses, followed by abuse of dominance cases and collusion cases. Detecting cartels has proved to be complex except in South Africa because of the Corporate Leniency Policy recently introduced there.

Based on enforcement experience and international best practices, deficiencies have been identified in some competition laws, especially in the old regimes. For example, South Africa reviewed its law to enable it to deal with complex monopoly situations and criminalize cartels, among other major

---

[4] Report of the First SADC Regional Training Workshop on Competition Law and Policy, held in Gaborone, Botswana, August 2008; and presentations on the impact of competition law and policy in South Africa, Zambia and Zimbabwe by representatives of their respective competition commissions.

amendments.[5] In Zambia the law is being reviewed in order to make it more comprehensive and align it with international best practices, and Zimbabwe is also reviewing its law for the second time to provide for the separation of adjudicative and investigative functions and to make it more comprehensive.[6]

The major challenge currently facing many competition agencies still remains the lack of enforcement capacity due to the limited number of experienced staff capable of analyzing complex cases and inadequate budgetary support from central government.

3. SADC REGIONAL COMPETITION POLICY: OBJECTIVES AND CURRENT STATUS

According to UNCTAD,[7] competition provisions in regional trade agreements (RTAs) have many objectives. An often-stated objective is that such provisions are needed so that the benefits of trade and investment liberalization are not compromised by cross-border anti-competitive practices. With the opening of domestic markets to foreign competition, countries become susceptible to anti-competitive practices originating outside their national borders. These include cross-border competition concerns, international cartels and mergers and acquisitions that risk monopolizing or creating dominant power in the internal market. To ensure that full benefits of trade liberalization are realized, complementary measures to liberalizing trade policies must be taken in the area of competition policy.

A second reason for including competition provisions in RTAs is to create region-wide competition policies and institutions that seek greater levels of integration. If parties to an agreement are seeking an integrated common market, as envisaged under the SADC, then anti-competitive practices must not replace government-implemented restrictive schemes within the integrated market if the initiative is to bear fruit.

---

[5] PowerPoint presentation by participants from the South Africa Competition Commission at the First SADC Regional Training Workshop on Competition Law and Policy; see *supra* n. 4.

[6] PowerPoint presentation by participants from Zambia and Zimbabwe at the First SADC Regional Training Workshop on Competition Law and Policy; see *supra* n. 4.

[7] UNCTAD (2005), *Competition Provisions in Regional Trade Agreements: How to Assure Development Gains*. New York and Geneva: United Nations.

The promotion of trade and investment within SADC regional integration has placed increasing emphasis on the development of appropriate competition policy regimes.

Competition policy is provided for in the SADC Protocol on Trade, which came into force in 2000. Article 25 of the Protocol on Trade provides that 'Member States shall implement measures within the Community that prohibit unfair business practices and promote competition'. The provisions of Article 25 have been interpreted to embrace two concepts: (i) competition law, and (ii) consumer protection law. Also, the Protocol acknowledges that the establishment of a framework of trade cooperation among member states based on equity, fair competition and mutual benefit will contribute to the creation of a viable Development Community in Southern Africa.

Work on the SADC regional competition policy only commenced in earnest in July 2008 following approval by the region's trade ministers of a draft Declaration on Regional Cooperation in Competition Law and Consumer Policy. The Declaration was subsequently signed by the SADC heads of state and government in September 2009.

In noting the status, then, of competition law and policy in member states, and further noting that only five member states had operational competition regimes, SADC decided to adopt a *cooperation model* as opposed to establishing a supranational competition authority. The adopted cooperation model requires that all member states (or at least a critical mass) adopt and enforce competition law in tandem with the implementation of the integration agenda. SADC member states agreed to cooperate in the application of their respective competition and consumer laws.

The Declaration provides for effective cooperation and the establishment of a Competition and Consumer Law and Policy Committee/Forum. The main purpose of the Committee/Forum, which was formally established in August 2008, is to implement the formalized system of cooperation and also serve as:

(i) a forum for discussion, exchange of experience, consensus building and cooperation of the 15 member states' competition and consumer authorities;
(ii) a forum to promote dialogue and networking between competition policy makers and law enforcers and the identification of best practices in competition and consumer laws;
(iii) a forum to facilitate research, policy analysis and data collection;
(iv) a forum to facilitate provision of technical assistance tailored to the

specific requirements of member states, especially those yet to develop and adopt competition and consumer laws.

The need for a regional competition policy framework came from the realization that competition and consumer protection laws are national but the relevant markets can extend beyond national boundaries. It was also noted that the cross-border effects of business activities were increasing with the growing integration of SADC economies, market liberalization and globalization. This brings with it the risk that anti-competitive practices will likewise cross frontiers. Enterprises active in one market may seek to erect their own barriers to the free functioning of markets once official barriers are removed. They may also seek to exploit ill-informed consumers and thus cut away the benefits that should come from a wider range of choice in their transactional dealings. A regional competition framework will improve the climate for domestic, cross-border and foreign investment. It will also contribute to the improvement and effective implementation of competition policies by member states as an integral part of their economic reforms at the national and regional levels.

Effectively applied, national laws will be the first line of defense or means of reacting to anti-competitive practices that inhibit the full enjoyment of the opportunities from liberalized trade. But such national laws are designed to deal with anti-competitive practices that take place within a national jurisdiction, and that adversely affect domestic consumers. Most, if not all, competition laws in the region explicitly exclude from their scope those anti-competitive practices that have no effect on the domestic market. They need to be supplemented by initiatives at regional level. There is no legal basis to investigate firms located in another country without the explicit consent and, preferably, cooperation of that country.

A regional framework provides for a mechanism for technical cooperation among national competition and consumer agencies, the strengthening of information exchange, consultations and joint operations in the enforcement of competitive standards and the thwarting of anti-competitive practices at the bilateral and regional levels. Competition and consumer authorities must cooperate in order to successfully identify and prosecute cross-border anti-competitive practices.

Given the short period that the regional competition policy program has been in existence, not much has happened. The Competition and Consumer Law and Policy Committee/Forum has only met twice to deliberate mainly on administrative issues associated with the formation of the Committee. The Committee agreed to meet at least once a year and a serious network of cooperation on actual competition issues commenced in 2011, now that there is a critical mass of operational competition authorities in the region.

The Committee adopted a phased regional policy program roadmap covering the period 2008–12. The focus in this period will be on capacity building and cooperation in the enforcement, harmonization and soft convergence of laws. One of the key functions of the SADC Secretariat during this period will be to facilitate the development and implementation of competition laws in the member states through capacity building and technical assistance. In this regard, the Secretariat over the last two years has organized two regional training workshops on competition policy, deployed short-term experts to new competition authorities and mobilized resources from cooperating partners to support development and implementation of competition policy in member states.

4. REGIONAL COMPETITION PROBLEMS

There can be little doubt that cross-border competition problems are widespread in SADC member countries. Some of the anti-competitive practices and unfair trade practices cited as common in the SADC region include:

(i) the inability of firms to access supply chains in new/foreign markets;
(ii) bid-rigging;
(iii) cartels;
(iv) the selection of a single distribution channel by a dominant firm;
(vi) deceitful, misleading representations and product safety standards;
(vii) mergers and acquisitions involving multinational companies operating in more than one SADC country, e.g. British American Tobacco/Rothmans of Pall Mall, Coca-Cola/Cadbury Schweppes, Total/Mobil, etc. There have also been a lot of mergers involving big and dominant South African firms.

South Africa's economic leadership in the region is well documented and accepted. The competition authority of South Africa has uncovered, and in some cases prosecuted and issued fines to cartels in the steel, pharmaceutical, milling and airline industries, among others. Most of the firms involved have subsidiaries in other SADC countries. What remains to be proved is whether their subsidiaries have also engaged in cartel activities. There have also been allegations of abuse of dominance by large South African firms operating in other SADC countries.

As part of the process of consolidating the SADC Free Trade Area, and to address all forms of barriers to trade including those in the area of competition policy, the SADC Secretariat recently embarked on an assessment exercise of the existence of, and possible remedies for, cross-border anti-competitive business practices. Though the assessment is not yet complete, similar allegations of cartels and abuse of dominance by South African firms in the fertilizer, construction, and food and beverage sectors have been made. The challenge, should these allegations be proved true, is how to address the practices in the absence of regional competition regulations/law. These challenges seem insurmountable, especially when one considers the different sizes and levels of development within SADC and the absence of competition law in some countries.

There have also been allegations of market allocation arrangements in the SADC region by multinational companies operating in the motor vehicle, cement and other industries. Other related issues, though in the area of consumer protection, are expired products, substandard goods and counterfeit products flooding the region. These are only some of the areas where the SADC Secretariat intends to institute studies in order to establish the nature and extent of the problem in the region.

5. CONCLUSION AND THE WAY FORWARD

The importance of competition law and the benefits of competitive markets, at least in the abstract, are now well appreciated in the SADC region. The fact that the few remaining member states without competition laws are now actively preparing their respective laws is concrete evidence that the region is now ready for a paradigm shift. Appropriate technical assistance will continue to be offered to member states to develop competition legislation and strengthen enforcement capacity. To be effective, the agreed cooperation model requires the active participation of every competition agency, particularly in cases with cross-border effects. The competition committee/forum will develop arrangements and ground rules, for instance, to deal with issues such as the notification of cases to other member states, the exchange of information and the coordination of investigations.

Overarching all these issues is the biggest challenge, that of the conflicting interests of different SADC member states in the way the law is applied, given their diversity and the different stages of their development, that is, the challenges of bringing together unequal partners. The SADC Secretariat has already embarked on a process of harmonizing the national laws. The first step in contributing to the harmonization process was the preparation of a manual for competition authorities, or the guide book or reference book now being used in member states for case investigation and analysis. The second stage will involve engagement of a consultant to prepare a harmonization framework. The exercise will entail identification of areas to be harmonized, for example, systems and procedures. The objective will be to ensure that member countries are in a position to implement the provisions of Article 25, whatever the differences in the structure of national laws; certain common core features must be included in the laws and enforced to an acceptable common standard.

The question of whether SADC will continue with its cooperation model or graduate to a higher and more binding level of developing regional competition regulations or law enforced by a supranational regional authority will be guided by a study to be undertaken and other developments taking place within the context of the SADC-EAC-COMESA tripartite arrangements. The three regional economic groupings have agreed to work together and implement joint programs in trade, customs and economic liberalization, among other areas. The draft tripartite agreement already expresses the need to establish a Tripartite Competition Forum.

4. Competition policy in the SADC: a South African perspective

Kasturi Moodaliyar

1. INTRODUCTION

The South African Competition Act[1] has been in effect since September 1999. Over the past ten years, competition law and policy have grown in stature and the competition authorities have become a respected force to be reckoned with.

The South African story of competition implementation took a dynamic turn with the change of government in the 1990s. It was recognized that, due to our previous apartheid laws, industries were favoured based on racial bias. These laws allowed for a high concentration of white-owned firms in formal domestic markets and a separate and rather informal trade restricted to the black population.[2] This separate and unequal duality thus hindered the ability of *all* citizens to compete fairly in the domestic and international economic markets.

In order to redress the injustices of the past, the 1998 Act was promulgated to promote a wider spread of ownership, with special attention given to those who had previously been disadvantaged, as well as on the promotion of economic efficiency in South Africa.[3] The purpose of the Act is to promote and maintain competition in South Africa in order to:

(a) promote the efficiency, adaptability and development of the economy;
(b) provide consumers with competitive prices and product choices;

---

[1] Act 89 of 1998 (as amended); hereinafter referred to as the '1998 Act'.
[2] See also Hartzenberg, T. (2004), 'Competition Policy and Enterprise Development: Experience from South Africa' (August), available at: http://www.competition-regulation.org.uk/conferences/southafrica04/Hartzenberg.pdf
[3] Preamble to the 1998 Act, p. 2.

(c) promote employment and advance the social and economic welfare of South Africans;
(d) expand opportunities for South African participation in world markets and recognize the role of foreign competition in the Republic;
(e) ensure that small and medium-sized enterprises have equal opportunities to participate in the economy; and
(f) promote a greater spread of ownership, in particular to increase the ownership stakes of historically disadvantaged persons.[4]

To fulfil these aspirations the 1998 Act also created three institutions. The Competition Commission employs *inter alia* lawyers and economists to investigate the competitiveness of mergers that fall within the Act's threshold and it investigates restrictive practice complaints that are filed with the Commission. The Commission has two core divisions, namely Mergers and Acquisitions, and Enforcement and Exemptions (which investigates restrictive practices). Other divisions assisting are the Legal Services, Policy and Research Division (economists who assist with investigations) and the Strategy and Stakeholder Relations Division (dealing with compliance, advocacy and international and media relations). The Commission can compel parties to furnish information either by letter of request or summons, or it can exercise its powers to search and seize evidence (i.e. dawn raids). Once the Commission has concluded its investigation, it then makes recommendations to the Competition Tribunal, which adjudicates on the cases.

The Tribunal has the power to conduct hearings, which include requesting documents and having witnesses testify under oath, and it may grant interim relief or deliver judgement after conducting the hearing. Firms can be fined up to 10 per cent of their annual turnover should they be found to be in contravention of the Act. The third institution created by the Act is the Competition Appeal Court (CAC), which is comprised of specialist high court judges. Cases from the Tribunal can be reviewed or appealed at the CAC. The CAC has heard appeals on both substantive and procedural issues and has dealt with over 60 cases to date.

The respect for these competition authorities has arisen due to their independence from each other and from the state when it comes to their decision making and the manner in which cases have been investigated and decided.

---

[4] Section 2 of the 1998 Act.

Before engaging with the question of whether regional competition policy would benefit the countries of the Southern African Development Community (SADC), it is imperative that each member country work towards implementing its own policy and achieving a functional agency with adequate capacity and capabilities. It will help the harmonization process if there is a common goal in mind.

This chapter focuses on South Africa and its developments over the last ten years, from which lessons can be learned by our fellow SADC members. The historical, economic and political context of South Africa has resonance in its competition policy. The consideration of the public interest in merger evaluation is a striking example. I describe below how this provision has been dealt with by the competition authorities. The competition agencies have also made significant progress in the last five years with regard to enforcing prohibited practices. In addition to the provisions of the Act, the Commission has also used the corporate leniency policy as a tool to detect cartels. The revised policy has been quite successful in uncovering cartels in a variety of industries. I focus here on South Africa's involvement in the SADC region especially with regard to the technical assistance and development of competition law within the region.

I then explore the possibility of the SADC incorporating a regional competition authority and the numerous concerns that this hypothesis may raise. This section does not provide any definitive answers, save the observation that member states in this region may not be prepared for a regional authority but rather work towards a strengthened national authority through greater regional cooperation.

I show that regional integration of competition law is not an easy feat. It requires contributions from stakeholders in each individual member country. The challenges that member countries face may be similar or different, but the basic principles of competition law, which enhances efficiency and creates product choice and innovation as well as competitive prices, can be achieved through cooperation.

2. PUBLIC INTEREST

A feature of the 1998 Act that arose due to the uniqueness of South Africa's political and economic history was the introduction of public interest considerations in merger analysis. All mergers that meet the required asset and turnover threshold as stipulated in the Competition Regulations have to file a compulsory pre-merger notification. Competition authorities evaluate whether the merger is likely to result in a substantial prevention or lessening of competition. If this is proved then the merging parties bear the onus to show whether there are any efficiency, technological or pro-competitive gains that outweigh the anti-competitive effect. The balancing test does not end there. On a separate account, the analysis goes a step further to determine whether there are any public interest considerations that arise as a result of the merger. This means that regardless of the outcome of the balancing test, it is possible for a merger to be prohibited if it fails on public interest grounds alone.[5] To ensure that proper consideration of the public interest is taken, the merging parties have to notify the affected trade unions and employees of the intended merger. The trade unions and other third-party interveners have the option to approach the competition authorities and make their submissions.

The Act stipulates:

> When determining whether a merger can or cannot be justified on public interest grounds, the Competition Commission or the Competition Tribunal must consider the effect that the merger will have on–
>
> (a) a particular industrial sector or region;
> (b) employment;
> (c) the ability of *small businesses*, or *firms* controlled or owned by historically disadvantaged persons, to become competitive; and
> (d) the ability of national industries to compete in international markets.[6]

To date there have been no cases that have been prohibited on public interest grounds alone. However, there have been a number of cases in which, in order to minimize the negative impact, the mergers were approved with conditions. These conditions are usually due to public interest considerations; in many cases, to reduce the number of job losses or to promote black economic empowerment.[7] Table 4.1 indicates that in the last financial year there have been a number of job losses in connection with merger activity. This could also be attributed to the global recession, which led to a downturn in the South African economy.

---

[5] See also *Anglo American Holdings Limited/Kumba Resources Limited (Industrial Development Corporation Intervening)*, Competition Tribunal case number 46/LM/Jun02 [2003] ZACT 4, 4 September 2003.

[6] Section 12A(3) of the 1998 Act.

[7] See *Shell South Africa (Pty) Ltd/Tepco Petroleum (Pty) Ltd*, Competition Tribunal case number 66/LM/Oct01.

Table 4.1 Job losses arising from mergers during the financial year 2009/2010

Primary acquiring firm	Primary target firm	Status	Sector	Effect on employment	Type
Bidpaper Plus	Pretoria Wholesale Stationers	Approved	Wholesale	24 job losses	15 skilled, 9 unskilled
Aquarius Platinum	Ridge Mining	Approved	Mining	8 job losses	skilled
Invicta Holdings	Criterion Equipment	Conditionally approved	Renting	117 job losses	11 skilled, 106 unskilled
ApexHi Properties	Ambit Properties	Approved	Property	10 job losses	skilled
Phomella Property Investments	Agri South Africa	Approved	Property	28 job losses	1 skilled, 27 unskilled
Redefine Income Fund	ApexHi Properties and Madison Property Fund Managers Holdings	Approved	Property	5 job losses	skilled
Shoden Data Systems	Faritec Holdings	Approved	IT	110 job losses	skilled
Astrapak Gauteng	The Flexpack business of Nampak Products	Approved	Packaging	138 job losses	unskilled
Imperial Group	The Midas Group	Conditionally approved	Retail	58 job losses	18 skilled, 40 unskilled
Tiger Consumer Brands and Tiger Food Brands Intellectual	The mayonnaise business of Nestlé South Africa	Approved	Manufacturing	8 jobs gained	unskilled

Primary acquiring firm	Primary target firm	Status	Sector	Effect on employment	Type
MIH Internet Africa	Korbitec	Approved	IT	20 job losses	skilled
Government Employees Medical Schemes	Medical Scheme for Correctional Services	Approved	Health	2 job losses	skilled
Harmony Gold Mining Company	Pamodzi Gold Free State	Approved	Mining	1600 job losses	unskilled
Nedbank	Imperial Bank	Approved	Finance	464 job losses	unskilled
Net1 Applied Technologies South Africa	MediKredit Integrated Healthcare Solutions	Approved	IT	24 job losses	23 skilled, 1 unskilled
Liberty Star Consumer Holdings	A&S Food Distributors	Approved	Wholesale	6 job losses	skilled
S.A. Leisure	Cadac	Approved	Retail	10 job losses	9 skilled, 1 unskilled
ARB Electrical Wholesalers	The Peragon group of companies	Approved	Wholesale	13 job losses	skilled

Source: Competition Commission South Africa, available at: http://www.compcom.co.za/merger-and-acquisition-activity-update/

The competition authorities have tried to minimize the impact in most of the merger cases over the last year. However, there are two cases indicated in Table 4.1 that had quite a grave effect on employment.

In the merger between Harmony Gold Mining Company and Pamodzi Gold Free State the Tribunal found that the merger would not substantially prevent or lessen competition. However, the merger did result in the loss of 1600 jobs, rather than the 3606 employees who could have lost their jobs if the merger had not been approved. Two trade unions representing employees of Pamodzi Gold negotiated a settlement with Harmony whereby Harmony undertook to re-employ 2400 employees within 24 months. The Competition Tribunal approved the merger subject to this condition.

The other case that had a major impact in terms of job loss was the merger of Nedbank and Imperial Bank, which was approved subject to conditions by the Tribunal. There were 464 job losses as a result of the merger (260 were permanent employees and 204 were temporary employees). The Tribunal took into consideration that this represented less than 1 per cent of the entire workforce of the merging parties. Also, many of the permanent employees who faced retrenchment were skilled and had extensive work experience and so were likely to find employment at other companies. The union also agreed to redeploy and re-skill staff in order to reduce the job-loss effect. The Tribunal made this agreement a condition of the merger.

These cases of high job losses may be exceptional; however, it is a concern when unskilled or semi-skilled employees lose their jobs, as it is more difficult for them to find similar employment. These are factors that the competition authorities have been considering and it is worth examining alternative options when unavoidable job losses are on the table.

By incorporating these non-competition factors such as public interest considerations into competition policy and legislation, socio-economic factors, which drive government objectives, can also be achieved.[8] This is a model for other developing countries that face similar consumer and workforce issues. It should also not simply be imported into legislation without being properly considered.[9]

---

[8] Chetty, V. (2005), 'The Place of Public Interest in South Africa's Competition Legislation: Some Implications for International Antitrust Convergence', paper presented at the American Bar Association Section of Antitrust Law 53rd Spring Meeting, Washington DC, 30 March–1 April 2005, available at: http://apps.americanbar.org/antitrust/at-committees/at-ic/pdf/spring/05/aba-paper.pdf.

[9] Afifa, T., J. Berger and T. Hartzenberg (2006), 'The Ability of Select Sub-Saharan African Countries to Utilise TRIPS Flexibilities and Competition Law to Ensure a Sustainable Supply of Essential Medicines: A Study of Producing and Importing Countries', available at: http://www.iprsonline.org/unctadictsd/docs/Trade%20and%20Competition%2030%203%2006%20final%20Edit1%20_2_%20_2_.pdf.

3. ENFORCING RESTRICTIVE PRACTICES PROVISIONS IN THE COMPETITION ACT

The Competition Act prohibits restrictive horizontal practices,[10] restrictive vertical practices,[11] abuse of a firm's dominant position[12] and price discrimination.[13] The Commission has a year within which to investigate complaints or for the Commissioner to initiate a complaint. Once the investigation is complete, and it is found that there is a contravention of the Act, the case is referred to the Tribunal for a hearing. Table 4.2 is a record of the number of cases investigated by the Commission in the last year.

Table 4.2 Restrictive practice cases under investigation for financial year 2009/2010

Number of complaints received from the public	Number of cases initiated by the Commission	Number of cases carried over from previous years	Total
172	31	86	289

Source: Competition Commission South Africa Annual Report 2009/2010, available at: http://www.compcom.co.za/assets/Publications/Annual-Reports/Annual-Report-2009–10-Final.pdf

Table 4.3 The outcome of cases investigated for the financial year 2009/2010

Cases recommended for referral to the Tribunal	Cases that were non-referred at screening	Cases that were non-referred after further investigation	Cases withdrawn	Consent agreements
27	102	15	6	6

Source: Competition Commission South Africa Annual Report 2009/2010, available at: http://www.compcom.co.za/assets/Publications/Annual-Reports/Annual-Report-2009–10-Final.pdf

[10] Section 4 of the 1998 Act.
[11] Section 5 of the 1998 Act.
[12] Section 8 of the 1998 Act.
[13] Section 9 of the 1998 Act.

The number of cases dealt with by the Commission has increased over the last few years. Table 4.3 shows the number of cases actually referred to the Tribunal after the Commission had completed its investigations; investigations that are sometimes complex and lengthy. This has also put a strain on Commission resources, not just in terms of the human capital needed to conduct the investigations, but in legal costs as well.[14] Due to this constraint the Commission has thus focused on priority sectors such as food and agro-processing, infrastructure and construction, intermediate industrial products, and, to a lesser extent, other industries such as media, transport, packaging, glass, skin products, tyres, furniture, franchising and advertising.

4. NEW DEVELOPMENTS

In the first half of the Commission's lifespan, it had great difficulty detecting and prosecuting cartel offences, which include price fixing, market allocation and bid rigging. It is commonly understood that cartels operate in secret and thus are very difficult to detect. In addition, the high concentration of firms in a number of industries due to South Africa's legacy could also be a breeding ground for cartel activity. In 2004 the Commission published its corporate leniency policy[15] but did not have much success. The policy gave immunity to the first firm to reveal the details of the cartel and assist with the prosecution.

The policy was later revised in 2008[16] to include a marker system, which had been successful in other jurisdictions such as Australia and the United Kingdom. The marker system provides a place for the first applicant that comes to the Commission's door to reveal cartel activity, but does not have sufficient evidence at the time. The Commission will hold that first place while the applicant obtains further evidence. Table 4.4 indicates the increase in the number of leniency applicants over the three years since the introduction of the marker system.

---

14 In the financial year 2007/2008 there were 193 cases, and in 2008/2009 there were 210 cases (source: Competition Commission of South Africa, available at: http://www.compcom.co.za/assets/Publications/Annual-Reports/Annual-Report-2009–10-Final.pdf).

15 Corporate Leniency Policy GN 25963 of 6 February 2004.

16 Corporate Leniency Policy GN 31064 of 23 May 2008.

Table 4.4 Corporate leniency applications received

2007/2008	2008/2009	2009/2010
10	13	79

Source: Competition Commission South Africa Annual Report 2009/2010, available at: http://www.compcom.co.za/assets/Publications/Annual-Reports/Annual-Report-2009–10-Final.pdf

This revised leniency policy has been successful in uncovering a number of cartels operating in industries such as milk, air transport, steel, bread, milling, gas and construction, amongst others. There was a substantial increase in the number of applicants for the financial year 2009/2010 as compared to previous years. This attests to the success of the leniency policy.

A case worth mentioning that was uncovered as a result of the leniency policy involves bread-producing firms who colluded amongst themselves to fix the price of bread and allocate markets. Apart from the leniency applicant, all the other firms involved signed consent agreements and were subsequently fined, except for Pioneer Foods, who decided to defend their case at the Tribunal. The Tribunal found that Pioneer Foods had engaged in price fixing and market allocation and imposed the maximum fine of 195 million rand, which was 10 per cent of the Pioneer Foods baking division's annual turnover.[17] The Commission took this one step further, filing an appeal requesting that Pioneer Foods not just be fined based on the turnover of their baking division, but instead be fined 10 per cent of their annual *group* turnover, which would amount to R1.5 billion. The Commission and Pioneer Foods subsequently reached a settlement agreement before the matter could be heard on appeal. In addition to the above-mentioned fine, Pioneer also committed itself to:

- pay R250 million as an administrative penalty to National Revenue Fund;
- pay R250 million to create an *Agro-processing Competitiveness Fund* to be administered by the Industrial Development Corporation (IDC). The aim of this fund is to promote competitiveness, employment and growth in food value chains. The Fund will provide finance on favourable terms to small and medium enterprises;
- adjusting its pricing of flour and bread (i.e. 600g and 700g standard white

[17] It should be noted that fines payable to the Commission and Tribunal become part of the budget allocated by the National Treasury.

and brown loaves) over a defined period such as to reduce its gross margin by R160 million when compared to the similar period in 2009/2010 by;

- increasing its capital expenditure by R150 million over and above its currently approved capital expenditure (capex) budget;
- cooperating with the Competition Commission in the ongoing investigations and prosecutions of the cases that are the subject of this settlement; and
- stopping anti-competitive conduct and implement a competition compliance programme.[18]

This settlement agreement thus took a more creative approach. The Competition Commissioner explained further that:[19]

> This agreement has gone beyond just a penalty and includes price adjustment for the benefit of consumers and a Fund to promote competition in the agro-processing industry. The Commission welcomes Pioneer's approach, as evidenced in this agreement, to resolving the matters and agreeing to undertakings aimed at a more competitive and dynamic economy in these crucial sectors.

The 1998 Competition Act has undergone further amendments to contend with competition law infringements. The new Competition Amendment Act was passed in 2009 and has been signed by the President, but has not come into effect as of early 2012. The Act has introduced new concepts such as complex monopolies (where there are a number of firms whose conduct restricts or distorts competition and at least one firm with 20 per cent of the market that is engaged in complex monopoly conduct). The Commission will have to prove that the conduct resulted in:

- high barriers to that market;
- exclusion of other firms from the market;
- excessive pricing within the market;
- refusal to supply other firms within that market; or
- other market characteristics that indicate coordinated conduct.

The Act also formalized market inquiries (which will serve as an explorative tool for the Commission to enquire into competition inadequacies). On the basis of its findings after such inquiry, the Commission can:

---

[18] Competition Commission Media Release 'Competition Commission settles with Pioneer Foods' (2 November 2010), available at: http://www.compcom.co.za/assets/Uploads/AttachedFiles/MyDocuments/Commission-settles-with-Pioneer-Foods2.pdf.

[19] Ibid.

- initiate a complaint and enter into a consent order with any respondent;
- initiate a complaint against any firm for further investigation;
- refer the complaint to the Tribunal without further investigation;
- take any other action within its powers; or
- take no action.

A new and challenging aspect of the Competition Amendment Act of 2009 is that it now criminalizes cartel conduct. Under the 1998 Act a firm found to be in contravention of the Act could be fined an administrative penalty of up to 10 per cent of its annual turnover. The 2009 Amendment Act now makes individuals criminally liable if found to be involved in cartel conduct. The Act states that:[20]

> A person commits an offence if, while being a *director of a firm* or while engaged … in a position having *management authority* within the firm, such person–
>
> (a) caused the firm to engage in a prohibited practice in terms of section 4(1)(b);[21] or
>
> (b) *Knowingly acquiesced* in the firm engaging in a prohibited practice in terms of section 4(1)(b).

The Act defines 'knowingly acquiesced' to mean having acquiesced while having actual knowledge of the relevant conduct by the firm. A person will only be prosecuted if the offending firm has signed a consent order indicating its involvement in cartel conduct or if the Tribunal finds that the firm has engaged in prohibited cartel activity. The criminal case will not be heard at the Competition Tribunal, but rather fall within the jurisdiction of the criminal courts, where the National Prosecuting Authority has the discretion to prosecute the matter. The individual can apply for leniency and the Commission can make submissions to the Prosecuting Authority in support of such leniency, although this does not prevent the individual from being sued in a civil court. If found guilty in a criminal court, the individual can be fined up to R500 000 or serve up to ten years' imprisonment or both. A new dynamic to the Act that is not common in other criminal legislation is that:[22]

---

20 Section 73A(1) of the Act; emphasis added.

21 Section 4(1)(b) refers to the provision prohibiting cartel conduct.

22 Section 73A(6) of the Act.

A firm may not directly or indirectly–

(a) pay any fine that may be imposed on a person convicted of an offence in terms of this section; or
(b) indemnify, reimburse, compensate or otherwise defray the expenses of a person incurred in defending against prosecution in terms of this section, unless the prosecution is abandoned or the person is *acquitted.*

This places a heavier burden on the individual and means a greater deterrence from engaging in cartel conduct.

5. SOUTH AFRICA'S COMPETITION JURISDICTION

The Competition Act is a creature of statute and can only be applied within the boundaries allowed in terms of the Act. The South African Act follows the effects-based test and states that '[t]his Act applies to all economic activity within, or having an effect within the Republic'.[23]

The extent to which the Act has an extra-territorial reach was argued in the *Ansac* cases.[24] Ansac is a group of soda ash companies from the United States of America who formed an association to export their product. A competitor, Botswana Soda Ash, complained to the Competition Commission of South Africa that Ansac was a cartel engaging in restrictive horizontal practices. Both South Africa and Botswana are members of the Southern African Customs Union (SACU), as well as the SADC, and have common import and tariff agreements.[25] Ansac was granted an exemption as an export cartel in terms of the US Webb-Pomerene Act.[26] The issue before the South African authorities was whether this exemption also extended to Ansac's operations in South Africa and whether the conduct was also exempt in terms of the South African Competition Act. The Tribunal held that the economic *effect* of the conduct has to be considered; thus, whether it had a positive or deleterious effect in South Africa. The Act does not distinguish between conduct by domestic or international firms if the economic effect is felt within South Africa.

---

23 Section 3(1) of the 1998 Act.

24 *Competition Commission and Botswana Ash (Pty) Ltd et al. v. American Natural Soda Ash Corporation et al.*, Competition Tribunal case numbers 49/CR/Apr00 and 87/CR/Sep00.

25 Hartzenberg, *supra* n. 2.

26 The Webb-Pomerene Act, 15 U.S.C § 61–65 (1982), which is an exemption for an association of competitors to engage in collective export sales.

This section of the Act also limits the reach of the South African competition authorities with regard to their jurisdiction beyond its borders. If a South African firm is abusing its dominance or engaging in other anti-competitive conduct in a neighbouring country, unless the economic activity has an effect in South Africa, the competition authorities would not have jurisdiction to prosecute the matter in terms of the Act. This statutory limitation nevertheless does not prevent the South African competition authorities from exercising an advocacy role in these neighbouring countries where their resources permit.

6. THE ROLE OF THE SOUTH AFRICAN COMPETITION AUTHORITIES IN SADC

South Africa is a member of SADC that shares common principles with its neighbouring countries. South Africa is seen as having one of the most 'important trading economies' in the SADC region.[27] Regionally-based communities such as SADC are focused on breaking down trade barriers between member states.[28] Having over ten years of experience in competition matters, the South African competition authorities have engaged with a number of neighbouring countries with regard to training, development and technical assistance. For example, in 2004 there was a mutual staff exchange between South Africa and the Monopolies and Practice Commission of Kenya. In 2007 the Commission hosted a merger review skills workshop that was attended by 14 members from eight African countries. In 2008 the Tribunal and Commission hosted a study tour on competition law for commissioners from Zambia and Swaziland.[29] More recently, in 2009, a senior analyst from the South African Commission was seconded to the Competition Commission of Mauritius to render technical assistance. Other delegates hosted over the 2009/2010 financial year were from Botswana, Tanzania and Gambia. The South African competition authorities have also

---

27 Ng'ong'ola, C. (2000), 'Regional Integration and Trade Liberalization in the Southern African Development Community', **3** (3) *Journal of International Economic Law* 485.

28 Mwase, N. (1998), 'Regional Economic Integration and Inter-Regional Trade in Post-Apartheid Eastern and Southern Africa: The South African Dimension', **21** (4) *World Competition* 77.

29 South African Competition Commission and Competition Tribunal (2009), *Unleashing Rivalry: Ten Years of Enforcement by the South African Competition Authorities*, p. 79.

been active participants of the Southern and Eastern Africa Competition Forum, and involved in the formation of the African Competition Forum which will focus on African projects, activities, and challenges in the competition arena.

The South African authorities are also part of a Joint Food Project with Egypt and Zambia. Competition issues in food and agro-processing have been of grave concern in most African countries. Problematic industries – namely, maize milling and fertilizer – were examined by South Africa and Zambia, and the pertinent issue of edible oil was examined by Egypt. Competition analysis in these food markets, including the informal sector, has also been done. The outcome of these studies will be a persuasive factor in transforming and promoting pro-competitive policies in future regional trade agreements.

7. CHALLENGES TO HARMONIZATION AND REGIONAL INTEGRATED POLICY

In 2008 the members of the SADC countries who had agreed to adopt a regional competition policy met to discuss the way forward.[30] Although details of the policy still need to be ironed out, the approach taken is for the policy to facilitate cooperation between members rather than to create a regional competition authority. This policy has been viewed as a step in the right direction to enhance regional trade and promote competition and consumer policy.

Enhancing regional integration would require all SADC countries to adopt competition policies. However, we know that not all member countries have competition policy or an active competition agency. Competition agencies need to develop a competition culture, which arises not only from the successful outcomes of cases, but also intensive and continuous advocacy, compliance and engagement with stakeholders such as Government agencies, the business forum and the public. This groundwork of promoting the benefits of competition and efficiency enhancing outcomes, through the development of competition agencies within the member countries, should be prioritized as a necessary precursor to the effective advancement of regional integration. Regional integration of competition policy is unlikely

[30] Toka, G. (2008), 'SADC Countries Adopt a Regional Competition Policy Blue-print', *Sunday Standard* online edition, 31 August, available at: http://www.sundaystandard.info/print_article.php?NewsID=3692.

to be effective if these member countries do not first ensure that competition policy is implemented successfully in their own countries. This requires creating a workable legislative framework and establishing well resourced and independent agencies.

We must also consider the commonalities and diversity of the member countries in SADC. Many African countries face the same issues of high unemployment, high concentration of industries, lack of consumer protection or awareness of protection rights, and low domestic and foreign investment.[31] These challenges can be overcome by enforcing competition policy and promoting competition policy in regional trade agreements to strengthen trade between the member countries.[32] However, the diversity amongst member countries may also pose challenges. Not all countries have the same economy or the same historical and political context. This challenge can also be overcome by customizing the legislation and policy within the affected country.

8. SHOULD THERE BE A REGIONAL COMPETITION COMMISSION AND TRIBUNAL FOR THE SADC?

This section presents a range of hypothetical questions to consider if the SADC countries were contemplating implementing a regional competition commission and tribunal to respectively investigate and adjudicate on cases.

For example, the Common Market for Eastern and Southern Africa (COMESA) has its own regional competition authority which decides upon cases that affect trade between member states. There are a few members of COMESA who also have an overlapping membership with SADC. Should there be two such regional competition authorities in existence? If so, would this result in endless battles over jurisdiction or concurrent jurisdiction to the extent that we will never get to hear the merits of the cases before these authorities? Or is the solution to have one regional competition authority, which reigns over all the members of all regional bodies?

As mentioned above, implementing competition law would require buy-in from stakeholders within the respective member states. Creating an overarching regional authority may provide an incentive for individual

31 Hartzenberg, *supra* n. 2.

32 See Cunningham, R.O. and A.J. LaRocca (1996), 'Harmonization of Competition Policies in a Regional Economic Integration', **27** (4) *Law and Policy in International Business* 883.

states to issue their own policy.[33] This has been the top-down approach taken at the European Commission. However, one should be wary of pressuring member states into enacting laws when they may not necessarily be ready to do so.

One should also be wary of merely adopting an existing approach, such as that taken by the European Commission. Developing countries in the SADC region have many variations among themselves, for example in terms of economy size, political climate, and legal and administrative systems.[34] Therefore, having one policy governing all the member states in the region may not be a cure-all to their competition problems. Competition requires not only the buy-in of their policy makers but also the will of the people to be educated and make use of the policy. 'Small jurisdictions suffer serious practical and motivational deficiencies.'[35] Younger democracies that are just in the process of establishing their own competition laws and political and economic identity may have different needs and challenges to older ones in the regional system. Competition law should be created to suit those individual needs first before embarking on a regional competition authority pursuit.[36] 'The adoption of a competition law within a new jurisdiction can raise difficulties concerning its proper placement within the existing framework.'[37] Timing of these laws from inception to implementation can also be a lengthy process.[38]

'Regional integration has long been seen in Africa as a means of achieving industrialization and modernization through encouraging trade

---

33 Alvarez, A.M., S.J. Evenett and L. Wilse-Samson (2007), 'Anti-Competitive Practices and the Attainment of the Millennium Development Goals: Implications for Competition Law Enforcement and Inter-Agency Cooperation', in UNCTAD, *Implementing Competition-Related Provisions in Regional Trade Agreements: Is it Possible to Obtain Development Gains?*, New York and Geneva: United Nations, p. 86, available at: www.unctad.org/en/docs/ditcclp20064_en.pdf.

34 See also Tavares de Araujo Jr, J. and L. Tineo (1998), 'Harmonization of Competition Policies Among MERCOSUR Countries', **24** (2) *Brook Journal of International Law* 456.

35 Gal, M.S. (2010), 'Regional Competition Law Agreements: An Important Step for Antitrust Enforcement', **60** *University of Toronto Faculty of Law Review* 3, at 3.

36 Alvarez et al., *supra* n. 33, at p. 84.

37 Ibid. at p. 82.

38 Ibid.

and securing economies of scale and market access.'[39] Regional trade agreements could also reflect the needs and requirements of member states to protect competition, efficiencies and consumer welfare.[40]

A difficult question arises where a regional authority would handle cases which may have a positive effect on one member country and a negative effect on another member country. Gal refers to this as the 'hard cases',[41] whereby each country experiences different effects, for example, an export cartel conducting business in another member state. It is difficult to determine what test should be applied and in whose favour the scales should tip.

Funding is a critical issue for any successful organization. How would a regional competition authority sustain itself in the SADC region? Perhaps membership fees may provide some comfort but may not be nearly enough to employ experienced staff. The agency could turn to other global agencies but they should not be entirely dependent on external funding because there is always a danger of the fund running out or being pulled. The relationship should also not undermine the agency's independence.

Other technical aspects to consider would be the institutional design of the regional agency – for example, how will employees of the Commission and Tribunal members be appointed, where would the agency be located, how can they attract and pay experienced staff, how should company fees and fines be managed and who would benefit from those payments, and would there be an avenue to appeal or take a decision on review and would all decisions be binding. Also, what would be the consequence of non-compliance with a decision by the regional authority?

Another consideration is whether experienced competition jurisdictions such as South Africa and Zambia would be willing to surrender their jurisdiction in favour of a regional agency. This should not be a problem if there is an outlook towards a greater good of competition and consumer welfare that is enhanced as a result of a regional agency. However, if the regional agency does not, or is unable to, use its resources effectively, or

---

39 Khandelwa, P. (2004), 'COMESA and SADC: Prospects and Challenges for Regional Trade Integration', IMF Working Paper WP/04/227, p. 6, available at: www.imf.org/external/pubs/ft/wp/2004/wp04227.pdf.

40 See Puri, L. (2007), 'Executive Summary' in UNCTAD, *supra* n. 33, p. vii; and Weiss, F. (1999), 'From World Trade Law to World Competition Law', **23** (6) *Fordham International Law Journal* 250, 254.

41 See Gal, *supra* n. 35, at 7. Gal also makes reference to 'easy cases' where the motivations between member states are the same – for example, the effect of an international cartel.

make decisions expediently, the more mature competition jurisdictions may not want to be party to such an agency.

In countries where non-competition related public interest concerns are on their agenda, would it be possible to reach a harmonious decision at the regional level if these social goals vary amongst the member states?[42] One member state's policies and priorities should not be allowed to dominate another's. Drawing this balance can bring about its own complexities.

The above concerns allow for further debate as to whether or not SADC should implement a regional competition agency. In an era of globalization, regional integration will become increasingly important if small developing countries are to find markets for their goods and services and compete effectively in a global market.[43]

The goal of ensuring cooperation among states, as proposed by SADC members, should ideally be to strengthen national competition regimes. Regional integration of competition policy and its inclusion into regional trade agreements does not necessarily have to be done under the auspices of a regional competition authority.

9. CONCLUSION

To create better harmonization there must be cooperation. The converse is true as well. Enacting a regional policy with its own competition agency may not be the answer, due to the complexities and challenges that each of these countries face. Making sure that each member country develops its own effective competition law using the basic principles of competition law would be a step towards harmonization.[44] A quick glance at competition policies in most competition jurisdictions shows aspects such as pre-merger notification, prohibition of restrictive horizontal and vertical practices and abuse of dominant position. The South African competition agency could lend its assistance to other young competition agencies in the form of technical assistance, training, and development and advice on institutional growth and development.

---

42 See Fox, E.M. (2007), 'World Competition Law: Conflict, Convergence, Cooperation', in Dhall, V. (ed.) *Competition Law Today: Concepts, Issues, and the Law in Practice*, New Delhi: Oxford University Press, p. 238.

43 See also Gal, M.S. (2009), 'Antitrust in a Globalized Economy: The Unique Enforcement Challenges Faced by Small and Developing Jurisdictions', **33** (1) *Fordham International Law Journal* 1, 47.

44 See also Cunningham and LaRocca, *supra* n. 32, at 881.

Recommended best practices giving agencies guidance on how to deal with cases at a practical level would form a welcome advancement to the development of competition integration. 'Competition agencies in member countries can develop a reciprocal relationship, helping each other with technical assistance, experiences and advice on how particular cases were dealt with, as well as facilitating a method of information exchange that promotes co-operation and harmonization within the region.'[45] Hearing about other agencies' experiences is a great learning tool. I have shown here how South African competition policy has developed over the last ten years, more so in the last five years. There has been development in merger cases and specific reference to public interest, as well as more recently in enforcement cases, which warranted a call for a corporate leniency policy and harsher criminal penalties. Younger competition agencies should also monitor whether these types of developments win the battle against anti-competitive conduct and whether they would suit their country's needs.

'Appropriate and effective competition regimes must also take into account countries' institutional capabilities.'[46] Not only are resources a constant challenge, but also, as in the case of South Africa, there is a statutory limitation on the competition agencies' jurisdictional reach. The penalties imposed on companies in South Africa should also serve as a warning that such anti-competitive practices will not be tolerated here or anywhere else in the region.

A stronger cooperative relationship amongst member states in the region will not only promote harmonization but also facilitate the strengthening of competition agencies at a national level.

---

[45] See Puri, L. (2007), 'Introduction' in UNCTAD, *supra* n. 33, at p. 2.

[46] Roberts, S. (2004), 'The Role For Competition Policy in Economic Development: The South African Experience', **21** (1) *Development Southern Africa* 227, 231.

PART II

Institutional coherence, regional integration and competition policy

5. Institutional coherence and effectiveness of a regional competition policy: the case of the West African Economic and Monetary Union (WAEMU)

Mor Bakhoum and Julia Molestina

1. INTRODUCTION

In the context of globalization, the shift from the *national* to the *global* has become an economic reality. The process of the 'rearrangement of the global legal environment, a result of the market economy',[1] has led to the emergence of new normative landscapes, which 'seem to be orientated towards a collective administration of national interests'.[2] The emergence of regional integration groups, especially in developing countries, is a result of this dynamic.

The creation of a common market, a tariff union or a free-trade zone, which leads to the opening of trade barriers, goes hand in hand with the necessity to protect free competition in these newly created 'common economic spaces'.[3] When competition expands from the national to the regional level, the legislation also has to follow this shift. In developing countries, the turn to regional economic integration is thus accompanied by the regionalization of their competition policies.

---

[1] Cissé, A. (2004), 'L'Harmonisation du droit des affaires en Afrique: l'expérience de l'OHADA à l'épreuve de sa première décennie', *RIDE* n° **2**, p. 198.

[2] Ibid.

[3] On the issue of economic integration and competition law in developing countries, see Drexl, J. (2012), 'Economic Integration and Competition Law in Developing Countries', in this volume, Ch. 11.

The objectives of regional competition policies are manifold and not necessarily mutually exclusive: protection against international cartels, economic integration, pooling of limited resources in order to foster enforcement, promotion of foreign direct investment, and so on.[4] Being more than a mere regulatory tool, for developing countries competition policy and economic integration have the potential to enable the countries' participation in the global economy.[5]

Despite the great potential of regional competition policies to foster economic development,[6] experience has shown that the implementation of those regional laws is still limping.[7] The promised results in terms of openness of national markets, promotion of trade between states and protection of free competition in the national markets, as well as in the common market, have yet to be seen. Different factors can explain the meager enforcement results.[8] Among other things, the institutional design of a regional competition policy plays a central role. Particularly, reconciling and finding an even balance of competences between the community and the national level is the crux of a regional institutional design. Hence, the distribution of competence between the regional competition authority and the national competition authorities may impede or foster the effective implementation of a regional competition policy, as evidenced by the experience of the West African Economic and Monetary Union (WAEMU).

WAEMU started its integration process as a monetary union whereby the former French colonies of West Africa adopted the same currency in the

---

[4] See on the objectives of regional competition policy, Bakhoum, M. (2011), 'Perspectives africaines d'une politique de la concurrence dans l'espace OHADA', *RIDE* n° **3**, pp. 356–361. See also Drexl, this volume, Ch. 11.

[5] Drexl, this volume, Ch. 11. Here Drexl states: 'Hence, the role of economic integration may well have to be redefined in times of globalization. Whereas, traditionally, economic integration has mostly been justified by the economic benefits that accrue from intensifying intra-regional trade, regional integration may nowadays seem much more important as a response to economic globalization.'

[6] See on this aspect Fox, E. (2012), 'Competition, Development and Regional Integration: in Search of a Competition Law Fit for Developing Countries', in this volume, Ch. 13.

[7] Gal and Wassmer, in their contribution in the present volume, discuss the obstacles to an efficient regional competition policy; see Gal, M. and I.F. Wassmer, 'Regional Agreements of Developing Jurisdictions: Unleashing the Potential', in this volume, Ch. 14.

[8] Ibid.

framework of the Monetary Union of West Africa (UMOA).[9] In 1994, a common market was created with the signing of the Treaty of Dakar,[10] which transformed the Monetary Union into an economic and monetary union. This constitutive treaty also comprises the core competition law interdictions of agreements and abuse of dominant position, Articles 88 and 89, while Article 90 vests the Commission with the competence to enforce the community law. There are further regulations and directives that specify the primary competition law.[11]

The WAEMU has adopted a centralized approach to its competition policy.[12] The Union has the exclusive competence to legislate on anti-competitive practices (agreements, abuse of dominant position and state aids) and the Commission enjoys exclusive decision-making power in dealing with anti-competitive practices. The member states' original competences have thus been limited to what one could call the 'secondary law' of competition: to restrictive practices and unfair competition.[13]

---

[9] Union Monétaire Ouest Africaine (UMOA). The UMOA treaty was signed on 14 November 1973. It created a uniform currency, the CFA franc (Franc de la Communauté Financière de l'Afrique), which is managed by the Banque Centrale des Etats de l'Afrique de l'Ouest (BCEAO).

[10] The WAEMU treaty is available at: http://www.uemoa.int/Documents/TraitReviseUEMOA.pdf.

[11] Règlement n° 2/2002/CM/UEMOA du 23.5.2002 relatif aux pratiques anti-concurrentielles à l'intérieur de l'Union; Règlement n° 3/2002/CM/UEMOA du 23.5.2002 relatif aux procédures applicables aux ententes et abus de position dominante à l'intérieur de l'Union Economique et Monétaire Ouest-Africaine; Règlement n° 4/2002/CM/UEMOA du 23.5.2002 relatif aux aides d'Etat à l'intérieur de l'Union Economique et monétaire Ouest-Africaine et aux modalités d'application de l'article 88(C) du traité; Directive n° 02/2002/CM/UEMOA du 23.5.2002 relative à la coopération entre la Commission et les structures nationales de concurrence des Etats membres pour l'application des articles 88, 89 et 90 du traité de l'UEMOA; Directive n° 1/2002/UEMOA du 23.5.2002 relative à la transparence des relations financières entre d'une part les Etats membres et les entreprises publiques, et d'autre part entre les Etats membres et les organisations internationales ou étrangères. The legal texts are available at: http://www.uemoa.int.

[12] See generally on the competition policy in WAEMU, Bakhoum, M. (2007), *L'articulation du droit communautaire et des droits nationaux de la concurrence dans l'Union Economique et Monétaire Ouest-Africaine (UEMOA)*, Berne & Brussels: Stämpfli/Bruylant.

[13] One has to highlight the fact that most member states of WAEMU combine anti-competitive practices with practices in restraint of competition, unfair competition, and in some states even consumer protection, in their competition legislation. All member states have a national competition law except Guinea-Bissau. Senegal:

However, the national competition law authorities have to fulfil certain cooperative functions, which are set forth in Directive 02/2002/UEMOA.[14] Firstly, the Commission has to inform the national competition authorities about ongoing or envisaged investigations in the member states. The national authority then has to assist the Commission during these investigations and inquiries in the member states. Furthermore, the national competition law authorities are involved in the decision-making process through the Advisory Committee on Competition, which is designed after the European Competition Network. The Advisory Committee has the competence to give an opinion on pending cases. However, its opinion does not bind the Commission.[15] In order to make the transfer of competence to the regional level effective, member states are obliged to reform their national competition laws and to limit the competences of their national competition authorities in accordance with the new centralized community competition system.[16]

Actually, the Treaty of Dakar does not explicitly centralize the competition law competences. Divergences already appeared during the elaboration of the community legislation. While the Commission supported an exclusive competence of the Union, the experts of the member states defended their domestic right to legislate on competition matters. Finally, it was an

---

Loi 1994/63 du 22 août 1994 sur les prix, la concurrence et le contentieux économique; Burkina Faso: Loi n°15/94 du 15 mai 1994 relative à la concurrence; Mali: Ordonnance n° 07–025 du 18 juillet 2007 portant organisation de la concurrence; Togo: Loi n° 99–011 du 28 décembre 1999 portant organisation de la concurrence au Togo; Bénin: Ordonnance n° 20/PR/MFAEP du 5 juillet 1967 portant réglementation des prix et des stocks; Niger: Ordonnance n° 92–025 du 7 juillet 1992 portant réglementation des prix et de la concurrence; Côte d'Ivoire : Loi n° 91–999 du 27 décembre 1991 relative à la concurrence. The various legislations have one common feature: besides the affirmation of freedom of trade and competition, the states are allowed, in exceptional circumstances, to intervene on the determination of prices.

[14] On the cooperation between the Commission and the national competition authorities, see Bakhoum, *supra* n. 12, pp. 223–226.

[15] The Commission usually follows the opinion of the Advisory Committee on Competition. There is no case yet in which the Commission and the Advisory Committee have had different opinions on a pending matter.

[16] The modalities of the obligation to reform are defined in Directive 2/2002/ UEMOA, *supra* n. 11.

opinion of the WAEMU Court of Justice[17] that ended the debate by deciding in favour of an exclusive competence of the Union.[18]

Almost eight years after the entry into force of the community competition law, the centralized approach of WAEMU has shown its flaws. The expected reforms in the member states are still pending, the collaboration of national structures and the community is not effective and the regional institutional level, which was supposed to constitute a strong authority, faces severe constraints in terms of resources and flexibility. The effectiveness of the community competition law thus far has failed to live up to its expectations.[19]

This chapter analyses the coherence of the institutional approach of WAEMU and its impact on the effectiveness of the community competition policy. It is based on eight years of experience that demonstrate the incoherencies of the institutional approach (section 2). In the third part of the chapter, a number of criteria that we have termed 'competition constraints' will be developed. These criteria, which influence the institutional design of a regional competition law structure, have to be taken into account when allocating the competences between the regional level and the member states. The theoretical analysis of the 'competition constraints' will then be applied to the case of WAEMU (section 3.2).

---

[17] Opinion n° 003/2000/CJ/UEMOA, unpublished. The Court of Justice stated in this opinion that the Union has the exclusive competence to adopt regulations on agreements, abuse of dominant position and state aid.

[18] The opposition to strong centralization did not end with the community competition law's entry into force. When the regulations were being drafted, the Senegalese competition authorities issued an opinion going against WAEMU's centralized approach. See *Rapport 2002–2003 de la Commission Nationale de la Concurrence du Sénégal* (unpublished, on file with the authors). For a critical analysis of the centralized approach, see Bakhoum, *supra* n. 12, pp. 228–243. In general, national competition authorities still do not accept the fact that they are deprived of all decision-making power.

[19] Community jurisprudence also remains limited; see section 2.3 below ('The Institutional Architecture and Efficacy of the Community Competition Policy in WAEMU: Overview of the Community Jurisprudence').

2. INSTITUTIONAL COHERENCE AND EFFECTIVENESS OF WAEMU'S COMPETITION POLICY: THE LIMITS OF A CENTRALIZED SYSTEM

The effectiveness of a regional competition policy depends considerably on the institutions that are in charge of the enforcement of competition law. However, in WAEMU, there are institutional flaws at the community level (section 2.1) as well as on the national level (section 2.2).

2.1 Incoherencies on the Regional Level

As in the EU, the competent competition law agency in the WAEMU is not an autonomous institution detached from the Commission. The WAEMU Commission is organized into departments,[20] which are arranged around the President of the Commission. Each department is led by a commissioner. The departments themselves are divided into directorates. As regards the application of community competition law, the Directorate of Competition, which is part of the Department of the Regional Market, Trade, Competition and Cooperation, is the competent agency.[21] However, it was not until 2007 that the specific Directorate of Competition was created. Prior to the creation of the Directorate, it was the Department of the Regional Market, Trade, Competition and Cooperation that dealt with competition-related matters without a particular focus on such issues. The competition law agency therefore lacked visibility.

Today, a heavy administrative burden limits the effectiveness of the actions of the Competition Directorate. As in most administrations, every action by the Competition Directorate is subject to the formal approval of the hierarchy. In the WAEMU, every inquiry, investigation or action has to be authorized by the President of the Commission: the Competition Directorate has to submit an application before the President, who decides on the possibility of initiating a proceeding before giving the 'go ahead'. This formal requirement applies to all procedural actions (requests for information, communication with the parties, search in the companies, etc.). The

---

[20] See Décision n° 0157/2007/PCOM/UEMOA portant création et organisation des services de la Commission de l'UEMOA, unpublished.

[21] See Décision n° 345/2008/PCOM/UEMOA portant organisation du département du marché régional, du commerce, de la concurrence et de la coopération, unpublished.

centralized bureaucracy around the President of the Commission limits the flexibility of the Commission itself considerably and slows down the procedures, thereby reducing the efficiency of the actions of the Competition Directorate.

The effective functioning of a competition agency requires sufficient material, financial and human resources. In terms of staffing, the Competition Directorate only has three agents. One must recall that the Commission, due to the centralized approach, is also appointed to deal with anti-competitive practices that are located in only one member state. The member states' support in terms of staffing and other means during investigations in their territory, despite their obligation to collaborate with the Commission, remains limited and cannot overcome the lack of human resources of the Competition Directorate.

An often-stated argument in favour of the regionalization of competition policies in developing countries is that creating a strong agency and supplying it with sufficient means on the regional level is better than coping with weak national competition-law structures that lack the essential resources. In the case of WAEMU this argument does not hold due to its lack of resources. The Commission, in principle, has sufficient financial means. However, the Competition Directorate lacks the necessary flexibility to use them.

2.2 Flaws on the National Level: Lack of Collaboration in the National Competition-law Structures

The design of the institutional framework to apply the competition policy of WAEMU requires reforms on the national level and effective collaboration between the regional and the national competition authorities. However, the national reforms are still not effective and the collaboration between the Commission and the national competition authorities remains weak.

2.2.1 Ineffectiveness of institutional reforms on the national level

A certain lethargy in the functioning of the national competition structures and an impediment of the national legislative dynamic have followed the entry into force of the community competition law. Hence, member states have not yet initiated the reform process of their national competition laws.

2.2.1.1 Centralization of competences and the decline of national initiative? Before the entry into force of the community competition law, certain national competition structures were more or less successfully operative. The national competition commission ('Commission Nationale de la Concurrence') in Senegal is often cited as an illustration of the national dynamism in the control of the market. The authority issued some decisions,[22] among them the famous *Air France* case.[23] In this decision, the air company was convicted of abuse of economic dependence.

However, since the entry into force of the community law, the national competition authority is no longer competent to hear competition cases.

While it is certainly true that the centralization of the community competition law has led to a decline in domestic competition law activities,[24] the case of Senegal by itself cannot justify the general assumption that the effect of the community competition law regime on the functioning of the national competition authorities is negative. In fact, the lethargy of the national antitrust authorities is endemic and congenital. Before the community law entered into force, although national competition law authorities had complete discretion on the implementation of competition policy, not a single domestic competition law authority effectively enforced its competition law. Even in the case of the competition commission in Senegal, its dynamism in the control of the market is to some degree exaggerated. The Senegalese competition commission, in similar circumstances to the other member states of WAEMU, faces capacity constraints that limit the efficacy of its actions.[25]

The national competition commission in Ivory Coast is an interesting example in this regard. Created in 1992 with the Law on Competition, the commission was operative until 2002. It was equipped with sufficient means and issued more than 30 opinions.[26] However, due to a sociopolitical crisis, its activity was decelerated.

---

[22] For example: *CIBA* v *FFSA and SARL Micro Doses technologies*. The cases are available in *Rapport 2002–2003 de la Commission nationale de la concurrence du Sénégal* (unpublished, on file with the authors).

[23] Ibid.

[24] Weick even argues that 'Senegal's National Competition Commission has collapsed since the Court of Justice judgment': Weick, D.P. (2010), 'Competition Law and Policy in Senegal: A Cautionary Tale for Regional Integration?', **33** *World Competition* 521, 522. This statement is, however, questionable.

[25] See *Rapport 2002–2003 de la Commission nationale de la concurrence du Sénégal* (unpublished, on file with the authors). The Commission has neither its own venue nor permanent staff.

[26] See the respective reports of 1994, 1998 and 2001 of the national competition commission in Ivory Coast (unpublished, on file with the authors).

Generally, national antitrust authorities have fulfilled their obligation of abstention: their obligation not to issue decisions on competition law issues subsequent to the entry into force of the community competition law.

The centralized approach has had a negative impact on the diffusion of the competition culture in the member states. While it also impeded the potential development of the national expertise of the competition authorities, one cannot assume a complete decline of national expertise. Apart from Senegal and Ivory Coast, specific competition law knowledge was already very limited in the majority of the member states before the centralized system came into force.

2.2.1.2 The centralization of competences and reforms of national competition laws Notwithstanding their obligation to do so, no member state of WAEMU has yet adapted its domestic law to the community law. In Senegal, Ivory Coast, Niger, Burkina Faso and Benin, reform projects are in progress, though not yet effective. This lack of effectiveness results from lethargy on the part of the member states in pursuing the legislative reforms, not to mention supplying the national competition authorities with the necessary means to fulfil their obligation to control the national markets.[27] Deprived of all competences for the regulation of anti-competitive practices, the member states fail to see the necessity to invest in reforms of their national competition law regimes, or, in case the domestic structure previously did not possess a competition law regime at all, to implement a domestic competition law. The latter is the case in Guinea-Bissau, which even today has not yet enacted a domestic competition law. As pointed out in the doctrine, strong centralization slows down the domestic legislative dynamics and endangers the development of a competition culture in the member states.[28]

The obligation to reform also applies to the sectoral legislation and authorities. The approaches to sectoral competition regulation differ from one member state to another.[29] While in some member states, such as Mali, anti-competitive practices in specific sectors fall under the scope of the

---

27 Generally the community competition law expects national competition authorities to monitor the national market and detect potential anti-competitive practices. This permanent surveillance is referred to as 'veille concurrentielle' in Directive 2/2002/UEMOA.

28 See on this aspect Drexl, this volume, Ch. 11.

29 The telecommunications sector serves as an example because competition-related provisions are frequently included in its sectoral regulation.

general competition authority (or tribunal),[30] other states have a specific regulatory authority that is competent in such sector-related anti-competitive practices. The latter is the case in Senegal, where anti-competitive practices are explicitly dealt with in the Code of Telecommunication.[31] The Regulation Agency of Telecommunication and Postal Services[32] holds the competence to deal with anti-competitive practices in the telecommunication sector through the derogation of the Law of 1994 on prices, competition and economic litigation.[33] However, this approach is not in conformity with the exclusive competence of the WAEMU Commission.

In Togo, the Law on Telecommunication regulates anti-competitive practices and it is enforced before the competent courts.[34]

In Benin, although the Telecommunication Regulation also includes provisions on anti-competitive practices, enforcement takes place before the competent courts. The regulatory authority's competence does not include litigation. The same approach is adopted in Niger: anti-competitive practices are regulated in the Telecommunication Regulation; however, they are enforced before the competent courts. In Ivory Coast, on the other hand, the Law on Telecommunication does not specifically govern anti-competitive practices and its telecommunication agency does not have competence on antitrust issues.

2.2.2 Ineffectiveness of collaboration with national competition law authorities

A few years ago, we warned that the domestic competition authorities – deprived of all decision-making power – would not be inclined to cooperate with the Commission and would not accept being reduced to the role of an

---

30 See Article 1, Ordonnance n° 99–043 du 30 septembre 1999 régissant les télécommunications en république du Mali. The provision states that the application of the telecommunications regulation does not pre-empt the application of the general competition law.

31 See Article 5 of the Code des télécommunications, which prohibits agreements and abuse of a dominant position. The Code des télécommunications is available at: http://www.gouv.sn/spip.php?article769.

32 Agence de Régulation des Télécommunications et des Postes (ARTP).

33 See Article 5 of the Code des télécommunications.

34 Article 35, Loi sur les télécommunications.

intermediary regarding the transmission of complaints to the Commission.[35] These 'predictions', based on the analysis of WAEMU's institutional community framework, have turned out to be true.

2.2.2.1 Resistance of national authorities to the centralization of decision-making power The national antitrust authorities were always opposed to the centralization of decision-making power.[36] In practice, this divergence from the institutional approach has not only hardened into a resistance of many national antitrust authorities against cooperating with the Commission, but also into a style drafting of national antitrust law that skilfully tries to exploit loopholes on the regional level. The distribution of competences regarding the substantial law contains a certain imprecision. The notion of abuse of dominant position, which falls within the scope of community law, is closely related to the notion of abuse of economic dependence, which falls under the member states' competence. Thus, by 're-qualifying' certain facts, the controlling agents in the member states are able to circumvent the exclusive competence of the Union.

The national antitrust authorities do not fulfil their role of monitoring the national markets; the number of complaints filed with the Commission remains limited; and in certain cases, there is even a complete absence of collaboration during inquiries.[37] Aside from the competition law authority in Burkina Faso, which has been very cooperative, the national antitrust authorities are not inclined to cooperate with the Commission.

2.2.2.2 The institutional weakness of national competition law institutions The institutional system of WAEMU still relies on the national institutions. Although the national competition authorities have been deprived of their decision-making power, they are still 'mobilized' as an intermediary during the surveillance of the national markets. This assigned role as an intermediary assumes that a national competition law authority exists and that it is equipped with the necessary means. However, Guinea-Bissau has neither a domestic competition law authority nor a domestic

---

[35] See Bakhoum, *supra* n. 12, p. 229 et seq.

[36] One has to recall the diverging opinions between the experts of the member states and the Commission when the regional regulations were discussed.

[37] This applies to the collaboration between the WAEMU Commission and the national competition commission in Senegal. During inquiries in the member state, the Commission mostly worked with the Direction du Commerce Intérieur (DCI), which is the branch of the Ministry of Trade in charge of economic investigations at the national level.

competition law. Even in member states where a competition law regime exists, the national competition law institutions lack the necessary resources to adequately fulfil their assigned role. These structural contingencies apply in all member states of the WAEMU. The following section presents an insight into the difficulties with which the member states are confronted.

THE INDEPENDENCE OF NATIONAL COMPETITION AUTHORITIES The member states have adapted different approaches regarding the institutional structure of their competition law agencies. In Benin, Mali, Niger and Togo, the competent competition authority directly depends on the administration. The agency often consists of a directorate in the ministry of trade, which assumes legislative control on prices, consumer protection and the enforcement of the competition law *stricto sensu*. One should note that these different states all have competition laws.[38] However, the conferral of decision-making powers on the administration considerably reduces their independence.

Other states, such as Senegal, Burkina Faso and Ivory Coast, have taken a different approach by creating 'independent' competition law institutions that are detached from the administrative apparatus. However, despite their structural independence, the actual operational framework of an agency calls for a reconsideration of this supposed independence. Usually a governmental commissioner in the competition law agency works as a 'spy' for the executive authority. Since the executive authority funds and staffs the agency, it effectively controls it. This situation can be seen in Senegal, Burkina Faso and Ivory Coast. In the case of Senegal, Benin and Mali, the agents of the competition commission simultaneously work for the Directorate of Internal Trade. In Ivory Coast, the competition commission cannot even make a decision. Its function is limited to issuing opinions on litigation on which the Ministry of Trade then decides at its own discretion.

AVAILABILITY OF RESOURCES All national competition law authorities in WAEMU lack the necessary material and human resources, such as sufficiently skilled staff, to deal with competition law issues.[39]

---

[38] See, on the different national competition laws in the member states, *supra* n. 13.

[39] See *Rapport 2002–2003 de la Commission nationale de la concurrence du Sénégal* (unpublished, on file with the authors).

2.3 The Institutional Architecture and Efficacy of the Community Competition Policy in WAEMU: Overview of the Community Jurisprudence

Eight years after the entry into force of the community competition law of WAEMU, the results in terms of effectiveness have not met expectations. While the Commission issued some opinions and observations related to state aids and anti-competitive practices imputed to member states, the core competition domains of agreements and abuse of dominant position have not been tackled. In fact, there has been no decision in either domain. However, there are ongoing cases related to the abuse of dominance.

In the case *SOCOCIM* v *the State of Senegal and Cement of Sahel*,[40] the Commission of WAEMU held that the exoneration from taxes of the Société les Ciments du Sahel on the importation of clinker constituted a distortion of competition. It ordered the State of Senegal to cease the exonerations.

In another case related to exonerations given on the importation of packaging in craft paper,[41] the Commission of WAEMU also instructed the State of Senegal to cease its exonerations. The Commission held that the exonerations created a disadvantage for locally produced craft paper, because it fell under the scope of a less favourable fiscal regulation.

In a decision from 2010, the Commission instructed the State of Senegal to retract its legal provision NS 03–072.[42] It was held that provision NS 03–072 concerning palm oil had resulted in a foreclosure of the Senegalese market in terms of quantity of community imports of palm oil and had therefore affected the trade between member states.

In each of the three recent cases, a member state of WAEMU was actively involved. This fact demonstrates that, despite market liberalization, the member states are still active market participants, either through legislative actions or state aids that conflict with the community law. Yet the cases also show that actions on the regional level are more effective in ordering a state to act in conformity with the community laws than are the national authorities.

Furthermore, other ongoing cases before the Commission confirm the tendency of the competition litigation to focus on restrictive practices initiated by member states.

---

40 Available on WAEMU's webpage: www.uemoa.int/.

41 Available on WAEMU's webpage: www.uemoa.int/.

42 Available on WAEMU's webpage: www.uemoa.int/.

However, only a few cases before the Commission deal with the crux of competition provisions: agreements and abuse of dominant position. In the case of *Sotelma-Malitel* v *Orange Mali*, Sotelma-Malitel felt excluded from a cost-free reciprocal roaming service between Senegal and Mali (unified network) that some mobile phone companies offered. Sotelma-Malitel argued that its exclusion from the service was based on its not being a member of the network. The Commission was called in on the grounds of an illicit agreement. The case is still pending before the regional competition authority.

The case of *CANAL Overseas* concerns the abuse of dominant position in the audiovisual sector. In this legal affair, CANAL Overseas, a French film production and distribution enterprise, refused to place its bundle of television channels at the disposal of its distribution clients, MMDS, in the region. The Commission was approached following the refusal to supply. The case is still pending.

In the case of *Staf* v *Sonapost* in Burkina Faso, an abuse of dominant position resulted from an administrative monopoly, which the State of Burkina Faso had assigned to Sonapost Burkina in 1988. The predominant company, Sonapost, initiated procedures and fined Staf, its rival, for illicit transportation and distribution of mail. The case is in progress before the Commission.[43]

One can draw some conclusions from the Commission's jurisprudence. As already pointed out, the member states take an active part in the distortion of competition. On the other hand, they do not hesitate to invoke community legislation in the case of violation by another member state. This signifies that the member states are generally aware of their competition-law-related obligations.

The number of cases upon which the Commission has decided, remains limited. However, one has to bear in mind that the community law is still a young jurisdiction. It is still in the process of implementation in the member states. The growing number of cases demonstrates that the economic actors, as well as the member states, are at least conscious of the advantages of community law and apply it more frequently.

---

43 These ongoing cases have not been published yet.

3. DESIGNING A COHERENT REGIONAL INSTITUTIONAL FRAMEWORK: THE DEFINITION OF A POSSIBLE APPROACH

Designing a coherent regional institutional framework should not be done in the abstract. It requires taking into account the specificities, objectives and constraints of the hosting jurisdiction. The following reflection of Professor Eleanor Fox with regard to institutions is very enlightening. She writes:

> Good institutional design is a critical component of good competition policy and competition law enforcement. The design of the institutions is like the design of a house: it must facilitate life within the house. Good institutional design takes account of the family's values and empowers life within its walls. Designs cannot be conjured in the abstract; they must fit the family that lives in the house, its aspirations, possibilities, and practical limits. Therefore, the good architect lives with the family before conceptualizing the design.[44]

This part of the study goes beyond WAEMU's experience to identify, with a more transversal and theoretical approach, the possible orientations of a regional institutional design, taking into account what we have termed the 'competition constraints' that influence the design of the institutions.

3.1 Competition Constraints to Take into Account When Designing the Regional Institutional Approach

We identify five factors that influence to a certain extent the design of regional institutions: the number of states and the level of integration of the regional market; the fluidity of trade between member states; the respective institutional capacities of the member states and the Union; the existence or lack of a competition culture in the member states; and the time dimension. These different criteria will be briefly discussed.

---

[44] Fox, E.M. (2010), 'Antitrust and Institutions: Design and Changes', **41** (3) *Loyola University Chicago Law Journal* 473, 487, available at: http://www.luc.edu/law/activities/publications/lljdocs/vol41_no3/pdfs/fox_design.pdf.

3.1.1 The size of the regional market

Size matters in competition law.[45] This is also true when one considers the regional dimension. Hence, the size of a regional market is a criterion one has to take account of when designing the regional institutions. This is also true of the degree of integration of the regional integration group. If the regional integration group is very limited in size with a limited number of member states it could be feasible to have a centralized approach. Hence in a regional integration group with a relatively small market, a limited number of states, a similar cultural background, and relatively similar levels of economic development, having a centralized approach would be advisable.

On the contrary, if the regional integration group comprises a relatively large number of member states with diverse economic characteristics and levels of development, differentiated competition cultures and uneven institutional capacities, a centralized approach with regard to the substantive law and decision-making power would disregard the national competition specificities and undermine the promotion of competition culture in the member states. A centralized approach would be disastrous for the national competition dynamic.

The experience of the Economic Community of West African States (ECOWAS) is very useful in this regard. ECOWAS has 15 member states, including a country as large and economically advanced as Nigeria, which is the economic leader of the organization, and a country as small as Gambia. In this context, a centralized approach would have a negative impact on the effectiveness of the community law. It would also prevent national competition authorities from addressing national restrictions of competition and developing their own competition culture. Although WAEMU is a relatively small organization with a lot of synergies between its member states in terms of the levels of economic development and culture, in addition to sharing the same currency, the over-centralized approach has had a negative impact on the effectiveness of its community law. In the Common Market for Eastern and Southern Africa (COMESA), which is comprised of states with different characteristics, a centralized approach would undermine the development of a national competition culture.

---

[45] Gal, M. (2003), *Competition Policy for Small Market Economies*, Cambridge, MA: Harvard University Press; see also Gal, M. (2001), 'Size Does Matter: The Effects of Markets Size on Optimal Competition Policy', **74** *Southern California Law Review* 1437.

3.1.2 Degree of integration of the regional market and fluidity of trade between member states

Another criterion of paramount importance is the degree of integration of the regional market. This is firstly determined by how far the member states commit to the regional integration process. For instance, creating a common market with a customs union and the guarantee of free movement of goods and services, people and capital, and providing firms with the freedom of establishment, is the most advanced level of regional commitment. The successful case of the EU evidences the benefits of such an advanced degree of economic integration. However, this advanced level requires time to become a reality. Setting up a regional economic cooperation framework with a customs union or a free-trade area is another, less advanced, approach to integration. WAEMU and ECOWAS have set up common markets that, theoretically, should facilitate the fluidity of trade between member states. Is it the case in practice? The mere fact of guaranteeing the free movement of goods and people and the freedom of establishment does not guarantee an advanced degree of fluidity of exchanges in practice. In sub-Saharan Africa, for instance, experience has shown that the fluidity of trade between member states is very limited in the framework of the regional integration groups. North–South trade is more advanced than South–South trade. This is in part due to historical reasons.[46] In the former French colonies of West Africa, the infrastructures were set up in such a way as to promote North–South trade and not South–South trade. The theoretical creation of a common market with fluid exchanges between member states is thus not yet a reality.

In addition, the prerequisite for fluid trade between member states of a regional integration group is the existence of firms big enough to do business in different states. In West Africa, for instance, the activities of the so-called informal economy, which represents, according to some statistics, more than 50 per cent of the economy,[47] are limited to national boundaries; and few national firms are big enough to expand their wings to more than one state. In a regional market populated by small and medium-sized companies and an informal economy, anti-competitive practices are likely

---

[46] On the development of competition law and policy in sub-Saharan Africa, see Gerber, D. (2010), *Global Competition: Law, Markets, and Globalization*, Oxford: Oxford University Press, pp. 248 et seq.

[47] See wa Mpungu, G.B. and B. Remiche (eds) (2010), *D'une économie populaire à une économie fiscalisée: INEADEC – Actes du colloque international de Kinshasa du 19 septembre 2008*, Brussels: Larcier.

to be more common within the member states. It is therefore essential to set up the institutional framework in a way that allows national competition authorities to address such national restraints on competition. The limited fluidity of trade between member states should not exclude the control of cross-border restrictions of competition. Though limited in theory, such control should be vested in the regional authority.

3.1.3 Institutional capacities of the Union and the member states

Assessing the respective institutional capacities of the regional authorities as well as the national competition authorities is a prerequisite for the design of a regional institutional framework, especially with respect to the distribution of competence between the community and the national levels. In the debate on regional competition policies in developing countries, it is often contended that pooling resources together at the regional level would help developing countries offset their resource constraints and make enforcement more effective.[48] This is especially true with regard to international cartels, cross-border restrictions of competition and anti-competitive practices originating within member states. The argument is sound in theory. In practice, however, a regional competition authority is not immune from resource constraints or the lack of independence and flexibility that national competition authorities often face. As this analysis has evidenced, the WAEMU Competition Commission faces the same constraints as its national counterparts. It does not have the power to conduct an inquiry, its independence is limited, and it is understaffed. The theoretical argument of pooling together the resources at the regional level for improved enforcement is not operative in the case of WAEMU. A case-by-case analysis, taking into account the practical constraints of the regional competition authority, should be undertaken.

The institutional capacities of the member states have also to be taken into account. Member states that have an independent and functioning competition authority should be vested with the power to exercise control at the national level. Limited institutional capacities at the national level could, at first sight, justify a centralized enforcement approach. In the case of WAEMU, for instance, the limited institutional capacities of the member states is an argument put forward to justify the centralized approach. However, the issue is more complex and the objectives multiple.

---

[48] Gal, M. (2010), 'Regional Competition Law Agreements: An Important Step for Antitrust Enforcement', **60** *U Toronto LJ* 239.

Hence, in addition to enforcement concerns, creating and diffusing a competition culture in the member states and fostering the enforcement capacities of the national competition authorities is another objective of a regional competition law. This objective is crucial especially for developing countries. If it is possible to have a centralized approach at the initial stage of enforcement of a regional law, as was the case in the EU, it is crucial to keep in mind the necessity to spread competition culture in the member states in the long run. This could only be done by recognizing a limited decision-making power to the national competition authorities or having them involved in the decision-making process. Differentiating between the member states is also important. The absence of national competition authorities in some member states (e.g. Guinea-Bissau in WAEMU) should not result in depriving all the member states of the competence to enforce their national competition laws.

3.1.4 The existence of competition culture in the member states

The presence or lack of a competition culture in the member states is another criterion that enters into consideration when designing the enforcement approach at the regional level. The 'cultural competition element' is related to other elements such as the institutional capacities of the member states and the involvement or not of the states in the market. In member states with strong competition culture, for instance, the states are less likely to interfere with the market and to distort the competition process. Such states are also more willing to supply funds and make national competition authorities functional. In a regional integration group where a strong competition culture exists at the state level, and the member states have well-funded and functioning national competition authorities, it would be possible to grant extended decision-making power to those national authorities. A weak competition culture at the regional level could justify a centralized approach at the initial stage. However, the absence of a competition culture should not lead to denying national competition authorities any decision-making power.

3.1.5 The temporal aspect: time and distribution of competences

The temporal aspect is also important in the design of the institutions, which are not static. Institutions evolve over time, taking into account experience and learning. The time dimension is also intertwined with the competition culture criterion, which becomes a reality over time. Institutions, therefore, should be designed in a way that allows member states to learn and have strong enforcement capacities in the long run. Let us recall that in the case of the EU the absence of a competition culture within the member states justified the centralization of certain competences by the Commission, particularly the power to allow exemptions. Decentralized enforcement took place when it was justified by the existence of a competition culture within the member states. Hence, the respective domains to centralize and to decentralize relate to the *temporal element* of each member country developing a culture of competition.

The regional integration experiences in developing countries are still young. Competition law is still unknown in the countries, the competition culture is limited and the institutional capacities of the countries are weak. In this context, the institutions should be designed in a way that gives the regional authority the possibility to centralize certain competences while recognizing the national competition authorities' power to take decisions that will not undermine the coherence in the enforcement of the community law.

3.2 Competition Constraints and Institutional Design: Redefining WAEMU's Institutional Enforcement Approach?

The interface between competition constraints and institutional design will first be briefly discussed before applying it to the specific case of WAEMU.

3.2.1 Preliminary remarks: interfacing competition constraints and institutional design

The competition constraints discussed in this paper shape to a certain extent the institutional design of a given regional competition policy. Taking them into account, one can identify a number of orientations for the design of the regional enforcement approach. In his contribution to the present volume, Professor Josef Drexl has put forward several such principles of orientation. Some of our observations are in line with his conclusions.

3.2.1.1 The applicable (substantive) law Drexl has identified three possible orientations with regard to the substantive law: (1) a centralized approach with a unique substantive regional competition law applicable directly in all member states, even for practices affecting only the national markets. This approach is the current option in WAEMU. Another option is (2) the harmonization of the national competition laws according to competition standards defined in the regional legislation. With this option, each member state would be able to enact and enforce its national competition law in line with the principles defined in the regional law. The regional competition law would be applicable only to practices affecting inter-state trade. The last option is (3) the 'downloading' approach, applied in the Andean Community,[49] which allows member states that do not have a competition law to directly apply the regional law (as a national law) to practices affecting the national market. Drexl gives preference, where developing countries are concerned, to the harmonization approach and the 'downloading' approach.

Which competition constraints could justify the choice of the unification, harmonization or 'downloading' approach, or a combination of more than one? Let us briefly consider this question.

In a regional integration group comprising a limited number of member states with relatively fluid trade between them, where there is political will on the part of the member states to surrender competences in favour of the Union and there exists a strong regional competition authority, it is advisable to undertake a unification approach with a single regional law applicable in all member states and a regional competition authority in charge of enforcing it. The fewer the member states and the smaller the common market, the more justified is the centralized approach. If the regional competition authority is able to effectively address national restrictions of competition, it is possible to have a single law applicable in all member states. As Drexl rightly pointed out, however, the risk with this option is of undermining the development of a local competition culture.[50] WAEMU has evidenced the limits of this approach. WAEMU is not, however, the best regional integration group to justify the unified approach. Its regional market is relatively large and the member states are able to develop their own competition law that could cohabit with the regional law. This centralized option might be more suitable to the Organization of Eastern Caribbean States (OECS) countries in the Caribbean.[51]

In a large regional integration group, for example ECOWAS or COMESA, a decentralized approach whereby the national law is harmonized in accordance with the standards of the regional law would be more respectful of the national specificities and the need to address effectively

---

[49] See Cortázar, J., 'Andean Competition Law: Looking for the Private Sector, or the Quest for the Missing Link in Antitrust', in this volume, Ch. 7.

[50] See Drexl, this volume, Ch. 11.

[51] Drexl argues in this vein: 'The best case for full harmonization is therefore those regions that only consist of micro-states, such as the Organization of Eastern Caribbean States (OECS).' See Drexl, this volume, Ch. 11.

local restrictions of competition. In the harmonization process, it is possible, for instance, to oblige member states to integrate certain prohibitions in their national laws. The guidelines set in the regional law could concern the obligation to prohibit anti-competitive restrictions, the obligation not to discriminate between public and private enterprises and the regulation of the exemptions. With regard to the exemptions it is crucial that the national law does not stretch the exemptions so as to shelter certain sectors from competition. Such exemptions are common in national competition legislations in West Africa. The intervention of the member states in the market should also be regulated by the regional law. It is common in West Africa that in exceptional circumstances the states have the authority to regulate prices or to exempt certain sectors from competition. This risk of limiting competition using the national laws should be dealt with by community law. As rightly pointed out by Drexl, contrary to the EU, in developing countries the regional law should be concerned with the quality of the national laws.[52]

The 'downloading' option is a transitory mechanism that could be applied in a centralized or decentralized approach. This mechanism provides the possibility of filling a juridical void in member states that do not have competition laws. In the case of WAEMU, for instance, it would make it possible for Guinea-Bissau, which does not have a competition law, to apply the regional law directly to national anti-competitive practices.

3.2.1.2 The distribution of competences The distribution of competences between the national level and the community level should be organized taking into account certain principles. In this regard, Drexl identifies the relevant factors. The anti-competitive practices affecting intra-state trade should be monitored by a regional competition authority. Drexl contends that in developing countries a decentralized enforcement of the community law, even for practices affecting intra-state trade, could be detrimental to the uniform application of the community law. In this regard, the decentralized approach of the EU, which requires member states' competition authorities to apply European law to practices affecting interstate trade, is not suitable for developing countries.

The exemptions should also be applied or monitored by a regional competition authority. A decentralized application of the exemption could endanger the uniform application of the law. WAEMU's members' national competition laws have evidenced the trend of the member states to use the

---

52 Ibid.

exemptions as a tool to shelter certain sectors or certain companies from competition.

It is crucial in the distribution of the competences, to give the national competition authorities the possibility to apply their national law or to participate in the decision-making process. The danger of excluding the national competition authorities is that the competition culture in the member states could be undermined.

With regard to substantive law, the distribution of competences would be different. A centralized approach with a uniform regional competition law, as is the case with WAEMU, could accommodate a unique enforcement authority. But the pertinence of this option is questionable. WAEMU's eight years of enforcement has proven that a centralized enforcement option can leave national restrictions of competition unaddressed.

However, the harmonization and 'downloading' approach would require vesting national competition authorities with decision-making power.

Of course, these general orientations are only guidelines that need to be tailored to the specific case of the region.

3.2.2 Guidelines for the redefinition of WAEMU's institutional enforcement framework

The debate in the framework of WAEMU is currently engaged on the revision of the institutional enforcement framework. The WAEMU Commission has mandated a study with the clear objective of identifying the flaws in its institutional design and the necessary reforms that need to be enacted. It is no surprise that the terms of reference of the study[53] put a special emphasis on the redistribution of competences between the Commission and the national competition authorities. Eight years of enforcement have demonstrated the limits of WAEMU's centralized approach. Specifically, the centralized approach has impeded the enforcement capacities of the national competition authorities,[54] slowed down the national legislative process in competition law, and diminished the competition culture in the member states. National competition authorities have always opposed the centralized approach of the WAEMU competition policy. Some

53 The study is being conducted by the Max Planck Institute for Intellectual Property, Munich, Germany.

54 See Weick, *supra* n. 24.

of them refuse to collaborate with the Commission. It is common to hear national competition authorities stating that 'not everything can be done in Ouaga'.[55]

If one agrees on the imperative to redefine the competences between national competition authorities and the Commission, a question that has to be addressed at the outset is in which direction the reform project should go. A *controlled decentralization* of WAEMU's regional competition policy has been defended elsewhere.[56] The reforms proposals put forward in this chapter are in line with our previous reform proposal, which basically calls for greater involvement of the national competition authorities in the decision-making process.

Two principles could guide the redefinition of the competences between the national competition authorities and the Commission: the *centralization of the standards of the substantive law* and the *decentralization of the decision making*.

3.2.2.1 Centralizing the standards of the substantive law WAEMU's centralized approach with unification of the rules regarding the prohibition of agreements and abuse of dominant position had the consequence of depriving member states of the competence to legislate on those domains. It is crucial, in order to effectively address national restrictions on competition and to develop the national expertise, that member states be allowed to develop their own laws. However, the development of national competition laws should be done following standards set up in the community law. In this regard it is possible to require member states to prohibit in their national competition laws anti-competitive practices such as agreements and abuse of dominant position. Most of the national competition laws already encompass such prohibitions, though they are no longer operative since the community law is exclusively applicable.

Exemptions should also be regulated according to standards set up by the community competition law. Member states should not have any leeway in defining practices or sectors that could be exempted from competition. The integration of the standards of the community law into the national laws

---

55 Referring to Ouagadougou, the capital of Burkina Faso, where the Commission has its headquarters.

56 See Bakhoum, *supra* n. 12, pp. 248 et seq. See also Bakhoum, M. (2006), 'Delimitation and Exercise of Competence between the West African Economic and Monetary Union (WAEMU) and its Member States in Competition Policy', **29** (4) *World Competition* 653, esp. 674 et seq.

could be done by expressly referring to the community law in the definition of the anti-competitive practices in the national laws. Benin has adopted this approach in the reform project of its national competition law. Member states could also redefine expressly the interdictions in their national law following the principles of the community law. A distinction should, however, be made between member states that have a national competition law and member states that do not. Member states with a national law would only have to integrate the prohibition of the anti-competitive practices following the community law. Guinea-Bissau, which does not have a competition law, could directly apply the community law as a national law, as was done in the Andean Community.

In addition to regulating the anti-competitive practices *stricto sensu*, member states should also continue to develop their unfair competition laws and the regulation of practices restricting competition.

Although it is important to centralize the standards of the substantive law at the regional level, member states should enjoy the freedom to develop their own national competition laws. Recognizing the possibility of member states to develop their own competition laws allows them to participate in the diffusion of the competition culture.

3.2.2.2 Distribution of competences between the Commission and the national competition authorities The distribution of competences between the WAEMU Commission and the national competition authorities is the most contentious issue in the WAEMU enforcement approach. The centralization of the decision-making power has evidenced its limits. National competition authorities should enjoy the freedom to protect national markets by directly addressing national restrictions of competition.

The following five principles could guide the redistribution of competences between the Commission and the national competition authorities.

- The competence to deal with anti-competitive practices affecting inter-state trade, exemptions and state aids should be the exclusive competence of the Commission.
- Anti-competitive practices that have effects limited to the national markets should be dealt with by national competition authorities.
- Collaboration mechanisms between the Commission and the national competition authorities should be created. The cooperation should concern inquiries and instruction, as is currently the case. In this respect, the Commission should be informed about the ongoing cases

before the national competition authorities and should also be authorized to pre-empt the cases that have a special interest for the community.

- The possibility should be created to appeal before the Commission the decisions issued by the national competition authorities.
- The WAEMU Court of Justice should be vested with the competence to deal with appeals against the decisions issued by the Commission.

4. CONCLUSION

Five competition constraints, generally and in the case of WAEMU, influence to a certain extent the design of regional institutions: the size of the regional market, including the number and heterogeneity of the member states; the degree of integration, particularly economic integration which implies the fluidity of trade between member states; the institutional capacities of the regional and national entities; the existence of a competition culture in the member states; and the aspect of time.

Based on these competition constraints, one can propose guidelines on the application of the substantive competition law and the distribution of competences between the national and regional level in an integration group.

Three different orientations regarding the application of the substantive law are possible: (1) a centralized approach with a unique substantive regional competition law applicable directly in all member states, even for practices affecting only the national markets; (2) the harmonization of the national competition laws according to competition standards defined in the regional legislation, while the regional competition law remains applicable only to practices affecting inter-state trade; or (3) the 'downloading' approach, which allows member states without a competition law to directly apply the regional law (as a national law) to practices affecting the national market.

In a regional integration group comprising a limited number of homogeneous member states with relatively fluid inter-state trade, strong commitment to the integration process and a strong regional competition authority, it is advisable to take a centralized approach with a single regional law applicable in all member states and a unique regional competition authority. However, WAEMU's experiences have shown that the pertinence of this option is questionable since such circumstances are rare, and, in particular, because of the risk of undermining the development of a local competition culture.

In a large regional integration group, a decentralized approach, in which the national law is only harmonized in accordance with the standards of the regional law, is more respectful of the national specificities and more capable of addressing local restrictions of competition.

The 'downloading' option is a transitory mechanism that can be applied in a centralized or decentralized approach. This mechanism can fill a juridical void in member states that do not have competition laws. The harmonization and 'downloading' approach require vesting national competition authorities with decision-making powers and thus according resources.

In developing countries a decentralized enforcement of the community law, such as in the EU, could be detrimental to the uniform application of the community law. Practices affecting inter-state trade should be monitored by a regional authority. In the same vein, exemptions should also be applied or monitored by the regional authority to prevent member states from using the exemptions as a tool to shelter certain sectors or certain companies from competition.

However, excluding national competition authorities completely from decision-making processes, in particular regarding solely national anti-competitive practices, bears the danger of undermining the evolution of a competition culture in the member states.

Applying the guidelines on the system in WAEMU, we propose a controlled decentralization, including on the one hand a centralization of its substantive competition law standards and on the other hand providing the national authorities with more decision-making powers in order to deal with practices that affect their national markets.

6. Regional integration and competition policy in the Economic Community of West African States (ECOWAS) region

Mbissane Ngom

1. INTRODUCTION

The opening of national economies to competition has become a fundamental necessity and in many respects a condition for economic development. The experiences of the South East Asian countries have sufficiently proven this. Unquestionably, in a few cases, this development, whose pace was sometimes forced, was detrimental to human rights. However, the economic progress achieved by such Asian 'tigers' remains, and can inspire other developing countries. The creation of the World Trade Organization (WTO) and the globalization of the economy have led to the necessity for all countries to enact a competition policy to enhance the rivalry between economic operators. Developing countries, and especially the West African countries, have adopted a collective approach towards disciplining the market. Hence, the Economic Community of West African States (ECOWAS)[1] also strives for an implementation of a competition law and policy, following the example of the West African Economic and Monetary Union (WAEMU).

ECOWAS was created in Lagos on 28 May 1975. The constitutive treaty was modified in Cotonou on 24 July 1993. Its main objective was to create an intra-regional West African market. In order to achieve this, ECOWAS

[1] ECOWAS has 15 member states: Benin, Burkina Faso, Cape Verde, Ivory Coast, Gambia, Ghana, Guinea, Guinea-Bissau, Liberia, Mali, Niger, Nigeria, Senegal, Sierra Leone and Togo. ECOWAS has approximately 290 million inhabitants. For more information on ECOWAS see: http://www.ecowas.int/.

has adopted a legal instrument to harmonize the legislations and to elaborate a common policy.

However, from 1975 until the beginning of the twenty-first century, ECOWAS did not genuinely concern itself with the elaboration of a competition policy, which is indispensable for the existence of a common market. While some economic policies were enacted, there remained a lack of a legal apparatus to guarantee the freedom of competition.[2] It was only in 2007, when the policy document was elaborated, that the framework for a competition policy in ECOWAS was constituted.[3] It provides the necessary instruments to guarantee the creation of a competitive market and to define the objectives of a competition policy in ECOWAS.

Like every policy, a competition policy can follow several objectives, which the competition law then has to reflect. Thus, the Sherman Act and the Clayton Act in the USA addressed the concern of combating the monopolies of railway companies and their negative influence on the American economy. After the Second World War, the overriding concern was the reconstruction of the war-ravaged countries and how to face the general shortage of resources. Nowadays, in most countries, the declared objective is to guarantee the freedom of trade and industry, the freedom of competition and the transparency of the market. More specifically, modern competition policies aim at protecting the freedom to exercise economic activities and the freedom of competition.

One might ask which of these objectives the competition policy of ECOWAS follows; a region that consists of developing, generally poor and debt-ridden countries. A first answer can be given based on the texts of the community competition legislation in ECOWAS. The document, titled *ECOWAS: Regional Competition Policy Framework*, states that 'ongoing efforts to facilitate economic integration in the ECOWAS sub-region and to promote regional economic growth will be meaningfully enhanced by the adoption of a sound regional framework for competition law'.[4] Regional integration and economic development thus seem to be the objectives of ECOWAS's competition policy. Apparently, competition policy was not

---

[2] One of the reasons is perhaps the diversity of the legal systems in the member states. Created in the cold-war context, ECOWAS has countries with different economic systems: communist, socialist and more or less capitalist regimes.

[3] ECOWAS (2007), *ECOWAS: Regional Competition Policy Framework*, available at: http://www.ecowas.int/publications/en/actes_add_commerce/1.Regional_Competition_Policy_Framework-final-P.pdf.

[4] Ibid., p. 4.

supposed to be at the stock of harmonization, even if Articles 50 and 60 of the Treaty could serve as a legal basis for this. However, due to the strong connection between competition and development, and the necessity to enact a regional common market, it was impossible to ignore the importance of a common competition policy. Without the implementation of such a common policy, private agreements or practices could endanger the free circulation of goods and services, hence the development of intra-community trade.

Additionally, the implementation of a competition policy in ECOWAS was strongly recommended by the Ministerial Committee for the Follow up of Economic Partnership Agreements (EPA). This influenced certain orientations of the adopted competition law. The Additional Act No A/SA.1/12/08 of 19 December 2008 comprises the community competition regulations and the modalities of their application within ECOWAS, at least concerning its substantive part. The procedural competition law is partially regulated by Additional Act No A/SA.2/12/08 of 19 December 2008, which organizes the creation, the attributions and functions of the regional competition authority of ECOWAS.

The fact remains that the competition law and policy of ECOWAS should reflect the strong interaction that exists between competition and development. The implementation of a policy entails choices of goals, of methods and of support. It requires a good knowledge of legal methods in order to effectively identify the prevailing and crucial issues and to find the best legal solutions in order to address them efficiently. From this point of view, an analysis of the competition policy in ECOWAS will demonstrate that efforts should be made regarding the rationalization of the competition framework in West Africa.

The underlying idea that 'law is the translation of a political project'[5] also influences ECOWAS's legislation process. If ECOWAS reaches its development goals through its regional competition policy (section 2), then the law, which is the legal translation of this political project, is doubly burdened, on normative and institutional counts (section 3).

---

[5] Aubert, J.-L. (2004), *Introduction au droit et thèmes fondamentaux du droit civil*, Paris: Armand Colin, Collection U, Foreword.

2. A COMPETITION POLICY DEDICATED TO REGIONAL INTEGRATION AND ECONOMIC DEVELOPMENT

The objectives assigned to the competition policy in ECOWAS clearly accentuate the main policy issues at stake related to the dynamism of its economy. The economic and social development in the area appears as a priority. However, to this primary objective, ECOWAS adds the objective of regional integration. In fact, ECOWAS's competition policy aims at the creation of a common regional market capable of guaranteeing the states within the region access to the globalized economy of the twenty-first century.

2.1 A Competition Policy Serving a Regional Integration Goal

The promotion, the preservation and the stimulation of competition in order to enhance the economic efficacy of trade on the regional level are some of the designated objectives of the competition policy of ECOWAS. Economic integration requires further definition and the implementation of common economic policies relating to aspects of agriculture, energy, telecommunications, environment and human resources. However, these policies by themselves are insufficient for the realization of a common market in an area consisting of cultural and linguistic diversity and different stages of development.

2.1.1 Promoting the creation of a regional common market by implementing a common regional competition policy within the ECOWAS region

Even if a common market is created, the affirmation by its participants of the freedom of circulation of persons, goods, services and capital cannot guarantee the efficacy of regional integration. This can only be achieved through a harmonization of the participants' competition law rules. Defining the community competition policy, which accompanies the economic and trade policies, is thus indispensable. In a global economy the economic function of a region depends on its competition policy's suitability. The region has a vital need for a competition law. This will complete economic integration.

The competition policy in ECOWAS, on the one hand aims at contributing to the freedom of circulation and, on the other hand, at the creation of a common market.

A common competition policy in ECOWAS is crucial for the effective realization of integration by guaranteeing to the population freedom of circulation and freedom of cross-border trade; hence a progressive abolishment of the barriers that were inherited from colonial times. This free circulation and exchange between peoples, who were once fragmented, allows the populations, especially the traders and tradespeople, to learn from each other and to trade.

The implementation of an ECOWAS-wide competition policy forms part of the creation of a common market. It signifies an elimination of barriers to free circulation, barriers that were created through the preponderance of small national markets – sometimes even micro-markets. It also justifies and fosters the ambition of national enterprises to conquer new markets in their immediate geographical area before proving their ability on the global market. In fact, global trade differs strongly from the tightness of the markets of the West African states. Thus, regional integration will allow the national enterprises to prepare themselves for international competition. The competition policy in the ECOWAS region should contribute directly to the welfare of the consumers – by providing them with a multiplicity of similar, competing or directly substitutable goods. It should equally profit the enterprises, in that their number of clients increases, as do their innovations, thereby increasing their competitiveness.

In general, it appears that economic integration cannot be achieved without a common competition policy. In other words, integration would be weakened by companies' anti-competitive and rent-seeking behaviour, which would thereby create obstacles to innovation. Hence, the chances of achieving the envisaged objectives of regional integration would be considerably reduced without a viable competition policy.

2.1.2 A complex common market

The development of a competition policy in ECOWAS took place during the process of installing a common market for investments in the integration zone. This common market of investments is presented as 'a crucial part of the economic integration process' in West Africa.[6] The communitarization of the investment laws therefore signified a big step in the process of regional integration, and it provides the investors with an equal legal infrastructure, which defines the conditions of their intervention. In this

---

[6] Ibn Chambas, M. (2009), *Vision du Marché commun des investissements de la CEDEAO*, p. v, available at http://www.ecobiz.ecowas.int/fr/pdf/CIM-Vision-French-Version.pdf.

context, the Heads of State of ECOWAS adopted the Supplementary Act A/SA.3/12/08 of 19 December 2008, which constitutes the community rules on investment-related matters. Such a unification determines the framework of legal rules for the competition between the enterprises, which will be created through investment.

However, in addition to the common market of investment, there incontestably exists a connection in trade, whether it is practised on the national, the community or the international level. The recognition of the interaction between international trade and competition can be traced back to the 1927 Conference of the Society of Nations held in Geneva.[7] The European Commission emphasized that 'there exist an increasing number of competition problems, which are of a cross-border nature: international cartels, export cartels, agreements on by their nature purely international matters ... concentrations of a global dimension, and even abuses of dominant position in several large markets'.[8] Economic integration, which leads to the opening of markets and simultaneously to the creation of a common market for the concerned parties, consequently has to be accompanied by a community competition policy that has the ability to counteract anti-competitive practices, irrespective of their origin (private or public).

However, the implementation of a community competition law regime is not an easy task for the West African countries, not only due to differences regarding their legal systems, but also in terms of the differences related to the level of economic development of the states. Another particularity of the West African region is its linguistic diversity, a diversity that was accentuated by colonization, which furthermore left the colonized states with a legal system based on a historical heritage. Thus certain West African states have adopted the 'common law' system, while others follow the Romano-Germanic system of 'civil law'. This cohabitation of legal systems, which may even entail the application of different styles of logic, can be difficult to reconcile. In fact, in the Romano-Germanic system, which ascribes to the state the role of a producer, economic intervention of a state is much more frequent than in the Anglo-Saxon system, where the state is only attributed with the function of an arbitrator between the economic actors who produce

---

[7] Society of Nations Conference, Geneva, 4–23 May 1927, publication of the Society of Nations, n° 1927, II.52.I and II.

[8] European Commission (1995), 'Competition policy in the new trade order: strengthening international cooperation and rules' (COM(95)0359 – C4–0352/95), OJ No C 362 02/12/1996, p. 0243.

and distribute goods.[9] From this it follows that ECOWAS is to incorporate this diversity, which could constitute a veritable threat to the existence and economic efficacy of a community competition law. To this difficulty is added the diversity of development levels of the member states of ECOWAS. The less developed states have to deal with a deficit of private initiatives and insufficient production capacities. This leads to an inclination towards strong economic intervention by the state, which is therefore called upon to produce and distribute, or to regulate certain sectors, sometimes to the detriment of all economic rationale and the development perspective of the state. On the other hand, more advanced states with a higher level of development have a tendency to favour the private sector. Generally, the common-law countries, Ghana and Nigeria, are rated among the latter category. Nigeria is the richest and most developed country in the entire region.

However, irrespective of the potential and actual difficulties, the economic development of the member states remains the main objective of the competition policy in ECOWAS.

2.2 A Competition Policy Serving an Economic Development Goal

In order to use a community competition policy as an instrument for regional integration to enhance economic development, one has to recognize the following prerequisite: the existence 'of rules whose goal is the promotion of economic development'.[10] Incontestably, such rules exist in the framework of the African sub-regional organizations. In ECOWAS, however, although its competition policy is purported to have this mission of economic development, in reality, the competition policy seems to be directed towards the attraction of foreign direct investment.

---

[9] It is worthy of note that the historical process of the constitution of a state influences and somewhat determines the role and importance of the state in the economy. Germany, with its post-war ordo-liberalist approach, evidences the role of the state in the market. Bilger, V.F. (1964), 'La pensée économique libérale dans l'Allemagne contemporaine', *Librairie générale de droit et de jurisprudence*, Paris, p. 318; Commun, P. (ed.) (2003), *L'ordolibéralisme allemand: aux sources de l'Economie sociale de marché*, Centre d'information et de recherche sur l'Allemagne contemporaine (CIRAC).

[10] Salah, M.M.M. (1998), 'La problématique du droit économique dans les pays du sud', *RIDE* **12** (1), 19–33, at 21.

2.2.1 The central place of competition policy

ECOWAS's authorities have acknowledged the central place of competition policy as an instrument of modern economics. To possess an open and competitive market has become a requirement for all integrated regions in order to promote economic efficiency. Based on the ambition of ECOWAS's initiators to combine their efforts in order to enhance development, the creation of ECOWAS was a necessity.

The document on the regional competition framework affirms precisely that 'the member states of ECOWAS, which all strive for the development of durable economies and for the stabilization of their market conditions, have the common interest to adopt a framework which controls the competition on the regional level'.[11] This position is based on the presumption that competition law and competition policy have contributed in a decisive manner to the prosperity of the developed nations by supporting strong growth, dynamic entrepreneurship, advantages for the consumer and finally social stability, which results from the foregoing aspects. The competition policy of ECOWAS is thus also aimed at these results.

In fact, the creation of a common market responds to the imperative to harmonize the efforts of the states to reduce poverty and to assure the population's access to basic standards. It implies that economic development appears as the prioritized objective at the national as well as at the regional level. In this regard, the competition law of ECOWAS has incorporated the general objectives of the organization. Article 3 of the Treaty describes harmonization and coordination of national trade policies as a means of maintaining and strengthening economic stability in the subregion.

The regulations on the competition law in ECOWAS, which are set out in the preamble and Art. 5ff. of the Supplementary Act A/SA.1/12/08, rely largely on the objectives pursued by the member states. In fact, the text states 'that the promulgation of community competition rules is compatible with the objectives of development within the member states of ECOWAS'. Among these is the necessity to have a 'dynamic and competitive [economy] in order to promote and support the necessary conditions for an economic growth in the region'. The text establishes a connection between these elements: the achievement of economic growth within ECOWAS is influenced by the existence of a dynamic and competitive economy, which fosters and promises this growth. ECOWAS thereby explicitly underlines its choice for a liberal economy in order to guarantee its development.

---

[11] ECOWAS (2007), *Regional Competition Policy Framework*, *supra* n. 3, p. 5.

2.2.2 The regional competition policy and ECOWAS's development objectives

The competition policy of ECOWAS has the potential to serve as an efficient instrument for attaining a competitive level of the economic activities in the region, in particular in its ability to enhance profitable integration in the global economy. From this point of view, the competition policy is in conformity with the objectives of integration. Two consequences follow from this – one positive, the other bearing a risk.

Firstly, the competition policy bears the potential to prepare the local enterprises of the region to compete internationally and to constitute a sign of quality of the legal environment regarding the attraction of investments and their security. The competition policy therefore appears as essential for the realization of an internal market. In that it promotes economic efficiency, it will create a climate favouring innovation, technical progress, reduction of production costs and the maximal satisfaction of the consumers.

At the same time, it entails a second consequence for the economy of the region: the risk of lacking adaptability. The choice of a liberal economy not only implies considerable consequences for the status of enterprises and for their freedom to exercise economic activity, but also for their chance to survive fierce competition. In fact, the decision to open the market leads to increased and more intense competition. However, there remain doubts over whether the domestic enterprises are competitive enough to cope with this new situation due to the weakness of the intra-community trade.

One of the conclusions one can draw from these justified doubts is that the competition law of ECOWAS is not exclusively committed to the protection of competition, but rather to the promotion of foreign direct investment. It seems to provide a legal framework (namely the Supplementary Acts A/SA.1/12/08, A/SA.2/12/08 and A/SA.3/12/08) which is mostly focused outside the region and that serves as a rallying call – a panel bearing the slogan: 'Come, we are open to competition.' In fact, the foregoing analysis of the adopted competition law rules in ECOWAS suggests that the real objective is to satisfy the needs of the foreign direct investors by supplying them with a secure framework in which the equality of chances is guaranteed.

However, this signifies that the competition policy does not follow an endogenous conception of development, which would take into account the lives of its own populations. This perception is supported by the absence of a definition of a West African vision on development. In fact, despite the efforts made to integrate the different states of the African region, coherence between the enacted acts is lacking. Little effort is made to promote an industry of development and of local consumption. The most important enterprises are situated in the export sectors. Therefore, a large majority of the population is involved in negotiating and small business activities, or in the attempt to escape poverty in the informal sector.

Nevertheless, one of the intentions of regional integration is the promotion of a local industry, adapted to the requirements of development. The freedom of circulation, to which ECOWAS is dedicated, has to support trade between the member states. Such inter-state trade is only of real interest if there exists a dense net of small and medium-sized firms (SMEs) in the different member states. From this point of view, however, the programmes were developed merely by the community institutions, and their legal translation and their implementation in the member states was inadequate. One would have to find an efficient balance between the necessity to guarantee competition and the crucial requirement for the protection of local enterprises. In the absence of such a balanced legal framework, the impact of the informal sector becomes even greater, thereby nourishing fraud and smuggling. It also leads to the situation that a large part of trade between the member states of ECOWAS is not included in the official statistics.

ECOWAS's competition law is contained in two Additional Acts A/SA.1/12/08 and A/SA.2/12/08 of 19 December 2008, which lay down the competition law regulations and which install the regional authority, which is vested with the respective controlling competence. However, the enforcement of the competition legislation entails several difficulties.

3. CHALLENGES TO THE IMPLEMENTATION OF THE REGIONAL COMPETITION POLICY

One can rightly qualify West Africa as an integration zone of 'variable geography'.[12] The region's competition law is a patent example of this. In fact, there is not only a multiplicity of legal rules in this zone, but also a diversity of authorities in charge of the control of competition-related

12 Professor Alioune Sall analyses the historical formation of the regional spaces in West Africa and highlights the different objectives of the regional integration groups over time. See Sall, A. (2006), *Les mutations de l'intégration des Etats en Afrique de l'Ouest. Une approche institutionnelle*, Paris: L'Harmattan, Etudes africaines.

matters. This diversity by itself is not necessarily harmful; however, it becomes problematic with regard to the coherence and the hierarchization of the system.

3.1 Normative 'Competition'

The West African region is characterized by a diversity of existing integration organizations. These organizations were created on the basis of very different criteria, such as arid climate conditions,[13] the will to exploit a river[14] or a community of production of agricultural products. They were created in order to serve either a general or a sectoral purpose. ECOWAS and WAEMU are the sole organizations that are aimed at a general integration surrounding the harmonization of policies and legislations. This identity of objectives, added to the fact that all member states of WAEMU[15] also belong to ECOWAS, results in an increased risk of a situation of normative competition, which arises when states make parallel use of available laws in order to achieve their integration objectives.[16] In addition, one has to bear in mind that the diversity of legal systems in the region is aggravated by the coexistence of countries with a civil-law tradition and countries with a common-law tradition.[17]

---

[13] This is the case with the Comité permanent Inter-Etats de lutte contre la Sécheresse dans le Sahel (CILSS).

[14] This is the case with the Organisation pour la mise en valeur du Fleuve Sénégal (OMVS) and l'Organisation pour la mise en valeur du Fleuve Gambie (OMVG).

[15] Benin, Burkina Faso, Ivory Coast, Guinea-Bissau, Mali, Niger, Senegal and Togo.

[16] See my contribution, 'Concurrence des droits communautaires: UEMOA/CEDEAO', to the conference De la concurrence à la cohabitation des droits communautaires. L'environnement juridique des affaires mis en place par les droits communautaires (OHADA, UEMOA, CEMAC, CEDEAO, OAPI, CIMA, CIPRES), 24–26 January 2011, Cotonou, Benin, forthcoming.

[17] In addition there is the possibility of the creation of a competition law in the OHADA region. Competition law has been added to the list of the areas that are to be harmonized. However, it is very doubtful whether having a competition law is pertinent in the OHADA region. Having a regional competition law is the result of an economic choice. OHADA aims only at harmonizing the business law, not at creating a regional economic area. OHADA is not a regional economic area.

3.1.1 An improvable normative cohabitation

The different regional integration groups in West Africa also constitute different legal spaces, which are superposed by complex interferences because these groups do not cover the same geographical space. It follows that there is a difficult normative cohabitation, which is reconcilable in certain sectors.

This normative cohabitation has become a reality in competition law. In fact, WAEMU and ECOWAS have both adopted a legal framework that regulates competition in the market. The community competition legislations – WAEMU's entered into force in 2002[18] and ECOWAS's legislation in 2008 – are to a large extent applicable in the same geographical space, even if the ECOWAS legislation covers a larger geographic area. This means that on the community level, the coexistence of competition legislations only concerns those states that are a member of both regional integration groups. From this it follows that WAEMU's Article 88 of the Treaty of Dakar and the texts related to its enforcement[19] cover the same scope of application as the Additional Act that constitutes the ECOWAS competition law regulations. This cohabitation of legislations will lead to discussions, especially concerning the risk of legislative rivalry and conflicts over their applicability.

The drafters of the Additional Acts A/SA.1/12/08 and A/SA.2/12/08 of ECOWAS did not ignore this risk. Furthermore, they proposed considering the WAEMU region as a single state from the perspective of ECOWAS, at least regarding the competition legislation of WAEMU. However, in reality,

---

18 See, on WAEMU's competition law, Ngom, M. (2007), 'Droit et intégration économique dans l'espace UEMOA: le cas de la régulation juridique de la concurrence', doctoral thesis, Nantes et Saint-Louis, unpublished.

19 WAEMU's competition regulations are:

- Regulation n°2/2002/CM/UEMOA relatif aux pratiques anticoncurrentielles à l'intérieur de l'Union Economique et Monétaire Ouest Africaine;
- Regulation n° 3/2002/CM/UEMOA relatif aux procédures applicables aux ententes et abus de position dominante à l'intérieur de l'Union Economique et Monétaire Ouest Africaine;
- Regulation n° 4/2002/CM/UEMOA relatif aux aides d'Etat à l'intérieur de l'Union Economique et Monétaire Ouest Africaine et aux modalités d'application de l'article 88 (c) du Traité;
- Directive n° 02/2002/CM/UEMOA relative à la coopération entre la Commission et les Structures Nationales de Concurrence des Etats membres pour l'application des articles 88, 89 et 90 du traité de l'UEMOA.

Those regulations are available on WAEMU's website at the following address: www.uemoa.int/.

such a solution could not prosper, since WAEMU itself has not definitely resolved the issue of the distribution of competences between the national and the community competition law. Moreover, it is generally possible to have a cohabitation of community legislations in the African region. This does not necessarily lead to a situation of competing legislations that judges would be called upon to resolve.

In fact, one could specify the scope of application of the community competition rules. Article 4 of the Additional Act precisely states that the community competition rules are only applicable to practices that are 'likely to affect the trade within ECOWAS'. The text thus requires an incident analysis of the relevant behaviour regarding its impact on intra-community trade in ECOWAS. This is a difficult analysis, not only for the judge who has to resolve the matter, but also for the plaintiff who files a complaint. Also, it could be preferable to refer to the WAEMU system, which does not require an effect on the trade between member states in order to be applicable. Facing this dilemma of two community systems that are *a priori* similarly applicable, the best solution would be to enact the system that entails an easier enforcement. However, this is a solution based on mere laziness and neither of the two systems is clearly better than the other one.

Furthermore, ECOWAS acknowledges the possibility of a coexistence of national regulations and community rules. ECOWAS's community law is only applicable to practices that affect the trade between member states. It follows that practices whose anti-competitive effect is limited to the national territory fall under the scope of the internal legislation of the concerned country.

3.1.2 Partially diverging competition rules

Irrespective of their coexistence, the competition laws of ECOWAS and WAEMU also overlap regarding their normative content. They prohibit illicit agreements and abuses of dominant position, address public aids and subject public enterprises to competition law. One can thus note that the competition law system of ECOWAS covers the different aspects of anti-competitive practices, whether activities are conducted by private enterprises or are imputable to the public power. The fundamental principles of competition law are thus respected in the case of the legislation of ECOWAS.

However, there are notable differences in the definitions of the concepts, differences that can have major consequences in the actual control of economic activity. The following examples demonstrate this risk.

The first example relates to the different influences of the criteria of the effect on trade between member states. While the WAEMU legislation, Directive N° 04/2002, which organizes the cooperation between the Commission and the national competition authorities, does not require an effect on trade between member states, the application of ECOWAS's competition law depends on this condition. In other words, while WAEMU has decided to unify its competition law by substituting the different domestic legislations with a unified community legislation, ECOWAS has chosen to follow the system of double barriers by maintaining the domestic legislations, which are applicable to anti-competitive practices with a mere national dimension. These diverging choices are not without consequences since some member states belong to ECOWAS and WAEMU at the same time, and since in this affiliation their domestic competition laws are neutralized by the community law of WAEMU. For those countries, one will have to answer the question regarding the role of the criterion of 'effect on trade between member states'. Thereby one has to determine whether ECOWAS's or WAEMU's competition law will be applicable.

Furthermore, ECOWAS applies a very restrictive concept regarding the abuse of a dominant position. A dominant position depends on the effect on a substantial part of the market, which is determined by the ability of the company to control prices and exclude other competition.[20] In WAEMU, the definition, more suitably, also includes substitutability and the diversity of situations of dominance. The definition requires that there be 'a situation in which an enterprise has the capacity to impede effective competition on the relevant market, to increase barriers to entry to the market by playing a directing role on the market'.[21] This definition is thus more complete. It is also better adapted to the West African context because it has a greater flexibility. It can be adapted to the diversity of economic situations that prevail due to the duality of the economy in the region.

Another fundamental difference relates to the anti-competitive practices that could be subject to an exemption. The ECOWAS legislation provides that practices that contribute to social progress can fall outside the scope of the competition law, while WAEMU does not provide for this kind of exemption. Article 4(2) of Additional Act A/SA.1/12/08 explicitly includes agreements and activities that have to do with 'questions relating to

---

[20] Art. 6(1) Additional Act A/SA.1/12/08.

[21] Note 5 of annexe 1 of Regulation n° 3/2002/CM/UEMOA relatif aux procédures applicables aux ententes et abus de position dominante à l'intérieur de l'Union Economique et Monétaire Ouest Africaine.

employment, notably activities of the employees which legitimately aim at the protection of their interests' and 'to agreements of collective negotiations which are concluded between employers and employees in order to fix terms and modalities of services'. One can thus conclude by noting that the ECOWAS legislation is more focused on the requirements of the labour law than on the requirements of the competition law.

3.2 Non-hierarchical Institutional Architecture

The procedural competition law of ECOWAS is characterized by a diversity of institutional controls. This institutional structure bears the risk of inefficacy, yet it could be corrected by unifying the method of enforcement employed by the controlling authorities.

3.2.1 Diversified institutional control

Calling for a new composition of the legal landscape, Mireille Delmas-Marty invites us to consider 'discontinued hierarchies' and 'unachieved pyramids'.[22] The institutional landscape of West Africa is under perpetual construction; the integration groups are created and cohabit according to the political will of the governments of the member states. Yet a certain stability can be noted in recent years following the crystallization of a construction surrounding WAEMU and ECOWAS. However, the observer should ask whether there exists a hierarchy or some sort of pyramid of control of competition in West Africa. Several organs were created at the internal and community levels in order to assure control, but without bearing in mind the coherence of the overall structure.

Thereby, regarding the normative rivalry, the control of competition could be exercised by organs of ECOWAS or by organs of WAEMU that are vested with the specific competence. Incidentally, ECOWAS has chosen a different institutional structure regarding the control of competition than that of WAEMU. In fact, while WAEMU copied the European system by vesting the Commission with the controlling competence on competition, ECOWAS chose to create a specialized organ. In this context, Additional Act A/SA.2/12/08 created the Regional Authority, whose function is the surveillance of the common market of ECOWAS as regards competition-related matters. In a case of infringement it is entitled to sanction the anti-competitive practices. The creation of this organ, whose effective operation is still pending three years after the adoption of the Additional

---

22 Delmas-Marty, V.M. (1994), *Pour un droit commun*, Paris: Seuil, pp. 92ff.

Act, can be explained by the concern to avoid an ineffective competition law system, which occurred in WAEMU due to the lack of a specialized authority dedicated to competition law matters. ECOWAS has thus tried to draw some lessons from the failures of WAEMU in the field of competition law.

However, the question of effective control of competition in West Africa can also be raised regarding the multiplicity of implied authorities, at either the national or the community level. The risk that these different bodies will issue contradicting decisions requires careful attention. In this respect, the entry into force of a cooperation mechanism could be an efficient solution. The law of ECOWAS envisages such a mechanism. Article 13(3) of Additional Act No A/SA.1/12/08 declares that 'during the implementation of competition rules in the Community, the Regional Authority will collaborate with other existing competition law agencies (WAEMU)'.

'Intertwined hierarchies' and 'strange circles'; perhaps the implementation of competition law in West Africa will take place in a 'curved form'.[23] Furthermore, one cannot ignore the differences that exist among the member states of WAEMU, which also all belong to ECOWAS.

3.2.2 A unified method

Despite the complexity of the institutional architecture of the control of competition in ECOWAS, there are reasons to be optimistic. One such reason is the unification of methods to control practices, methods used by the authorities in charge of applying the community competition legislations.

Different by their nature, the controlling community and national authorities have one identical mission: to apply the competition law in the ECOWAS region. Therefore, they were attributed with specific powers in order to guarantee that competition is not distorted, and, in the case of infringement, to sanction possible threats to competition.

The methodology used is marked by the importance of teleological reasoning, which refers to the competitive process of the market.[24] That the common market of ECOWAS remains competitive has to be ensured by sanctioning all the actions that could endanger the existence of economic competition. The control of competition-related practices implies complex economic assessments. In fact, since 1969, the ECJ has affirmed that '[t]he

---

23 Ibid.

24 Frison-Roche, M.-A. (2002), 'Le juge du marché', *Le juge de l'économie*, special issue of *Revue de Jurisprudence commerciale*, at 45.

question whether such an agreement is in fact prohibited depends on the appraisal of economic and legal factors which cannot be assumed to be present in the absence of an explicit finding [on] the individual agreement in question'.[25] This affirmation also applies to the competition law of ECOWAS. The evaluation of anti-competitive practices, which is conducted by the controlling authorities with new competences, does not only require legal competences. One has not only to analyse the legality of behaviour, but also to evaluate economic activity, meaning, one has to undertake a legal and economic analysis. The mode of functions and the reasoning of a judge also have to be saturated with economic theories. Regarding the controlling function of the authorities this also entails that a judge 'fosters in his [or her] reasoning also other norms than those of the law'.[26] The fusion of legal and economic methods of logic is a necessary condition for effective enforcement of competition. The composition of the Regional Authority displays the efforts made to address this necessity.

The evaluation of anti-competitive practices in the ECOWAS area thus constitutes not only a legal but also an economic analysis. This double analysis results from the necessity to proceed on economical and competition-related assumptions in order to decide whether a practice should be prohibited or authorized. The economic analysis stimulates an objective appreciation of the economic situation. The advantage of this method, which is shared by all competition law organs, is that it guarantees relative objectivity without respect to the concrete intervening instance. The method also reduces the impact of the differences in the legal traditions of the member states; specifically, whether they have a civil or a common-law legal tradition.

From this point of view, the competition policy can be an efficient tool for the emergence of a law well adapted to the prevailing situation of underdevelopment in the region of ECOWAS.

---

25 ECJ, judgment of 9 July 1969, Case No. 10/69, [1969] ECR 309 – *Portelange v. Smith Corona Marchant International*, para. 13.

26 Frison-Roche, *supra* n. 24, at 48.

7. Andean competition law: looking for the private sector, or the quest for the missing link in antitrust

Javier Cortázar*

1. INTRODUCTION

At the end of the day more and better business is what competition law is all about. Therefore, sound competition law is in the interest of all: it matters not only to national authorities and some international agencies, but especially to the private sector, where businesses come from.

As I come from the private sector I will focus on its role in Andean antitrust law (Decision 608 of 2005),[1] especially because, as we will see, it is one of the pinions that urgently need to be assembled within the Andean system, which, though a very good system, paradoxically, has not yet been enforced.

The quality of Andean competition law is so high in part because of the legal system in which it was conceived, the Andean Community Law. For this reason, I will first refer briefly to its main features, before also briefly describing Decision 608, putting some emphasis on what Professor Francisco Marcos of the Spanish Instituto de la Empresa Business School

---

* Mr Cortázar is the author of the books *Hacia un Nuevo Derecho de la Competencia en Colombia* (Towards a New Competition Law for Colombia, Bogotá 2003), *Curso de Derecho de la Competencia* (Textbook on Competition Law, Bogotá 2011) and translator into Spanish of Professor David Gerber's latest book, *Global Competition: Law, Markets, and Globalization* (Oxford 2010), which will be published in Spanish-speaking countries in February 2012. Many thanks to the Max Planck Institute, its director and staff for the kind invitation to participate in this workshop and to express my ideas, which will hopefully find some echo.

[1] Decisión 608 (Marzo 29 de 2005) Normas para la protección y promoción de la libre competencia en la Comunidad Andina.

cleverly termed the 'downloading' option[2] for Ecuador and Bolivia: to have their own competition authorities apply Decision 608 to domestic cases until the enactment of their own national laws.

I will then analyse what I consider the big problem of Decision 608, which is its lack of use. This analysis will cover four reasons that explain the phenomenon and the manner in which the Andean Community is trying to deal with the problem, especially through the CAIPIR initiative within the project INTERCAN I, and why, even though this initiative is a good idea, it is not sufficient. Finally, I conclude that to put Decision 608 in practice the active participation of the private sector is crucial. To be done properly, this needs an activist non-government organization (NGO) in antitrust law in which engaged lawyers, economists and journalists could fight – with some chance of success – for the effective enforcement of antitrust law in the Andean countries.

2. A PRELIMINARY EXPLANATION OF ANDEAN LAW

Conceived following the European law model, there is a well-established body of doctrine and case law from both the Andean Tribunal of Justice and domestic courts relating to the law's main characteristics, amongst them supremacy, supranationality, direct effect, direct applicability, autonomy and state responsibility for the breach of Andean law.[3]

Another important feature of Andean law is its system of dispute resolution, in which individuals have extensive rights of standing. Briefly, this system comprises: (i) actions for nullity of the Community acts (Decisions and Resolutions) when they violate Andean law; (ii) actions for the breach of Community law when domestic governments violate Community law, which has two stages, one administrative, before the Secretariat General, and the other judicial, before the Andean Tribunal of Justice; (iii) preliminary rulings when domestic authorities have to apply Andean law domestically; and (iv) others rather related to the Community's internal affairs, as for instance actions related to labour matters.

---

[2] Marcos, F. (2008), 'Downloading competition law from a regional trade agreement (RTA): A new strategy to introduce competition law in Bolivia and Ecuador', paper submitted to UNCTAD's Seventh Session of the Intergovernmental Group of Experts on Competition Law and Policy – Geneva, 30 October to 2 November 2006 – mimeo.

[3] Tangarife, M. (2002), *Derecho de la Integración en la Comunidad Andina*, Bogotá: Biblioteca jurídica Dike, pp. 194–213.

The dispute-resolution system was drafted taking into account the rights of standing of individuals, so they do not need, for instance, to go to Lima, the city where the Secretariat General has its headquarters, or Quito, where the Andean Tribunal of Justice sits, to lodge complains, attend hearings and similar matters. They can act from their domicile and communicate with the Community's bodies through different means, such as by fax, and they do not need even a lawyer. Another interesting feature is that time limits are ample to bring appeals. In the administrative stage of cases on breach of the law, for instance, parties have 45 days to appeal if they do not agree with the decision.

Compared with the dispute-settlement mechanisms of other regional trade agreements of which Andean countries are a part, Andean law excels. In the Free Trade Agreements between Peru and the United States and between Colombia and the United States, agreements drafted following the template of the North American Free Trade Agreement (NAFTA), the situation of individuals (among many other things) is quite different. It does not, for instance, involve a tribunal like that of the Andean Community.

Despite the Andean region's long association with the legend of 'El Dorado', it seems that we have become accustomed to thinking that treasures do not exist at all, forgetting that beyond gold cities hidden deep in rain forests there are also other, more earthly and not so inaccessible treasures, for instance, cleverly conceived institutions. Andean law is one of these – paradoxically – actual but hidden institutional treasures.

3. THE ANDEAN COMPETITION LAW: DECISION 608 OF 2005

Even though, since the signing of the founding treaty, the Cartagena Agreement (Acuerdo de Cartagena), in 1969, competition was called on to play a crucial role, it was not until Decision 608 of 2005 that a sound regime in the matter was adopted. Before Decision 608 there were other regimes, such as the flawed Decision 285, which I will not refer to, since this kind of legal archaeology is not important for the purpose of this chapter.

The underlying principle of Decision 608 is regional integration. The preamble states that at that stage of integration a new law in competition was needed to prevent anti-competitive schemes from hampering the integration process.

Decision 608 appointed the Secretariat General as the competition authority, which acts in coordination with the domestic authorities both in the instigation of investigations and in the execution of decisions.

The Decision drew up an entire procedure to carry out investigations, in which the domestic authorities of the countries of the investigated enterprises have a special logistical role in the gathering of evidence and the execution of the rulings.[4]

In addition to cease-and-desist orders, the Decision endows regional authorities with the power to impose fines on economic agents acting anti-competitively. Such fines can be up to 10 per cent of the offender's last year's gross revenue.[5]

Decision 608 introduced competition-advocacy rules within the region. Article 36 prohibits member states from adopting regulations or implementing economic policies that hamper competition (unreasonably) within the region, a rule that, though susceptible to actions for breach of the Andean law, was considered by the Secretariat General only in relation to regulations of regional scope and with effects in two or more countries.[6]

Other interesting features are: (i) the establishment of the Andean Committee for the Defence of Competition as an advisory group formed by representatives of the competition authorities of the member countries in crucial matters such as injunctions, the imposition of fines or the issuing of recommendations to regulatory agencies to ease restrictions of competition;[7] (ii) the domestic authorities' duty of close collaboration;[8] and (iii) the 'downloading' option: that the Decision may be applied in domestic cases in Bolivia and Ecuador until their adoption of their own competition laws.[9]

3.1 Distribution of Competences between Regional and Domestic Authorities

As long as within the Andean Community domestic and regional antitrust laws coexist, one important issue is the proper allocation of competences, especially because, unlike the current European regime, in which since 2004 domestic authorities have been allowed to apply European law

---

4 Articles 10, 15, 16, 17, 18, 35.

5 Article 34.

6 Secretariat of the Andean Community – Dictámen (Opinion) 1 of 2007, Gazette No. 1489.

7 Articles 38–41.

8 Article 37.

9 Articles 49 and 50 for Bolivia and Decision 616 for Ecuador.

directly in cases of regional scope, the Andean authorities are not endowed with this power.

3.1.1 How it works

Article 5 of the Decision lays down the basic rules for allocating competences, which depend upon two factors: the origin and the effects of the anti-competitive practice. The Article comprises two options. The first applies when the practice originates within the region and the second when it comes from abroad.

Regarding the former, when the origin of the practice is in one or more member countries and it has effects in one or more member states, the competence is with the Community; otherwise the case is domestic. In the latter, when the practice has effects in two or more member countries, the Community law applies; otherwise the case is domestic.

Figures 7.1 to 7.4 help to explain when the regional law applies: Andean Community law would apply in all of the four cases.

3.1.1.1 Option one This option offers three possibilities. The first is when the practice originates in one member country and has effects in at least two other member countries. Figure 7.1 shows a practice that originates in Colombia with effects in Ecuador and Peru.

The second possibility is that the practice originates in two member countries and has effects in at least one member country. In Figure 7.2, the practice originates in Bolivia and Peru with effects in Colombia.

The third possibility is when the practice originates in one country and has effects within the same country and another member country. This is illustrated by Figure 7.3, with a practice originating in Colombia that has effects both in Colombia and Peru.

3.1.1.2 Option two The second option is simpler since the practice has to originate in a foreign country and its effects must be felt in at least two member countries. Figure 7.4 shows a practice originating in Brazil with effects in Ecuador and Bolivia.

3.1.2 The (likely) meaning of the term 'effect'

There is a common tendency to equate the origin with the effect of anti-competitive behaviour, considering that the Andean regime only applies when the practice at issue is performed at least in two member countries. This is a fallacy that has greatly contributed to the problem of the lack of use of Decision 608.

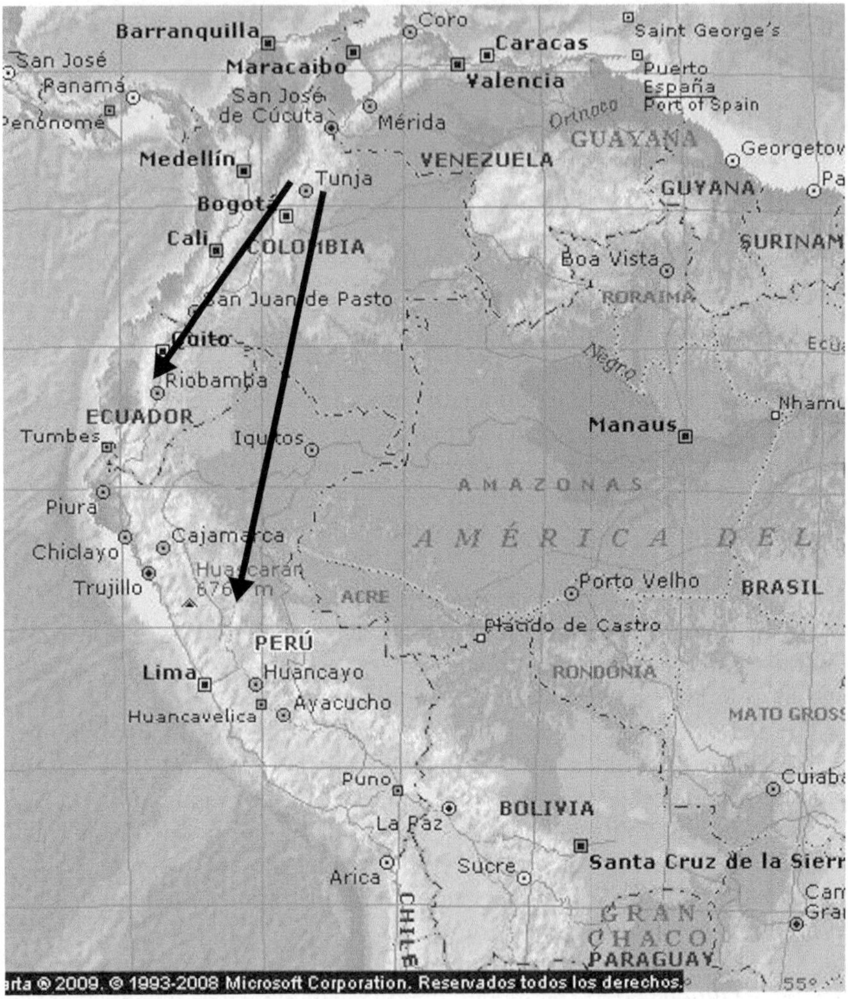

Figure 7.1

The meaning of the term 'effect' is very important in allocating competences between the different authorities because what counts is not only the origin of the practice but also its effects.

Since there is not any Andean case law in competition, we must turn to the European experience to look for precedents, especially those before the 2003 reforms that empowered the domestic authorities to apply Community law directly, which is not possible in the Andean regime.

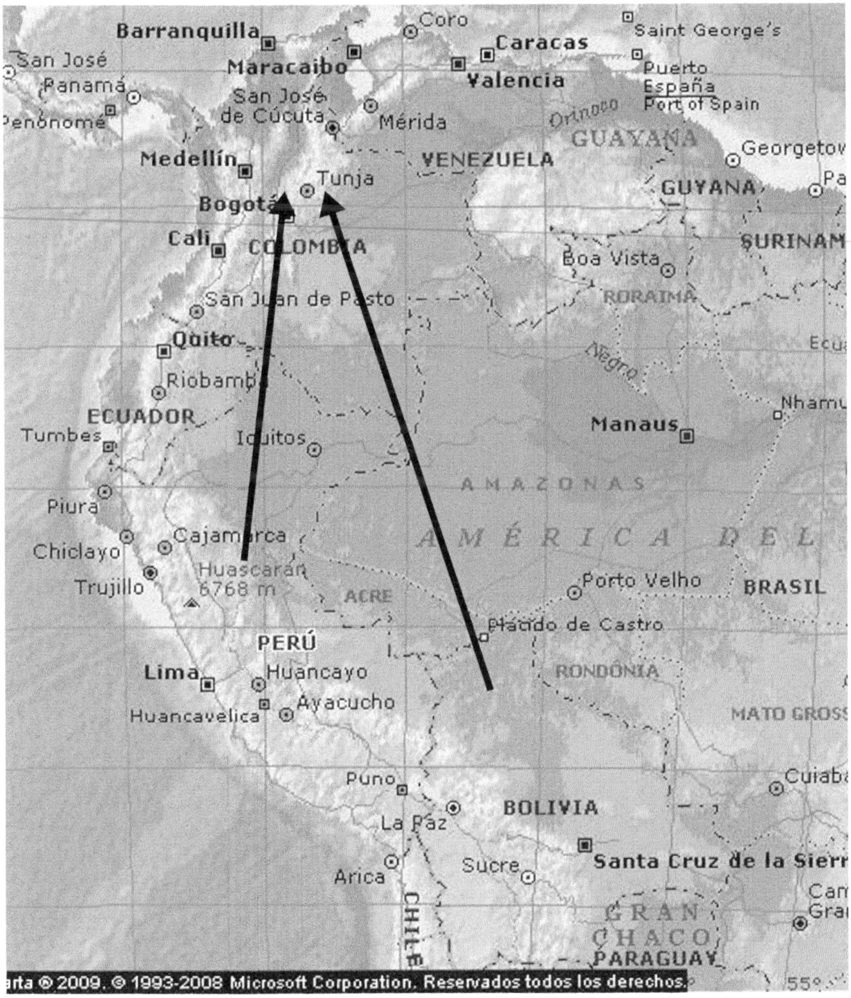

Figure 7.2

The case law of the European Court of Justice encompasses two standards. The first is the effects standard derived from the case of *Société Technique Minière* v *Maschinenbau Ulm*,[10] and the second is the standard of altered competition structure within the Union.[11]

---

[10] 56/65 [1966] ECR 235, [1966] CMLR 357.

[11] Whish, Richard (1989), *Competition Law*, London: Butterworths, p. 248.

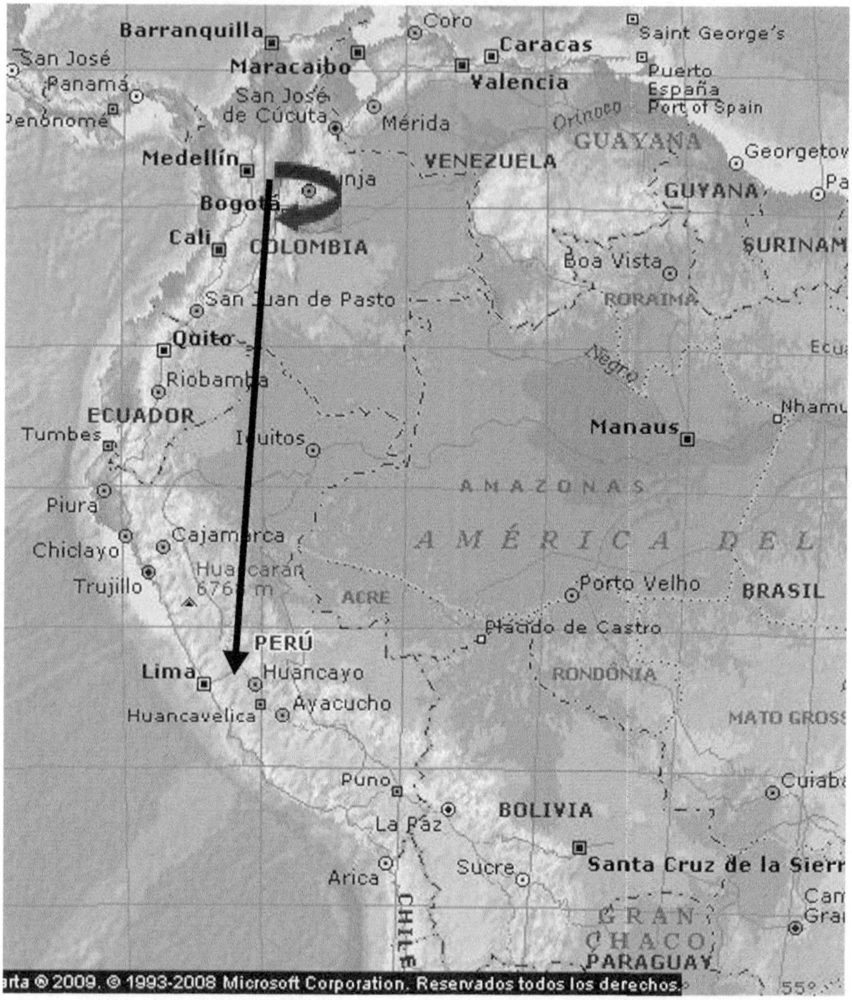

Figure 7.3

According to the former, an anti-competitive practice falls under Community law if it can influence, directly or indirectly, actually or potentially, the trade patterns of the member countries. This is a principle that has been developed by the European Court of Justice in various ways, such as in the possibility of scrutinizing the whole agreement even if only a tiny part of it

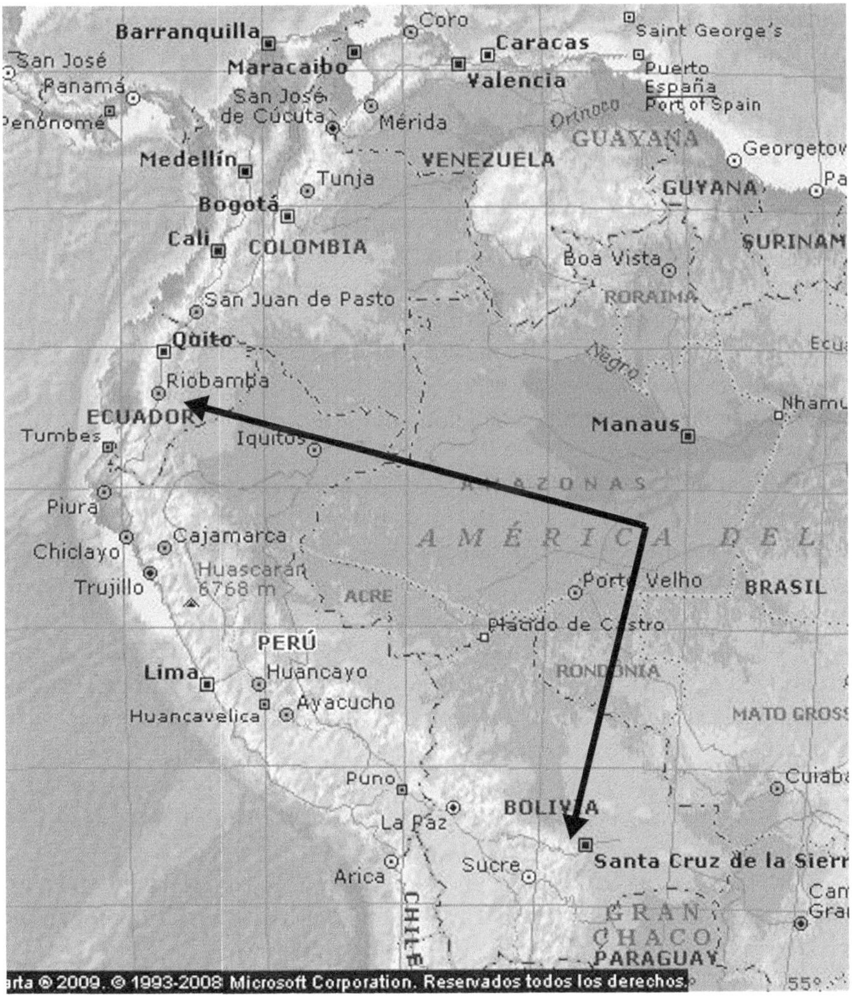

Figure 7.4

has effects on the Community (*Windsurfing International Inc* v *Commission*)[12] or when a domestic practice falls under Community law if it can hinder foreign trade, even potentially (*Cutsforth* v *Mansfield Inns*)[13] or when Community law applies, even if trade volume increases (*Consten and*

12 183/83 [1986] 3 CMLR 489.
13 [1986] 1 CMLR 1.

Grundig v *Commission*),[14] just to cite some of the main developments of this standard.

The latter standard is simpler, stipulating that any alteration of the Community's competition structures places the case under Community jurisdiction.[15]

It will foreseeably be quite difficult for the Secretariat General of the Andean Community not to follow the European lead, not just because of the 'European' mark but because it is a very serious body of jurisprudence that has been evolving for 50 years, and the only one the Andean authority can look to for strong guidance. As Professor Gerber states, 'European experience in coordinating national and transnational competition law efforts is the most extensive laboratory we have for studying the dynamics of transnational competition law development'.[16]

3.1.3 Practical results of the distribution of competences

Currently the significance of the distribution of competences is rather focused on the importance of safeguarding competition within the whole region as an issue of integration, since Community trade effectively could be (badly) hampered by anti-competitive practices.

Before the enactment of Law 1340 (2009)[17] in Colombia, which introduced healthy changes to the until then quite flawed antitrust law system, the application of Community law could have another level of meaning, as it was possible to impose harsher sanctions in cases in which Community rather than domestic law applied, but today this difference lacks the significance it once had, because the current Colombian regime also has harsh sanctions.

A brief review of the domestic and the Community regimes shows that, as is the case in Europe, the national regimes and the Andean one do not differ much, especially from the substantive point of view.

Table 7.1 shows a brief comparison of the Community and domestic regimes.

---

14 Cases 56–58/64 [1966] ECR 299.

15 Whish, *supra* n. 11.

16 Gerber, D. (2010), *Global Competition: Law, Markets, and Globalization*, Oxford: Oxford University Press, p. viii.

17 Republic of Colombia – LEY 1340 DE 2009 (julio 24) Por medio de la cual se dictan normas en materia de protección de la competencia.

Table 7.1

Factor	AC	Bolivia	Colombia	Ecuador	Peru
Catalogue of practices	• Agreements • Abuse of dominance • Mergers?	'Mexican style'	• Agreements • Abuse of dominance • Mergers	Same as AC	• Agreements • Abuse of dominance • No mergers
Authority's independence	More independent	Less independent	Less independent	Less independent	More independent
Length of procedures	• Certainty in preliminary inquiry • 2 years (estimated)	N/A	• Uncertainty in preliminary inquiry • Average 3 years	N/A	• Certainty in preliminary inquiry • Average 3 years
Sanctions	Up to 10% of gross revenue	Mixture of economic and administrative remedies	• Possibly higher	Same as AC	Up to 12% of gross revenue
Leniency	No	Yes	Yes	No	Yes
Competition advocacy	Yes*	Yes	Yes	Yes	Yes

Note: *Possible state responsibility

The catalogue of anti-competitive practices, for instance, is very similar. Decision 608 and the Colombian,[18] Peruvian[19] and Ecuadorian[20] laws follow the American and European pattern of prohibiting anti-competitive agreements and abuse of dominance (monopolization) separately, while, as we will see below, Bolivia has adopted the 'Mexican style' of distinguishing between absolute and relative practices, even though at the end of the day both approaches are similar.

The Andean regime has not established any express prior-notification procedure for mergers, which raises the question of whether or not they can fall under the Community's scrutiny, a question that is worth an answer since this issue could have huge consequences for the integration process.

Here as well, the Andean Community can learn from the European experience, where Articles 101 and 102 of the Treaty on the Functioning of the European Union (TFEU) likewise do not expressly include this issue, and yet the Commission has developed a whole regime on the matter.

Before Resolution 4064/89, which finally established the prior-notification procedure, the European Commission reviewed mergers *ex post* based on the consideration that they were the result of agreements or a consequence of domination. A whole case law was developed from the cases of *BAT* v *Commission*[21] and *Continental Cann* v *Commission*.[22]

From the point of view of the independence of the competition authority, the Community regime offers a clear advantage, especially for Bolivia, Colombia and Ecuador, where authorities depend upon the will of their respective presidents. In Peru things are somewhat different since the government structures of its competition authority, the National Institute for the Defense of Competition and Protection of Intellectual Property (INDECOPI), are more complex – one reason why they function at arm's length from the government.[23]

Though the length of the procedures may be similar (an estimated two to three years) for Colombians, the Andean preliminary inquiry offers more certainty. In the Andean scheme the Secretariat General has 15 working days to decide whether to accept or reject a claim, while in Colombia the

18 Law 155 of 1959, Decree 2153 of 1992 and Law 1340 of 2009.
19 Statutory Decree No 701 of 1991 and Statutory Decree No 1034 of 2008.
20 Executive Decree 1614 of 2009.
21 Case 142 and 156/84 [1988] 4 CMLR 24.
22 Case 6/72 [1973] ECR 215.
23 Law 25868 of 1992 and Decree 1304 of 2009.

authority has no time limit for preliminary inquiries, meaning they could last for years, as in fact has happened more than once.

In the matter of fines all the regimes are similar, with the exception of Bolivia, where the rules are somewhat different since the authority was endowed with the power of ordering the liquidation of the offender business and imposing remedies.[24]

The Andean regime does not contain leniency schemes; Ecuador likewise has none, while all the remaining member countries have them.

All the regimes contain competition-advocacy rules. In the case of the Andean regime, the rule of Article 36 of Decision 608 has the advantage that a breach brings the possibility of bringing infringement actions for the affected individuals against the member state and claiming for remedies.[25]

Another factor that counts within the region and that has had influence in the said similarities is the cultural identity of all the Andean countries, which broadly have the same language, habits, history and legal background. Indeed almost 200 years ago under Spanish rule, they had been part of the same country for 300 years, and after independence Colombia, Ecuador and Venezuela formed a single country for a while, the Great Colombia. Venezuela was a founding member of the Andean Community, and part of it for 30 years but departed in 2006.

So similar are the regimes that they would be prone to 'forum shopping' if the Andean regime were properly enforced. In the future, once forum shopping is possible (hopefully), a clear distribution of competences must be drawn up to avoid it.

Even though cultural differences and different legal backgrounds could be a very important factor in some regional integration processes, such as some of those in Africa in which countries of very different cultural and legal backgrounds are involved, in the Andean region this is not the case.

4. THE 'DOWNLOADING' OPTION

Using the term coined by Professor Marcos, the 'downloading' alternative refers to the possibility Decision 608 gave to Ecuador and Bolivia to use regional Andean law for domestic cases until the adoption of their own laws. The Decision instructed both governments to appoint their domestic enforcement authorities.

---

24 Supreme Decree 29519 of 2009.
25 *Supra* n. 6.

As long as it was adopted by the Community's Commission, which is made up of representatives of all the Andean countries, which unanimously voted this way, the 'downloading' option was not an imposition but an agreed alternative.

This kind of option is quite different from the current decentralized European regime in which domestic authorities are endowed with the power to handle Community cases by themselves and decide them in direct application of European law. What Decision 608 established was that only Bolivia and Ecuador were allowed to use the Decision domestically but never to decide Community cases.

Although the 'downloading' alternative could be seen as an ingenious way to introduce competition laws in countries that are reluctant to do so, this is not as original as one might think at first glance. The resource of introducing difficult innovations to a country through community channels is quite usual within the European Union, where countries have used this method more than once to adopt policies and take decisions that were domestically difficult and politically costly.

4.1 Evolution of the 'Downloading' Process

The development of this alternative, the actual 'downloading' of Community law to the domestic systems of Bolivia and Ecuador, has been different in each country.

By the time Decision 608 was enacted, Bolivia already had some competition provisions for utilities so the government decided to use the Decision for the remaining economic sectors and appointed the Vice Ministry of Industry as the enforcement authority. It also presented before the legislative body a bill establishing a brand new regime that was not passed.

In 2008 the Bolivian government issued Supreme Decree 29519 regulating various laws, amongst them Law 2495 of 2003, which was used to include a comprehensive body of competition provisions, both substantive and procedural.

As noted above, from the substantive point of view, the government decided to follow the Mexican model of categorical distinction between absolute and relative anti-competitive practices.

The Superintendence of Industries, which later become the Ministry of Productive Development and Plural Economy, was appointed as the enforcement authority and even empowered to decree the liquidation of offender businesses and to order remedies (Art 21(1)).

With Supreme Decree 29519, currently Bolivia has its own competition regime, so Decision 608 returned to its original role as the Andean regime in competition, as in Colombia and Peru.

Soon after the enactment of Decision 608 the Ecuadorian government appointed the General Direction for Foreign Trade Policy of the Ministry of Foreign Trade, Industry, Fisheries and Competitiveness as the enforcement authority, but also appointed CONATEL, the regulatory body of telecommunications, as the sectorial enforcement authority and drafted a whole competition law only for telecommunications, mirroring Decision 608, that in the end was not enacted.

In 2009 the government issued Decree 1614, in which it appointed the Ministry of Industry and Productivity as the enforcement authority and laid down the rules for the functioning of an internal competition law regime, mirroring Decision 608, until a new law could be enacted by the legislature. The Decree provided for the creation of the Sub-Secretariat of Competition within the said Ministry to deal with logistics and the legwork of competition cases. In February 2010 the Ecuadorian authority signed a cooperation agreement with the Colombian competition authority, the Superintendence of Industry and Trade, on technical assistance. Recently, in September 2011, the government sent to Congress a Bill in Competition.[26]

Though praised as ingenious, the 'downloading' option has raised questions too. Professor Marcos[27] has noted: (i) possible problems of compatibility with other laws or possible contradictions; (ii) possible interferences with other sectorial rules affecting competition; (iii) the risk of eroding the credibility of Andean law if subject to different interpretations according to the individual ideas of the incumbent authority; and (iv) the danger of spoiling the very idea of competition law because of the forcible way in which the legislation is introduced (bringing in by the window what did not pass through the door).

The problem of compatibility indeed could be a matter of concern, though not of competition law alone, but regarding any other law. We need to bear in mind the particularities of Andean law (supranationality, autonomy, etc.) that prohibit governments from enacting laws that are

---

[26] 'Proyecto de Ley Orgánica de Regulación y Control del Poder del Mercado'. For more detail on the draft bill see http://www.elciudadano.gov.ec – a digital newspaper of the Presidency of The Republic of Ecuador in which appear various notes about the Project and its trajectory through the legislative process.

[27] Marcos, *supra* n. 2.

incompatible with all the Andean law, the founding treaties and the decisions and resolutions based on them.

The interference with other sectorial laws in competition also could be a matter of concern since different and sectorial competition laws are sources of uncertainty, so it is important to try to avoid this tendency.

The problem of different possible interpretations does not arise within the Andean region, thanks to the preliminary rulings referred to above. These were drafted mirroring the European preliminary rulings that have assured uniformity and consistent interpretation of European law for decades, and this has happened within the Andean region as well. If there is something in which the Andean Tribunal of Justice excels, it is in its experience with preliminary rulings. Between 2005 and 2010, for instance, it dealt with around 900 cases.[28]

Finally, concerning the danger of jeopardizing competition law in itself, the 'downloading' option for the least developed countries, such as Bolivia and Ecuador, effectively could be considered as a gamble, with chances of success and of failure, in which the final verdict will be the enforcement record.

Another concern is the possible difference of goals between regional and domestic regimes, a concern, indeed, expressed by the organizers of the workshop on which this volume is based,[29] and an issue in which preliminary rulings, again, have a crucial part to play, even where, as in the Ecuadorian case, the Decision could be applied domestically. In another matter – intellectual property – the Andean Community has gathered extensive experience in the domestic application of Community law in which, when it comes to binding interpretations, the Andean Tribunal of Justice always has the last word.

Once Bolivia and Ecuador took their respective actions in 2008 and 2009, domestic criticism that was not sound was also voiced. A statement by Mauricio Ochoa, for instance, in an article published in the electronic journal *Boletin Latinoamericano de Competencia*, that Bolivia's Supreme Decree 29519 and Decision 608 are incompatible because of the Mexican style adopted by the former,[30] evinces a lack of familiarity with Andean law. Keeping in mind that the Bolivian government is obligated to not enact

[28] http://www.comunidadandina.org

[29] See the workshop's concept paper, on 'Regional Integration and Competition Law in Developing Countries', mimeo.

[30] Ochoa, M. (2009) 'Régimen general del Derecho de la Competencia en Bolivia', *Boletín Latinoamericano de Competencia*, **26**, 8–22.

legislation that is incompatible with Andean law, and considering that no action has been brought before the Community's authorities concerning Decree 29519, it seems that Bolivia has in fact honoured this principle.

In Ecuador the press criticized the lack of discussion leading up to the draft decree and the danger of government authoritarianism against businesses,[31] criticism that somehow forgot that since 2005 Ecuador has effectively appointed its domestic enforcement authority and since then the Decision has entered into force. On the other hand, and regarding the danger of authoritarianism, this is not a problem of competition law but of institutional framework. Today there are more than 120 countries worldwide with competition laws, and to my knowledge this has not led to rampant authoritarianism; on the contrary, these laws have led to other and quite opposite effects on public good.

The misuse of laws to exercise excessive control over businesses is not a matter related just to competition laws, but to many others as well: tax laws or even anti-corruption laws have sometimes effectively been used by some 'rough' regimes this way, as has happened in Russia with the Yukos affair over tax law, and corruption cases against opposition leaders in dictatorial regimes. Indeed, to my knowledge competition law has never been used this way.

To sum up, the 'downloading' option was good for the region as long as it gave Bolivia and Ecuador the opportunity to enjoy well-drafted competition laws earlier than otherwise thought possible.

By extension, 'downloading' could be a good alternative for some of the least developed countries' members of regional trade agreements, so that they would have their own competition laws and avoid unnecessary *tours de force*. This, however, does not mean that the 'downloading' alternative functions automatically. There are some necessary preconditions, such as the appropriate context. In environments like the Common Market for Eastern and Southern Africa (COMESA), for instance, cultural differences matter a great deal, while – as we have noticed – within the Andean countries they do not. Another very important issue is the risk of lack of uniformity, which arguably could arise if preliminary rulings are not in the hands of serious tribunals of justice.

Within the Andean region, then, the 'downloading' alternative was not a problem, which does not mean that the regime does not have shortcomings. This issue will be the focus of the next section.

---

[31] 'Sin autoridad ni diálogo decreto antimonopolio', *El Universo*, Quito, 19 March 2009, available at: http://www.eluniverso.com (accessed 19 April 2010).

5. THE REAL PROBLEM OF THE ANDEAN COMPETITION LAW

The more compelling problem of the Andean competition law is its lack of use.

It is difficult to believe what is happening with Decision 608. The Decision was the outcome of a project with European backing that took three years and cost €2 million,[32] and it included not only the drafting of the Decision but also a guide to its use,[33] as well as a great deal of capacity building. Its gloomy result is not a single case on anti-competitive practices and just one related to the breach of Article 36 (competition advocacy) brought by an individual. Not one competition authority has brought a single case before the Secretariat, which itself has not initiated even a single case.

5.1 Explanations for the Lack of Use

Why such a surprising outcome? It is a puzzling situation, much like having, not exactly a Ferrari (Decision 608 is good but not perfect), but perhaps a Porsche in the garage languishing and getting rusty while its owner needs a car to continue down the road, that is, to further the integration process. To really achieve economic integration, the Community indeed needs the vehicle that, although parked and ready to go, is not used.

---

[32] 'Proposal for a COUNCIL DECISION … on the signature of a Political Dialogue and Cooperation Agreement between the European Community and its Member States, of the one part, and the Andean Community and its member countries, the Republics of Bolivia, Colombia, Ecuador, Peru and the Bolivarian Republic of Venezuela, of the other part … Proposal for a COUNCIL DECISION on the conclusion of a Political Dialogue and Cooperation Agreement between the European Community and its Member States, of the one part, and the Andean Community and its member countries, the Republics of Bolivia, Colombia, Ecuador, Peru and the Bolivarian Republic of Venezuela, of the other part (presented by the Commission)' Document COM(2003) 695 Final, available at: http://eur-lex.europa.eu/LexUriServ/LexUriServ.do?uri=COM:2003:0695:FIN:EN:PDF (accessed 2 April 2012); European Commission 2007, *Andean Community – Regional Strategy Paper 2007–2013*, Document (E/2007/678) available at: http://eeas.europa.eu/andean/rsp/07_13_en.pdf (accessed 2 April 2012).

[33] 'Guía práctica para la aplicación de la Decisión 608: Normas para la protección y promoción de la libre competencia en la Comunidad Andina', Documento de trabajo SG/DT 396, 23 Oct 2007, 2.17.27.

At first glance, some possible explanations occur: a lack of anti-competitive practices within the region; the possible flaws or useless character of Decision 608; the possible uselessness of the Andean Community itself; or the possible lack of interest of the member countries' governments in competition law and policy. It happens, however, that all these explanations are wrong.

Firstly, anti-competitive practices abound within the region. As a practitioner I have witnessed it for a long time, but more convincing than this are the hundreds of cases that authorities of the member countries have handled domestically since the enactment of Decision 608 – and these hundreds were only domestic cases.

Secondly, as this chapter explains, Decision 608 is not an ill-crafted or wrongly conceived law. Decision 608 is a very good antitrust law, carefully drafted according to the standards of the most recognized competition regimes, such as the European one. Its quality is widely recognized; academic literature on the Decision tends to exalt it.[34]

Thirdly, the Andean Community in itself is not a useless construct, despite the criticism it has received,[35] even from Mr Robert Zoellick, former US Trade Representative, who once said that the treaties of the Andean Community existed on paper rather than in reality.[36] Most of its critics are quite unaware of the benefits it has brought to regional trade and integration during the last 40 years.

Fortunately, despite all the criticism, the governments of its member countries strongly support the Andean Community (though with some remarkable lapses, as we will see) and are quite conscious of its value. It is important to keep in mind, nonetheless, that the political process of the organization, with all its ups and downs, is one thing – a very different matter is the legal scenario in which Andean law has real force: it is a fully developed and binding legal system that all the member states are bound to honour.

Fourthly, it is not true that the governments have little interest in competition law and policy. Quite the opposite: the enforcement record and

---

[34] Marcos, *supra* n. 2.

[35] See e.g. Javier Garvich (2006), 'Por qué ha fracasado la Comunidad Andina de Naciones?', available at: http://www.terra.com.pe/noticias/articulo/html/act512774.htm (accessed 9 November 2011).

[36] Andean Community Secretariat (2004), 'Secretario General de la Comunidad Andina rebate críticas de Zoellick', press note, available at: http://www.comunidadandina.org/prensa/articulos/efe8–6-04.htm (accessed 9 November 2011).

the enactment and reform of competition laws in all the member countries during recent years refute completely such a contention, for example Bolivia in 2008 (Supreme Decree 29519); Colombia in 2009 (Law 1340); Ecuador in 2009 (Decree 1684) and Peru in 2008 (Decree 1304).

There is not, indeed, one single reason for the lack of application of the Andean regional competition law, but a mix of them: a combination of scepticism towards the Andean Community; unawareness of Andean law; a lack of competition culture; and budgetary constraints – shown graphically in Figure 7.5.

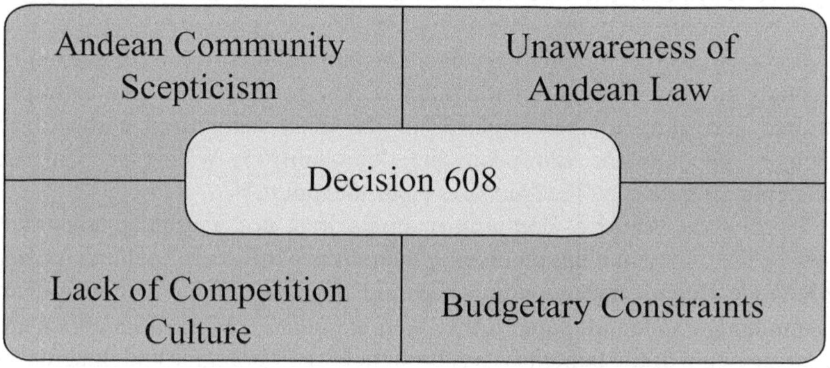

Figure 7.5

Each one of these factors plays its role, and though each one of them merits thorough analysis that exceeds the limits of this chapter, I would like to highlight one factor of the utmost importance: budgetary constraints.

All the possible parallelism between the European Union and the Andean Community simply disappears when the focus is on funds. Unlike the EU, which has various sources, including the custom duties of its member states, a portion of the value-added tax and direct contributions, the Andean Community only has the third, and this in a quite modest measure. In 2007, for instance, while the EU's budget was €138 billion (approx. US$160 billion), that of the Andean Community was US$6.7 million, not even a thousandth of the EU's budget.

Looking at this quite meagre sum, the real question is how the Andean Community has done so much with so little.

5.2 The Andean Response: Project INTERCAN I

Despite the abovementioned constraints, the Community has not been unaware of the problem, which in a wider scope relates not only to Decision 608 but also to other Decisions that are important for the integration process.

As a response, in December 2009 the Community launched, through Decision 723, the 'Project INTERCAN I' (Proyecto INTERCAN I de apoyo a la integración económica de la Comunidad Andina) to provide extra support for the integration process. The project, which has an estimated budget of €8,920,000 and an estimated length of three and a half years, is like a turbocharger, comprising a series of initiatives to boost the integration process.

One such initiative envisages a digital network linking all the member countries' customs offices, which once completed could allow the coordinated functioning of the customs union. Another is the initiative for the organization of the Andean Centre for the Implementation of Policies of Regional Integration (Centro Andino para la Implementación de Políticas de Integración Regional, or CAIPIR), with an estimated cost of €1.4 million.

CAIPIR is not a new body, but an ad hoc working group composed of one expert per country working very closely with the member countries' respective liaison authority and one coordinator, based in Lima, whose main function is the coordination with the national governments in the implementation and application of the Community decisions that are important for economic integration, amongst them Decision 608. One expressly mentioned strategy is the carrying out of 'visible' actions aimed at enhancing the awareness of the people about the benefits of the integration process and the Community's economic policies.

Without a doubt, the CAIPIR initiative, as well as the entire INTERCAN I project, is a good programme, since it aims to overcome some of the Community's biggest shortcomings (if not all of them, since the budgetary problem will continue), but in terms of giving full operation to Decision 608, it is insufficient.

The CAIPIR initiative has a wider scope than just Decision 608. It comprises many fronts that the Community needs to address. Additionally, although one expert per country is much better than none, it is not realistic to think that one person will be capable of solving the problem of Decision 608. Experts may provide great support, but they are not saviours.

5.3 Towards a Real (and Durable) Solution: The Missing Link of Private-sector Involvement

It is generally possible, and indeed common, for antitrust cases to be officially initiated. And yet many factors keep trustbusters from looking into all possible infringements. Not even the US Department of Justice and the Federal Trade Commission, the most powerful antitrust authority on earth, is able to investigate all offences. Indeed, in the US the majority of antitrust cases are brought by individuals seeking remedies.[37]

From this perspective, the Andean scenario offers a gloomy picture for both officially and privately instigated cases. Given the budgetary restrictions, the explanation for the former is relatively clear: it is certainly difficult for the Community to devote funds to such a new undertaking that could easily prove to be overwhelming.

The latter is more compelling, since it involves a sum of factors that form a vicious circle: lack of competition culture and lack of practitioners in which the outstanding balance is the lack of cases.

While big businesses, especially global enterprises, are quite aware of competition law, Andean small and medium-sized businesses, which shoulder the bulk of our economic activity, face various dilemmas before antitrust law.

When they become victims of the anti-competitive practices of big businesses, or indeed of other similar enterprises, these small enterprises face the David-versus-Goliath syndrome, in which – the Biblical story being one of the few remarkable exceptions – the former usually loses.

In antitrust the sling in such a confrontation should be in the hands of an expert, meaning a lawyer, who ought to be paid, which for the small entrepreneur most of the times is neither attractive, nor even an option. The most an entrepreneur can hope for, if successful, is a cease-and-desist order, perhaps accompanied by a fine; they must bear a heavy burden, both economic and legal. In Bolivia especially, the possibility of remedies is remote and complicated, not to say practically non-existent.

On the other hand, the small entrepreneur also bears the risk of retaliation of various kinds (boycotts, shortages, discrimination, etc.), thus further lowering the likelihood of medium and small entrepreneurs confronting big businesses that are behaving badly.

---

[37] Amongst the numerous references, see Commission of the European Communities (2008), *White Paper on Damages Actions for Breach of the EC Antitrust Rules*, document COM(2008) 165 Final.

In addition to these difficulties in bringing actions, the prevalent lack of a competition culture means that small entrepreneurs are often not even aware of antitrust at all. Naïve cartels usually come from these types of businesses.[38]

Thus the vicious circle that leads to the lack of cases continues to turn: though anti-competitive activities abound, the expense and difficulty of enforcement and the lack of awareness of competition law – except among major competitors – leads to a dearth of cases and thus of practitioners. As an academic discipline, Andean antitrust law has no market at all and domestic antitrust law is only slightly more in demand. Colombia, for instance, has 168 faculties of law and in only two is competition law part of the basic curriculum. In postgraduate studies there is little more, except as part of wider subjects such as commercial or economic law; the situation is much like that in the US in the 1930s, when the discipline started to be included in law studies.[39]

The promotion and defence of free competition is not an easy task, much less within a rather hostile environment such as the one depicted.

5.4 Breaking the Vicious Circle

Competition and competition law are important values for society, as has been extensively corroborated. This is why the defence of competition is so important. As experience has also shown, this is not a task for state action (antitrust authorities) alone. Civil society ought to be involved, but, as we have seen, it is not as easy as just leaving the burden to businesses, let alone to the medium and small enterprises which form the majority of businesses.

Other important values that are worth protecting also face constraints of this kind as well as hostile environments, but it is not only the state that rushes to their defence, but also non-government organizations (NGOs), the media and academia.

Examples abound: human rights have advocates in NGOs such as the UK-based Amnesty International or the Washington-based Human Rights Watch, which are active worldwide. Greenpeace has for decades fought for

---

[38] Cortázar Javier (2011), *Curso de Derecho de la Competencia (Antimonopolios)*, Bogotá: Editorial Temis.

[39] Waller, S.W. (2001), 'The language of the law and the language of business', *Case Western Law Review*, **52**, 238, http://papers.ssrn.com/sol3/papers.cfm?abstract_id=253732

the environment. Transparency International, another well-known organization, combats corruption. All these organizations play important roles within their own fields, whether complementing state action or confronting countries when the state has failed.

In competition law there are several private (mainly academically focused) organizations advocating competition law, as well as cooperation and capacity building, for instance the antitrust section of the American Bar Association,[40] the American Antitrust Institute,[41] the Global Competition Forum of Competition Lawyers,[42] the International Network of Civil Society Organizations on Competition (INCSOC),[43] the Competition Law Association[44] and various university groups, such as the Centre for Competition Law and Policy of Oxford University,[45] the Competition Policy Center of the University of Berkeley[46] or the Centro de la Libre Competencia of the University of Chile,[47] just to mention a few.

Notwithstanding the importance of all these organizations and their role in the development and consolidation of the legal discipline, there is no activist organization comparable with Amnesty International, Greenpeace or Transparency International in the field of competition law. Though INCSOC's mission is 'to promote and maintain a healthy competition culture around the world by coalition building among civil society and other interested organisations',[48] its work is rather of the traditional style.

Considering the activist NGOs' achievements in their respective fields, I believe that in competition law a more activist civil society or plainly an activist NGO is needed to complement the Community's actions in the promotion and defence of competition.

This activism needs not Rainbow-Warrior-style rock concerts or fashionable demonstrations, but simply to act with strong determination; it should be a serious and responsible organization with a character designed to raise credibility and respect.

---

40 http://www.americanbar.org/aba.html
41 http://www.antitrustinstitute.org/
42 http://www.globalcompetitionforum.org/about.htm#
43 http://www.incsoc.net/
44 http://www.competitionlawassociation.org.uk/new/
45 http://denning.law.ox.ac.uk/competition/home.php
46 http://iber.berkeley.edu/cpc/
47 http://www.lcuc.cl/?option=com_frontpage&Itemid=1
48 http://www.incsoc.net

To attempt a brief but concrete blueprint of what this organization could be like, there are four critical issues: independence, the careful selection of its activities, its organization, and funding.

The essential prerequisite is complete independence; the organization should be totally detached from any political interference and, more importantly, any populist tendency.

The NGO's activities should be twofold. One is to bring antitrust cases before the courts or administrative watch, cases carefully chosen using strict and objective methodologies and a serious and conscious decision-making process. The second is the public denouncing of anti-competitive practices – equally carefully and seriously chosen.

In many cases denouncing could be rather effective. We cannot forget the debt that antitrust law owes to investigative journalism. Had Henry D. Lloyd, for instance, not written what he did about the abuses of the rough capitalists of the American Gilded Age, antitrust law probably would not have come into being until much later.

The organization, thirdly, should be well organized, with a board of directors composed of respected individuals and a staff of committed lawyers, economists and journalists, all carefully appointed to assure respectability.

The most formidable obstacle preventing an NGO of this kind from coming into being is the funding. Without resources the idea will remain a chimera. Taking into account its characteristics, funding could likely come from international organizations and private donations from many sources, even businesses, provided that the NGO's independence is not compromised.

If an NGO of this kind came into being in the Andean region, the vicious circle could be exchanged for a virtuous one formed by a mixture of Community action (through the trustbusters' activities and such initiatives as CAIPIR) and private action that could bring more opportunities to enhance competition culture and involve more practitioners, which in the end could lead to cases being brought before the Andean competition authority.

6. CONCLUSIONS

First of all I must say that the Andean competition law is a good law. Nonetheless, so similar are Andean competition law and domestic laws that they could be prone to 'forum shopping', calling for the need to establish a clear allocation of competences.

The 'downloading' option for Bolivia and Ecuador has worked well. The importance of the context has to be considered if such method is to be used in other contexts.

The problem with Decision 608 is its lack of use. To overcome this problem public reaction is good but not enough. The participation of the private sector is very important and a necessary complement to state action. In addition to the CAIPIR initiative of the Andean Community, an activist NGO in competition law would raise awareness for Decision 608 and likely lead to its being applied in the region. If such an NGO is to be created, it will need adequate funding and must be organized under strict principles of transparency, accountability, professionalism and responsibility.

PART III

Economic structure, regional integration and competition law enforcement

8. Regional integration in the Caribbean: the role of competition policy

Taimoon Stewart

> The reality is that an efficient Single Market and Economy is this Community's best hope in relating to the international community and for its growth and prosperity and for the improvement in the standard of living for its people.
> (Edwin Carrington, Secretary General of CARICOM)[1]

1. INTRODUCTION

The perception of the Caribbean as a place where people have a relaxed way of life, basking in the sun and enjoying sand and sea is partly true, but there is an underbelly of tensions, poverty and disharmony that is a much more potent reality for the majority of people living in the region. Indeed, it is a very complex area, and one that has been shaped from the sixteenth century by European expansion and imperialism. To focus mechanically on the instruments of regional integration based purely on integration theory, and on the regional competition policy, would leave blind spots in the analysis that would result in a distorted picture and flawed conclusions.

This chapter provides an evaluation of the role of competition policy in the integration process, and suggests that there is a very real danger that the objectives of free flow of goods and services in the CARICOM Single Market (CSM) could be compromised by anti-competitive conduct by large firms in the region. In the process of this evaluation, the paper provides a snapshot of the societies and economies in the CSM, the tensions involved amongst member states in achieving the CSM, the extent of intra-regional trade, and who the big players in the region are whose conduct could have a

[1] Caribbean Community (CARICOM) Press release 387/2009, 'Single Market Working but More Commitment Needed', 9 October 2009.

substantial effect on intra-regional trade and investment. It provides a backdrop for the chapter that follows with a more in-depth look at legal issues in implementing the regional competition policy.

The major types of anti-competitive conduct that need to be targeted are linked to the historical legacy of concentration of capital in the hands of a few, many of whom inherited this capital from colonial ancestors. In this regard, then, this chapter argues that the major concerns for regional and national competition enforcers are the possibility of abuse of dominant market position and the effects on market structure of mergers and acquisitions. While the question of whether merger control regulation (MCR) is relevant for the region is still being debated, there is now substantial agreement in its favour.

The peculiarities of small economies that have an impact on competition processes, and how these could affect implementation of competition policy in the CSM, are addressed. So too are the limitations of the existing regional competition policy enshrined in Chapter 8 of the Revised Treaty of Chaguaramas (see sections 4 and 6 below), and the constraints to overcoming these limitations.

2. EXPLAINING THE CARIBBEAN TO THE WORLD

While 'the Caribbean' is sometimes used to describe all the countries bordering the Caribbean Sea (except the United States), we are here referring to the former colonies of Britain, the English-speaking Caribbean (mostly islands). Together with Suriname (formerly a Dutch colony) and Haiti (formerly a French colony), these territories form the Caribbean Community (CARICOM).[2] It is important to note that the imperial powers are still very present in the region: colonies/dependencies/departments of Britain, France, Holland and the United States.[3] Moreover, linkages among

---

[2] Countries in CARICOM are: Antigua and Barbuda, the Bahamas, Barbados, Belize, Dominica, Grenada, Guyana, Haiti, Jamaica, Montserrat, Saint Lucia, St Kitts and Nevis, St Vincent and the Grenadines, Suriname and Trinidad and Tobago.

[3] British overseas territories: Anguilla, British Virgin Islands, Cayman Islands, Bermuda, Turks and Caicos, Montserrat; French departments/overseas territories: Martinique, Guadeloupe, French Guiana, Saint Martin, Saint Barthelemy; Dutch territories: Aruba, Netherlands Antilles; United States territories: US Virgin Islands, Puerto Rico. With the withdrawal of Britain from the Caribbean, the US asserted control over the region, regarding it as their sphere of influence, and intervening militarily and politically to protect its interests and its 'underbelly'.

the islands of the Caribbean are truncated by the colonial heritage, with deeper linkages and a shared identity among those with a similar colonial past and cultural heritage, but far less connection between those with different former colonial history, with language differences being an important barrier.[4] Similarly, the physical landscape shaped by production structures created in colonial times (sugar and banana plantations, extractive industries in oil and bauxite), the ethnic composition of the societies and social stratification, concentration and ownership of wealth, and cultural expressions are all echoes of the specific colonial experience of the territories.

Indeed, the Caribbean is a microcosm of the world.[5] It was the first area to be penetrated and colonized by European powers (apart from Ireland), and it was a pawn in European wars of the seventeenth and eighteenth centuries, resulting in some territories having experienced, at some point, Spanish, French and English colonialism (e.g. Trinidad and Tobago). The populations of the Caribbean today are transplants from diverse areas of the world, largely brought to work on sugar plantations as slaves (Africans) or indentured labourers (Indians, Chinese, a small number of Portuguese/Madeirans). The indigenous population was completely eradicated (except in Guyana and Belize, and a sprinkling in Dominica). In addition, more recent migrants include Syrians and Lebanese (displaced after the area came under British 'protection' in the period after World War I), and new waves of Chinese, Vietnamese[6] and Indians. One therefore finds in the Caribbean descendents of Africans, East Indians, Chinese, Spaniards, Portuguese, French and British (from the colonial period), Syrians and Lebanese, Vietnamese, and others. There is a tension within these societies as each ethnic group clings to remnants of its cultural heritage while also moving towards forging a new shared identity with Caribbean roots.

The societies are extremely stratified, with a strong correlation between race, class, unequal distribution of wealth and income that creates a 'caste'

---

[4] Thus there is more shared identity between Trinidadians and Jamaicans than Trinidadians and Venezuelans, even though the two territories are adjacent to each other and separated by only a few miles at the nearest point. Similarly, the populations of Venezuela and the Dominican Republic have more shared identity.

[5] A theme explored by Herb Addo in various of his works. See, Addo, H. (1990), 'The Caribbean in the World-Economy', mimeo, Institute of International Relations, University of the West Indies, St Augustine Campus.

[6] Some of the micro-states sold citizenship in order to raise much needed capital, and this was utilized by the Chinese and Vietnamese, among others.

system and generates social tension and instability.[7] This social stratification is a direct result of colonization, slavery, and the plantation system. The role of colour is still very much a factor in social mobility.[8] The race factor impinges negatively on access to finances and other support systems, and stifles entrepreneurship. As pointed out by Maldonado and Sethuraman,[9] the marginalized face discrimination in access to productive resources, administrative harassment and systematic intimidation, among other exclusionary practices, which all affect competition in markets.[10] Access to loans from banks for business purposes is extremely difficult for the disadvantaged and this entrenches the poverty among the black population.

Not only is the region's population a direct creation of European colonialism, but so are the economies and the physical landscape shaped by colonial production systems. The Caribbean is the most intensively integrated region in the capitalist world economy, its indigenous production system having been destroyed and re-shaped to serve the needs of the imperial powers, producing for export and importing consumption needs from the metropolis, under rules of mercantilism. The 'plantation system'[11] defined economic

---

7 Beckford, G. and K. Levitt (2000), 'The Social Economy of Bauxite in the Jamaican Man-Space', in *The George Beckford Papers*, Jamaica: Canoe Press, p. 218.

8 One result of this, for instance, is the sad situation of young women today, particularly in Jamaica, bleaching their skins in order to be of lighter complexion and thereby increase their chances of climbing the social ladder.

9 Maldonado, C. and S.V. Sethuraman (eds) (1992), *Technological Capability in the Informal Sector: Metal Manufacturing in Developing Countries*, Geneva: ILO, p. 3.

10 The correlation between concentration of wealth in the white population and persistence of poverty amongst the blacks makes governments unwilling to facilitate full competition if it gives more power to the elite class at the expense of blacks. An example is the situation with St Lucian taxi drivers who are extremely inefficient, divide up the market and control the trade, but the government would not allow the Destination Management Company to transport their clients from the airport or hotels, despite requests and arguments about the inefficiency of the taxi service, because the Destination Management Company is owned by an elite family that also controls some 80 per cent of the import and distribution business in the country. Barbados is particularly notorious for its unequal distribution of wealth in favour of the white plantocracy class. See Stewart, T. (2004), *Competition Policy in CARICOM Countries: An Empirical Study*, available at: http://www.idrc.org/competition/

11 Originally referring to the organizational structure and composition of the actual sugar plantation, the term has been used by Lloyd Best and Kari Levitt metaphorically to mean an economy that displays the essential elements of a

activity, demographics, transportation linkages, social stratification, cultural hegemony and de-culturalization strategies, but most importantly, the ownership of wealth. It also evoked resistance strategies, rebellions and revolutions, which still have echoes in these societies. The footprints of this violent past are everywhere to be seen, for those who understand this history.

These economies are very open, with major production primarily for export, and imports of most consumables. This pattern of production and trade was established in colonial times. The major sectors of the economies in the region are a product of their factor endowments, thus sugar in the larger territories, bauxite in Jamaica and Guyana, petroleum in Trinidad, and tourism in the coral islands of the rest of the Caribbean. However, the production of bananas in the Windward Islands was started solely to provide Britain with fruit during and after the Second World War. Indeed, these islands are not suited to the production of bananas, being hilly and having difficult terrain.

The major economic activities remain commodity producing and are mostly foreign-owned (including the majority of large hotels in the tourist destinations), with the price of the major exports externally determined, and generally declining (except oil), while the prices of imports, particularly food and fuel, have escalated in recent times, rendering these economies extremely vulnerable. Because of the severe erosion of preferential market access for bananas and sugar, these products are being phased out in some territories but not replaced by production structures that are more self-reliant and have upstream and downstream linkages to the economy. Caribbean rum enjoys a good international reputation, but faces many barriers to entry into markets in the developed countries.

The economies remain open and extremely dependent on import of essential consumer goods (and therefore on earning hard currency for survival). This is reflected in the persistently negative balance of payments, as seen in Table 8.1 (except for Trinidad and Tobago, which is riding the wave of high oil prices). There is no hinterland in the island states, unlike other developing countries where groups of indigenous peoples and their production systems are retained. Major transport routes lead north to the former metropolis, rather than south. Physically dispersed across the Caribbean Sea, and therefore separated by water, the island states are highly dependent on intra-regional transport for exchange of goods, services and

---

plantation system of control by foreign firms that extract and leak surplus out of the economy, while being dependent on imports to meet consumption needs. It is no different with the tourism industry, for instance.

people. Yet there are numerous problems with the one intra-island air service, which is plagued by inefficiency and financial losses, no doubt attributable largely to its monopoly status.

Table 8.1 Statistical profile of CARICOM

State	Land area in sq. miles	Population (2009)	GDP (US$ million)	GNI per capita (US$)	Selected BOP current acct. 2006 (US$ million)
Antigua/ Barbuda	171	87,600	1,131.7 (2009)	12,070	–310.2
Barbados	166	255,827	3,681.5 (2008)	9,330	–269.8
Belize	8,867	333,200	1,358.7 (2008)	3,740	–25.4
Dominica	209	73,596	377.7 (2009)	4,870	–49.9
Grenada	133	103,930	626.5 (2009)	5,550	–198.4
Guyana	83,000	762,498	1,159.2 (2008)	1,450	–165.4
Jamaica	4,244	2,699,617	14,681.4 (2009)	4,990	–1,182.8
Montserrat	40	4,500	39.3	n/a	–7.9
St Kitts/Nevis	104	49,593	544.9 (2009)	10,100	–85.1
St Lucia	238	172,092	945.8 (2009)	7,170	–309.0
St Vincent & The Grenadines	150	109,209	582.6 (2009)	5,110	–117.9
Suriname	63,251	519,740	3,033.0 (2008)	4,760	+110.4
Trinidad and Tobago	1,980	1,338,585	21,087.0 (2009)	16,490	+ 7,270.5

Source: CARICOM Secretariat Statistical Databases 2005, 2006. Compiled from country data available at http://caricomstats.org/ – drop down on databases, Balance of Payments, under which is each country (www.caricom.org) for area and BOP statistics and world development indicators (World Bank) for population, GDP and GNI per capita.

Entrepreneurship in the Caribbean is extremely weak, with local savings very poor. This was the case throughout the colonial period (with planters borrowing from finance houses in London and becoming heavily indebted to them), and continued after independence. Arthur Lewis proposed that savings are so poor in 'backward' countries because the (local) capitalist sector is so small.[12] Lewis defined the capitalist class as that which thinks of investing capital productively. Certainly the Caribbean does not have a capitalist class, since the capital holders engaged essentially in commerce, importing, wholesaling and distributing. As Lewis stated, people invest in what they know, and the capital holders in the Caribbean at that time were the colonizers and subsequently the descendents of the colonizers, who were historically a merchant class, importing consumption needs. After independence, capital flight to more secure currencies became a feature of the behaviour of capital holders. There was, and still is, very little local investment in research and development, and so an essential ingredient for the growth of a capitalist class of Lewis's ilk was (and still is) absent. The lack of investment to diversify the economies away from bananas into self-reliant production can be understood in this context. Caribbean entrepreneurs are generally not good risk-takers.

Manufacturing has remained largely based on the import of intermediate goods for final production, using imported capital goods. Hence, there is little value added, employment generation is minimal, and the sector remains highly dependent on the commodity export sector to generate foreign exchange for purchasing supplies. It is really a carry-over of the import substitution industrialization (ISI) strategy that was embarked upon in Latin America and the Caribbean in the 1960s, as well as other developing countries.[13] Moreover, production systems remain highly similar across the region, thereby placing the economies in competition with each other, rather than being complementary. Tourism is one example, as is agriculture. Light manufacturing in Trinidad and Tobago, Barbados and Jamaica is similar, being generally assembly production. Trinidad and Tobago utilizes its relatively low cost of energy by using natural gas to produce steel, urea,

---

[12] Lewis, W.A. (1954), 'Economic Development with Unlimited Supplies of Labour', *Manchester School*, pp. 11–12, available at: http://www.globelicsacademy.net/2008/2008_lectures/lewis%20unlimited%20labor%20supply%201954.pdf

[13] Governments encouraged investment in the light manufacturing sector by erecting tariff and non-tariff barriers to imports of manufactured goods. Again, local capitalists did not invest in industrialization, and foreign direct investors were invited. For these investors, direct investment was a way to get around the barriers to entry of their products that were erected all over the developing world. Capital goods that incorporated much of the labour component of production were imported together with the intermediate goods that were fed into the machines. There was little demand in the local economies for labour and raw or intermediate goods and services, and little backward and forward linkages. This continues today in many of the light manufacturing industries.

methanol, ammonia (all foreign-owned enterprises), but none of these are linked to value-added downstream industries. There is some production of steel rods, but nothing more sophisticated, and no plastics industry, despite an abundance of raw materials, because the capital holders are not risk-takers.

To compound these structural rigidities and constraints, the Caribbean is extremely vulnerable to natural disasters, with dire consequences for its economies. One only has to recall the recent earthquake in Haiti, the volcanic eruptions in Montserrat and the numerous hurricanes that have devastated the region year after year, triggering floods and landslides and destroying homes (particularly those owned by the poor) and infrastructure. Hurricanes and flooding take a great toll on agriculture and make it a high-risk business. Banks are therefore unwilling to lend for agriculture, and people are increasingly unwilling to undertake agricultural projects. The Caribbean islands are amongst the most vulnerable to the effects of climate change, and given that their topography dictates that most of the airports are on the coast, there could be dire consequences for tourism and intra-regional linkages.

Another major challenge faced by the Caribbean is that it has become a major trans-shipment route to the USA for Colombian drugs, and this has generated within the societies drug gangs and gang warfare, with an exponential increase in violent crimes, fuelled by the domestic consumption of drugs and the accompanying extreme vulnerability of the citizenry. According to the *Caribbean Trade and Investment Report 2005*, 'The greatest danger facing the Region is the dramatic increase in very violent crimes. The threat to one's physical well being could cause a flight of entrepreneurs (along with their capital) especially if kidnapping is directed at them and their families, with adverse consequences for the intra-regional investment process.'[14]

---

[14] *Caribbean Trade and Investment Report 2005*, Georgetown Guyana: CARICOM Secretariat (available at: http://www.caricom.org/jsp/community/regional_issues/ctir2005_index.jsp), p. 116. For this reason, I have argued that the leniency programme will not work in the region, as the business sector will be exposed to violent retaliation, and the smallness of the societies means that individuals in the business sector are well known to each other, with close family or friendship ties, and are therefore unlikely to entertain whistle-blowing. It is not acceptable culturally. There are also implications for the effectiveness of competition law enforcement, given the lack of rule of law, Barbados being the exception. That also can be explained by the colonial history: Barbados was colonized continuously from 1630

The underbelly of the Caribbean is this drug trade and its ripple effects throughout society, plus a high level of poverty. A large informal sector thrives in the region, a direct result of lack of job opportunities and access to capital for the poor and underprivileged. This informal sector is as high as 50 per cent of the economy in Jamaica. The informal sector consists of several sub-sectors: the subsistence sector, the drug sector, more established businesses that evade taxes by not registering, etc. A study by the Inter-American Development Bank (IADB) in 2006[15] revealed that enterprises in the informal sector in Jamaica are concentrated in low-productivity, labour-intensive activities, with some 60 per cent of persons operating in the informal sector engaging in wholesale or retail trade or subsistence agriculture. This reflects the reality throughout the region.

It is interesting that intra-regional trade linkages throughout the Caribbean, spanning all language areas, are the most vibrant and established type of trade in the informal sector, whereby the 'higglers' (mainly women) buy supplies in one country and sell them back home, using various strategies to evade government charges at the border. There are serious challenges for competition law enforcement because of the elusiveness of the informal activities and the firms that engage in them, the penetration of the commercial sector (both formal and informal) by drug money through laundering, and the active participation and control exercised by drug lords. This challenges market analysis and enforcement of the law, where investigations may come too close to drug-related firms.

3. SUMMARY OF THE REGIONAL SITUATION

In sum, the island states that make up the CSM are all dependent on tourism for their major export earnings (except Trinidad), and thus compete with each other for the international tourists, having little intra-CARICOM tourist flow relative to the total flows. Trinidad, and to some extent, Barbados and Jamaica, have limited assembly production of light manufactured goods, and these products make up the majority of non-petroleum intra-regional trade in the CSM. The vast majority of intra-regional trade consists of exports of petroleum from Trinidad and Tobago to the rest of the

---

by Britain, endured the plantation system longest and most effectively, and had the ethos of British norms stamped indelibly on the society.

15 IADB (2006), 'The Informal Sector in Jamaica', available at: http://www.iadb.org/

CSM. The majority of economic activity outside the petroleum and light manufacturing sector is commerce: import, distribution and retail.

In most of the territories, there is high concentration of capital in the hands of mostly the white and near-white population, leaving the majority of the black population in poverty and engaging in informal economic activities to survive.

Because of the small size of the economies, firms need to achieve economies of scale in order to be viable. Link this to the fact that most consumables are imported and that the territories are mostly island states, requiring marine transport, thus necessitating bulk freight in order to reduce transport cost, and scale becomes more important. This has led to oligopolies in these small economies, largely owned by the white or near-white population, where there is a concentration of capital derived largely from colonial inheritance. Competition policy at the regional level is very important to ensure that the large capital holders do not engage in anti-competitive conduct with cross-border effects that can negate the objective of free flow of goods and services in the CSM.

Socio-structural and ethnic divides lead to lack of access to capital for a large segment of the population, thus stifling entrepreneurship and further limiting competition in the economies. The propensity for natural disasters hampers economic development, as does the social pathology resulting from the drug trade and its accompanying violence. These factors create great challenges for the process of integration because domestic issues can take precedence over regional ones.

4. THE IMPERATIVE OF INTEGRATION FOR CARIBBEAN STATES

> The natural state of our Caribbean is fragmentation. Without constant effort, without unrelenting perseverance and discipline in suppressing instincts born of tradition and environment, it is to our natural state of disunity that we shall return. (Sir Shridath Ramphal, 1975)[16]

Against this historical template and the current realities of fragmentation and disunity, what are the choices for the Caribbean in strengthening its position vis-á-vis the constantly changing global economy (which has been to its increasing disadvantage since the decline of sugar in the nineteenth

[16] Quoted in Mullerleile, C. (1995), *CARICOM Integration: Progress and Hurdles: A European View*, Jamaica: Kingston Publishers Ltd, p. 23.

century). Most of the Caribbean countries have populations of under one million, with annual GDP the equivalent of petty cash for the transnational corporations (TNCs) that dominate in their economies in the bauxite, petroleum and petro-chemical industries, and in the tourism industry in particular (see Table 8.1 above). Integration is not an option for these territories; it is a necessity for survival in the world economy.

Indeed, the British government recognized that these micro-economies were not viable as independent states, and created the West Indian Federation, keeping the unity of the Anglo-Saxon Caribbean. But, sadly, this lasted only four years, and collapsed in 1962 because of insularity, a narrow focus on 'sovereign rights', protectiveness of locally generated wealth and unwillingness to share such resources, and Caribbean leaders who were already smitten with the taste of power. The irony is that, ever since, the region has been working towards reunification, step by step.

This thrust to re-integrate economically (and hopefully, politically) started in 1965 with the formation of the Caribbean Free Trade Area (CARIFTA) and was strengthened in 1973 with the Treaty of Chaguaramas, establishing the Caribbean Community and Common Market (CARICOM), thus forming a customs union (with a commitment to effecting a common external tariff, rules of origin, and a harmonized scheme of fiscal incentives), and moving towards policy and functional cooperation. In 1989, the regional heads of government, in the Grand Anse Declaration, agreed to move towards a single market and economy,[17] and this was formalized in the Revised Treaty of Chaguaramas (RTC), which was signed in 2001 and came into effect in 2006. Chapter 8 of the RTC outlines a competition and consumer policy for the region, which will be elaborated upon in section 6 below.

There has been slow progress in implementation of the necessary provisions to effect the Single Market. Barbados's Prime Minister Thompson attributes the slow progress of implementation of the CSM to capacity constraint, not indifference, and tensions surrounding the free movement of labour, in which area there is little progress. Further, he argues that difficulties exist when trying to integrate countries with different levels of

[17] Signatories to the RTC are all members of CARICOM, listed in n. 2 above, excluding the Bahamas. Haiti is not yet part of the CSM because of its underdeveloped state.

development and legislative systems, varying cultures and languages, and which are separated by water.[18]

This integration movement faces many challenges, not least among them the fact that the area is dominated by three states (Jamaica, Barbados and Trinidad and Tobago) with the rest being micro-states. This disparity is taken into account in the regional arrangement, with special and differential treatment for the small states, termed less developed countries (LDCs) (meaning less developed within the regional grouping and not within the UN meaning of LDCs, or least developed countries). The more developed states (MDCs) are Barbados, Jamaica, Guyana, Suriname, and Trinidad and Tobago. The Eastern Caribbean countries,[19] together with Belize, are the LDCs. Within the regional grouping, there is a sub-regional grouping, the Organization of Eastern Caribbean States (OECS), created in 1981 as an inter-governmental organization dedicated primarily to the economic harmonization and integration of these countries. The purpose of this sub-regional grouping was to enhance its members' negotiating power within the wider regional group, to be able to pool their resources for development and to cope with regional disasters, among other goals. The OECS has achieved a greater degree of integration than CARICOM and the CSM to date.

Many institutions were created to support the regional integration effort (see the CARICOM website: http://www.caricom.org/), as were organs of the Community; among those of relevance to this paper are the Conference of Heads of Government and its bureau (the CARICOM Secretariat) and the Council for Trade and Economic Development (COTED), a political body with representatives from each state, with the responsibility for developing economic and development policies for the region. More recently, and accompanying the establishment of the Single Market, new institutions have been created, among them the Caribbean Court of Justice (CCJ) and the CARICOM Competition Commission (CCC). Of critical importance is the fact that, unlike the European Community, which has vested supra-national authority in its organs of government, in CARICOM there is no such arrangement. This has serious implications for the effective functioning of the regional institutions and the advancement of the integration

---

18 Feature address at the opening of the two-day Convocation on the CARICOM Single Market and Economy (CSME) at the Lloyd Erskine Sandiford Conference Centre, Bridgetown, Barbados, October 2009.

19 Antigua/Barbuda, Belize, Dominica, Grenada, Montserrat, St Lucia, St Vincent and the Grenadines, St Kitts, Nevis and Anguilla.

process, and reflects the continuing jealous guarding of sovereign rights. By extension, it also hampers the effective implementation of the regional competition policy (to be elaborated on in the following chapter).

In order to evaluate the role that competition policy can play in the integration process, it is useful to look at the intra-regional trade and investment that could be affected by anti-competitive conduct.

5. STATE OF PLAY IN ECONOMIC INTEGRATION

5.1 Intra-regional Trade

The verdict in the *Caribbean Trade and Investment Report 2005*[20] is that there is no significant difference in intra-CARICOM trade performance between the period of 1995–2000 and that of 2000–2005. The report puts this down to many of the structural rigidities referred to above, particularly similarity of production structures and a very limited range of intermediate and capital goods.[21] More recent data on the CARICOM website show an increase in intra-regional imports and exports, but this is largely due to the increased price of petroleum (from US$23 per barrel in 2001 to US$58.3 in 2006)[22] and petroleum products, and not quantum of trade. Indeed, intra-regional exports declined from 20 per cent of total exports in 2001 to 16.3 per cent in 2006 (see CARICOM Statistics at http://www.caricom.org/).

The MDCs dominate CARICOM's intra-regional trade, with Trinidad and Tobago being the leading exporter, and Jamaica and Barbados being CARICOM's top intra-regional importers. MDCs account for an average of 77.1 per cent of total intra-regional imports over the 2001–2006 period, while the LDCs account for an average of 19.9 per cent. Indeed, Trinidad and Tobago has a persistent positive balance of trade with the rest of the region, importing little from the region, while the reverse is the case for all other countries except Belize.[23]

Only two countries show a positive balance of trade in intra-regional trade: Trinidad and Tobago and Belize. Trinidad and Tobago's positive balance of trade is explained by its export of petroleum and petroleum

---

[20] *Caribbean Trade and Investment Report 2005*, *supra* n. 14, at p. xxiv.

[21] *Caribbean Trade and Investment Report 2005*, *supra* n. 14.

[22] http://www.inflationdata.com/: historical prices for oil.

[23] CARICOM Statistics: 'Value of CARICOM's Intra Regional Imports and Exports and Trade Balance by Country: 2001–2006', available at: http://www.caricomstats.org/Files/Publications/Quick_Ref2008/CARICOM.pdf

products, and light manufactured goods throughout the region. Indeed, Trinidad and Tobago accounted for 85.5 per cent of total intra-regional exports in 2006, of which mineral fuels, lubricants and related materials accounted for 66.7 per cent.[24] Light manufacturing exports include sweet biscuits, concentrated orange juice, processed foods, aerated beverages, beer, cigarettes containing tobacco, detergents, cartons, boxes and cases of corrugated paper or paperboards, toilet paper, nappies (diapers) and nappy liners for babies. Trinidad and Tobago is the largest and most dominating economy in the region.

Belize's positive balance of trade with the rest of CARICOM may be largely explained by its geographic proximity to Mexico and the fact that it accesses its petroleum from that source, petroleum accounting for the majority of intra-regional trade. Belize is not at all deeply engaged in intra-regional trade, its intra-regional exports being only 0.8 per cent of the total intra-regional exports in 2006 and its imports only 0.6 per cent of the total intra-regional imports in the same year. On the other hand, Belizeans informally access both goods and services across the border in Mexico.

The narrow range of products traded reflects the limited production structures in the region. Of the 15 most intra-regionally exported items (representing approximately 60 per cent of all intra-regionally exported items), the only ones that represent significant value added are rice, cane sugar, cement and, to some extent, petroleum (taking into account that Trinidad and Tobago has local reserves of oil, but also imports a substantial amount for refining and re-export). In the case of rice, Guyana is the only indigenous producer in large quantities. Interestingly, Guyana exports the products with the highest value added (fish, shrimp, prawns, rice, sugar, edible cane molasses, wood, plywood). Sadly, despite an abundance of tropical fruits, fruit concentrates are imported and mixed, to be sold as reconstituted juices, while the fruits grown domestically are consumed to the extent that is possible, and the rest go to waste; this is mainly because of a lack of efficient collection systems to provide a reliable source of supply to processing plants. Agro-processing and light manufacturing, capital-intensive products that rely heavily on the import of intermediate and capital goods, account for the rest (see above). Of these, the majority is exported from Trinidad and Tobago, followed by Barbados, and also, most

---

24 CARICOM Statistics: 'Intra Regional Trade, Imports, Exports & Trade Balance', available at: http://www.caricomstats.org/Files/Publications/Quick_Ref2008/CARICOM.pdf

of the imports go to Barbados and Jamaica. Progress in trade integration is still slow, and this is attributable to the structural rigidities elaborated upon above.

5.2 Intra-regional Investment

According to the *Caribbean Trade and Investment Report 2005*, more than two-thirds of intra-CARICOM capital flows emanate from Trinidad and Tobago. The other significant suppliers of cross-border capital are Barbados and Jamaica. The investment flows are largely limited not only to the three largest countries, but also to a few firms within these countries. There has been considerable increase in intra-regional investment over the last decade, but this by only a handful of firms. The vast majority of firms in the region are small (micro by international standards). The majority of Trinidad and Tobago's intra-regional investment is in the financial sector. Between 1999 and 2004, 57 per cent of direct investment out of Trinidad and Tobago was in banking and insurance – undertaken by a handful of banks (e.g. RBTT and Republic Bank) and an insurance company (Guardian General).[25] The openness of the economies and the high import bill creates a demand for hard currency, and in some economies, such as Belize, banks favour granting credit to firms that earn foreign currency because of its scarcity.[26] There is a mixture of locally owned and foreign-owned banks in the region.

In addition, the leading conglomerates in Trinidad and Tobago, a handful again, have been responsible for investment in non-financial services. Of the 16 leading investors in non-financial services, ten are Trinidad and Tobago firms, four are Jamaican firms (in tourism mainly), and two are from Barbados (in airline catering, trading and distribution mainly). Of the Trinidad and Tobago firms, there has been some shift in ownership of wealth, with Syrian and Lebanese descendants buying firms that were originally owned by the white plantocracy.[27] The original wealth rested in land ownership, granted by the crown to the plantocracy, and this was used in part to finance business ventures in commerce. Much of the privately owned land in the prime areas of Trinidad is still owned by the white

---

25 *Caribbean Trade and Investment Report 2005*, *supra* n. 14, 105–107, 174.

26 Stewart (2004), *supra* n. 10.

27 There is an interesting situation in Trinidad and Tobago, where the Syrian-Lebanese community hold themselves apart from the Indian and black populations, have inter-married with the whites, and are considered by themselves and the blacks as part of the 'white' ethnic group. The whites may have a different view.

plantocracy class, and the large conglomerates whose roots are in the colonial period, are still owned by the whites or have been bought over by the Syrian-Lebanese elites, 'the near-whites'.[28] The major Barbados conglomerates are unambiguously part of the inherited wealth of the plantocracy class. This concentration of capital in the hands of a few elite is relevant for competition policy because in small societies these families are closely knit, socializing with each other and inter-marrying. They control import and retail trade and the potential for collusion is very high, but very difficult to prove. Moreover, oligopolies make coordination of strategies easier.

The conglomerates chose modes of entry through joint ventures, wholly owned subsidiaries and equity ownership in companies, while financial-sector companies used mergers and acquisitions for cross-border expansion, thereby capturing existing customers. Some franchising of fast food outlets has also taken place. Cross-border ownership of shares in another conglomerate is also occurring (Neal and Massy of Trinidad and Tobago and Barbados Shipping and Trading). 'Subsidiaries tend to operate as stand alone entities catering to the host market, rather than as part of an integrated supply change. Integration of Caribbean markets tends to exist, but not integration of production, per se.'[29] There have been limited numbers of new ventures, and corporate integration rather than intrinsic production integration has been seen.[30]

---

28 For instance, the ANSA/McAl group, one of the two major conglomerates in Trinidad and Tobago, was originally owned by white families, the Alstons and the Wrights. In the early days the company dealt with the exportation of cocoa, and also imported products, serving as commission agents. Sometime in the 1970s or early 1980s the group, which at the time was expanding to include shipping agents, travel agents, insurance, clay products, etc., found themselves the object of a foreign takeover bid, and succeeded in having the group taken over by the then McAnerney group, another conglomerate owned by whites. That takeover saw the creation of the McAl group, which operated quite successfully for many years until the first recession, when oil prices dropped drastically. During this period, ANSA, a group owned by A.N. Sabga, a Syrian, was invited to invest in McAl; this investment allowed Sabga to own the majority of shares. With this power he eventually took control of the whole group, resulting in the birth of the ANSA/McAl group.

29 Odle, M. (2006), quoted in *Caribbean Trade and Investment Report 2005*, p. 117.

30 *Caribbean Trade and Investment Report 2005*, *supra* n.14, p. xxvi.

6. CARICOM COMPETITION POLICY

6.1 State of National Legislation

This brief analysis of trends in cross-regional investment and trade shows that only a few firms can engage in conduct that could have a substantial effect on the relevant market in two or more countries, and that these firms are largely from Barbados and Trinidad and Tobago. There is, therefore, a need for instruments to discipline particularly firms in Trinidad and Tobago engaging in cross-border anti-competitive conduct. Given the lack of supranational authority in the region, it is necessary for each territory to have a national competition law and institution. While strengthening the CCC by conferring supranational powers is an option, it is not politically feasible.

This is a fundamental obligation in the RTC. Chapter 8 of the RTC provides for a regional competition commission, the CCC, to investigate and discipline cross-border anti-competitive conduct in cooperation with the national authorities, with results enforceable by national courts, and to assist member states in developing national competition laws and institutions, among other responsibilities. The main objective of the regime is to ensure that the benefits to be derived from the creation of the Single Market are not frustrated by anti-competitive conduct by firms. The RTC prohibits anti-competitive agreements and abuse of dominance, but does not speak to MCR. Given the evidence presented above of mergers and acquisitions being a favoured mode of market entry by financial institutions, and that the largest share of investments has been in the financial sector, there is a pressing need for the region to adopt MCR as part of their competition regime.

Up until this point, implementation has been slow. The regional commission, the CCC, has been established and is in the process of completing its staffing and developing its rules of procedure and other operating instruments. It is also engaging in activities with member states to assist in developing national regimes. At this point, there are only four member states with competition laws enacted: Jamaica, Barbados, Trinidad and Tobago, and Guyana. Jamaica has had its law and a corresponding commission since 1993, but has encountered several problems that need to be addressed in a revised law (see the following chapter), and this is in progress. Jamaica also needs to revise its law to make the decisions of the CCC enforceable in the national jurisdiction. Barbados's regime is up and running, with a fully developed law that is compatible with the RTC and a fledging commission that is progressively finding its feet. Guyana has recently appointed its commissioners, and the CCC has conducted a training seminar for them. Trinidad and Tobago lags behind Guyana, but now that a new government has been elected, it is hoped that there will be movement on full proclamation of the law, appointment of commissioners and the setting up of the institution. It is the country that is most in need of a fully functioning competition regime, because of the size and reach of its firms.

Other countries are still in the drafting stage, some more advanced than others. The OECS countries have agreed to the establishment of a sub-regional competition commission to serve as a national commission in each of the countries in the OECS, with an agency in each country to facilitate the work of the commission. This is primarily because of severe constraints on both financial and human resources. The draft law is in the final stages of approval, and the most pressing constraint at present is the funding for the commission. Suriname has a draft law, but there seem to be problems getting consensus across the board in advancing the process. Belize is also at the drafting stage, and one expects some progress in the near future in enacting the law. The Bahamas is not a signatory of the RTC, and therefore has not assumed its obligations.

The major constraint to implementation of the competition regime in the Caribbean region is lack of resources, both technical and financial. The OECS has gone a long way towards setting up its regime, but does not have the money to cover the establishment of the Commission and recurrent expenditure. The governments are now hard-pressed to find that money, due to the severe economic contraction in these economies. There is a lack of a culture of competition throughout the region, and much advocacy is needed, not just among the stakeholders, but also with government officials and parliamentarians. Political will is very low, and since there are many pressing problems in the region, governments are prioritizing their focus, at the expense of competition law.

6.2 Some Glitches Discerned in the Regime

There is a need for convergence of the various national laws in the region. This is not difficult, given the infancy of those regimes that do exist, the fact that many of the states have not even passed their law as yet, and that each country has used the CARICOM Model Law as the template from which to draft their legislation. However, the inclusion of Suriname in the CSM introduces a country with a civil-law heritage, as opposed to the common-law background of the English-speaking Caribbean. This is not an insurmountable problem, but one that presents challenges, given the scarcity of expertise in the region.

Lack of harmonization could render the law very ineffective in critical cross-border situations. For instance, only Barbados and Trinidad and Tobago have MCR in their laws, and only Barbados is implementing MCR. We have seen from the empirical evidence provided above that firms from Trinidad and Tobago are penetrating the region through mergers and acquisitions, and the CCC has no authority to investigate the effects of a proposed merger on markets in the region. Financial institutions from Trinidad and Tobago are the ones using this mode of entry. Yet they are exempt from competition law in the Trinidad and Tobago Fair Trading Act. They fall under the supervision of the financial regulatory bodies. Competition provisions are incorporated into the Financial Institutional Act, but the Trinidad and Tobago Financial Regulatory Body only considers mergers that affect the domestic market. In addition, there is no effective system of cross-border supervision, collaboration and cooperation among the financial institutions of the host and the home country, according to the *Caribbean Trade and Investment Report 2005*.[31]

Another concern is the fact that Article 176 of the RTC limits the power of the CCC in cases of dispute between a member state and the CCC as to the nature and effects of the business conduct or the jurisdiction of the investigating authority. The Commission must cease any further examination of the matter, and refer the matter to COTED, a policy-making body that does not have dispute-settlement powers. At a recent workshop of competition commissions from small states,[32] CARICOM participants, primarily the Commissioners and staff of the Jamaican FTC and the Barbados FTC, felt that there was a need for further consideration of the full implications of this Article for the ability of the CCC to function effectively, and also for a re-evaluation of the role given to COTED by the RTC in the implementation of the regional competition regime. By contrast, in the EC regime, the European Commission has the authority to relieve a national authority of competence if the Commission initiates a proceeding.

COTED is authorized by Article 182 (Chapter 8) of the RTC to develop and establish appropriate policies and rules of competition within the

---

[31] *Caribbean Trade and Investment Report 2005*, *supra* n. 14, p. xxvii.

[32] Workshop on Competition Law and Policy in Caribbean Small States, Barbados, 26 and 27 October 2009.

Community, including special rules for particular sectors. COTED also has the authority to suspend or exclude the application of Article 177 (prohibition of anti-competitive conduct) if it determines that special rules apply to specific sectors of the Community. Given that the structure of trade and investment in the region is heavily skewed in favour of Trinidad and Tobago and, to a lesser extent, Barbados, there is the possibility that states may apply to COTED, and gain a favourable hearing, on exemption of sectors that are out-competed by Trinidad and Tobago firms, or that may be deemed to be in the public interest.

There is also concern that the CCC can issue negative clearance rulings under Article 180 of the RTC. In other jurisdictions, this has been found to place too great a demand on the limited resources of the commission. In Malta, for instance, the advance notification system was abolished in 2004, and firms were thereby encouraged to engage in self-assessment.[33] COTED's overarching power in the implementation of the regional competition policy is also a reflection of governments jealously guarding their sovereignty.

The CCC faces many challenges in fulfilling its mandate: it is constrained in its powers and faces incompatibilities and a lack of convergence of laws within the region that would hinder enforcement of the regional policy; particularly, it faces a lack of legal access to enforcement against domestic firms, while most member states are without a competition law or institution. On the other hand, the firms that can have a substantial impact on markets are from Barbados, Trinidad and Tobago and Jamaica; the Community decisions are enforceable in Barbados, and will soon be so in the other two states. Other member states and COTED could request that the Commission investigate suspected anti-competitive conduct. (These legal issues are addressed in the following chapter.)

---

33 Ibid.

7. THE CARIFORUM–EU ECONOMIC PARTNERSHIP AGREEMENT: IMPACT ON THE REGIONAL COMPETITION POLICY

The CARIFORUM–EU[34] Economic Partnership Agreement (EPA) was signed in 2009 and includes a chapter on competition policy. It is interesting that the EU tried very hard to force the CARICOM integration process to extend to the Dominican Republic. Both the Dominican Republic and CARICOM strongly and successfully resisted this pressure. However, in the competition chapter of the EPA, 'Competition Authority' is defined as referring to the European Commission, the CARICOM Competition Authority, and the Comisión Nacional de Defensa de la Competencia of the Dominican Republic (still to be established). While this simplifies institutional arrangements for interaction between the two parties to the agreement, and works for CARICOM, given capacity constraints, it does present a problem for the Bahamas, which is a signatory to the EPA. While the Bahamas is a member of CARICOM, it is not a signatory of the RTC, having chosen not to be part of the Single Market. This is understandable, since there is little trade between the Bahamas and the rest of CARICOM, and there was grave concern in the Bahamas about the free movement of labour, since it has the highest wages in the region. Now, with the CARICOM Competition Authority being the only recognized authority in the EPA, the Bahamas will have to find a way to come under its umbrella for purposes of the EPA.

The provisions of the competition chapter do not place further requirements on CARIFORUM other than those that its members have undertaken themselves (except the Bahamas). The Dominican Republic has passed its law and is in the process of setting up its institution. The EPA does, however, require that within five years of the signing of the agreement, the member states must have laws in force and give effect to the provisions of Article 128 (exchange of information and enforcement cooperation. Thus, external pressure is exerted on member states of the CSM and the Bahamas to enact competition law and comply with the obligations of Chapter 8 of the RTC, which is a requirement of the EPA.

---

[34] CARIFORUM consists of CARICOM plus the Dominican Republic, and was created purely for the purpose of facilitating relations with the EU in the context of the Lomé/Cotonou Agreements and now the EPA.

The cooperation provisions of the EPA are quite soft, with all provisions in that section preceded by 'Parties may' rather than 'shall'. There is no provision for substantial cooperation in investigation, which leaves the CARIFORUM countries with little ability to investigate the TNCs from Europe that engage in cross-border anti-competitive conduct affecting their domestic markets. While it is understood that more intense cooperation between competition authorities is the exception rather than the rule, and that a high level of convergence in the laws and maturity of the commissions is needed, it is also of concern that small developing states would be particularly vulnerable to the actions of international cartels, and furthermore have no recourse.

For example, in the EPA's chapter on tourism services, Article 111 addresses the prevention of anti-competitive practices. It states that

> appropriate measures shall be maintained or introduced by the EC Party or the Signatory CARIFORUM States for the purpose of preventing suppliers, in particular in the context of tourism distribution networks [defined as tour operators and other tourism wholesalers] to affect materially the terms of participation in the relevant market for tourism services by engaging in or continuing anti-competitive practices, including, *inter alia*, abuse of dominant position through imposition of unfair prices, exclusivity clauses, refusal to deal, tied sales, quantity restrictions or vertical integration.

Yet the perpetrators of such anti-competitive conduct affecting tourism in the Caribbean are the international tour operators, who operate in cartel-like fashion. A few international tour operators dominate the hotel reservation business, with links to airlines, travel agents and destination management companies. A recent UNCTAD study on tourism has identified biases in a network of computerized reservation system (CRS) that give the linked operators market power. The study points out the tied-in biases in hotel distribution systems, frequent flyer programmes and direct selling, concluding that market power in this sector centres on CRS display, airline alliances and competition, and access to distribution systems and computer displays. The result in the Caribbean is that:

- Large hotels, which are usually foreign-owned, get the business.
- Non-tied tourists have difficulty getting an airline seat.
- Local hotels and businesses suffer, and less money comes into and stays in the economy.

The EPA provision does not address the issue of jurisdictional constraint to investigating foreign firms and the power asymmetry between small economies and powerful TNCs. This provision in the tourism chapter has no teeth. One hopes that once the regime is fully established in CARIFORUM, and the agreement is re-visited, there will be fierce demands for more assistance in dealing with such conduct emanating from Europe.

8. CONCLUDING REMARKS

This chapter has evaluated the role of competition policy in advancing the integration process in CARICOM and concluded that introducing and enforcing competition law is vital to preserving market access and to preventing abuse of dominance and high concentration in markets. It was shown that regional trade and investment is dominated by a few firms, and these mainly from Trinidad and Tobago, and that wealth is concentrated in a few hands throughout the region, and this mainly in families who inherited from the plantocracy. This creates social tensions and political sensitivities that affect the formulation of competition policies.

It was also shown that while the states within the CSM (except Suriname) have a common colonial heritage, which allows for a sense of identity, the divisions caused by separation by water and claims to sovereignty have created problems that are not easy to overcome. To compound this, there is racial tension in the region, particularly in Jamaica, Barbados, Trinidad and Tobago, and Guyana, where the societies are more ethnically mixed.

The actual evidence of trade and investment showed that one country dominates in both areas, and in this country, only a few firms dominate. This has created resentment in the rest of the region, and exposes the smaller economies in particular to abuse of dominance by these firms. This can lead to friction among states, and erode the integration process. Competition policy at the regional level would protect the process of competition and thus ensure that the integration process is more politically acceptable to the smaller states, in particular, because they would be protected from anti-competitive conduct that could be exercised by the larger firms from the MDCs. This evidence also revealed that merger and acquisition is a preferred mode of entry for the financial services sector, but there is no MCR in the regional competition policy. Firms are not integrating at the production level. Indeed, apart from a few firms that are intensifying production processes, though still not at the cutting edge, the main activities of firms are still based on commerce.

In sum, the regional economic integration process is slow because of the limited amount of products that can be offered for exchange; there is not sufficient product differentiation in the various economies that generate vibrant trade, and the region is still heavily reliant on imports from the north. Be that as it may, competition policy has a vital role to play in preventing the big firms from eroding the benefits of the free flow of goods and services anticipated in the single market, and hurting consumers by engaging in anti-competitive conduct. The process of implementation of the competition regime is on-going, and the EPA now provides a push factor for getting the regime up and running.

9. Implementing effective competition policy through regional trade agreements: the case of CARICOM

Delroy S. Beckford

1. INTRODUCTION

In this chapter we examine the governance arrangements in CARICOM for the implementation of effective competition policy through a regional trade agreement (RTA), how the nature of the governance arrangements operates to achieve Community competition policy, and the challenges posed for implementing effective competition policy, not only in balancing competing objectives but in overcoming constitutional hurdles that affect administrative design and the implementation and enforcement of competition policy.

Our examination proceeds on the premise that effective implementation of competition policy for small developing countries with resource constraints requires some level of centralized enforcement to monitor and remedy cross-border anti-competitive conduct, but that decentralized enforcement may be necessary to give effect to development objectives or to discipline anti-competitive conduct that originates in, and whose effect is confined to, a particular member state.

For our purposes, competition policy refers to the 'full array of government policy measures that influence competition in domestic markets'.[1] These include instruments of trade policy such as tariffs but also effective implementation and enforcement of competition law. Here, competition policy is treated as the body of rules, regulations, decisions, administrative

[1] See paper by Hassan, Qaqaya (2009), 'Competition Policy and its Relevance to Trade and Development', Regional Seminar on Trade and Competition: Prospects and Future Challenges for Latin America and the Caribbean, Caracas, Venezuela, 20–21 April.

guidelines and other policy instruments whereby the integrity of the competitive process is safeguarded for market participants and consumers.

Effective competition policy through RTAs depends largely on the goals being pursued by the RTA. Several goals may be pursued simultaneously, subsumed under one overarching goal, or disparate goals may not be concretely delineated or clearly tied together, so as to avoid contradictions or conflict in the application of the regional competition law governing the RTA. Some of these goals include global competitiveness, market integration through harmonization, consumer welfare, efficient allocation of resources and enforcement of competition policy taking into consideration special and differential treatment.

Within an RTA, the governance structure chosen may be centralized, decentralized or a hybrid. The typology sometimes employed in this structure differentiates between voluntary and mandatory forbearance.[2]

The particular regional institutional framework adopted often signifies the goals being pursued or the overarching goal being promoted. Decentralized enforcement, for example, eschews or discounts harmonization and market integration and this may exemplify extant fissures among RTA partners, resonating distrust or a lack of commitment to regionalization and to the pooling or reduction of sovereignty envisaged.

2. COMPETITION PROVISIONS OF THE REVISED TREATY OF CHAGUARAMAS

The competition provisions of the Revised Treaty of Chaguaramas (RTC) and the governance arrangements established pursuant to the Treaty represent a hybrid structure in the enforcement of competition policy. In addition, although the governance arrangements for enforcement of competition policy in regional trading arrangements is often referred to as exemplifying a distinction between voluntary and mandatory forbearance, the governance arrangements in CARICOM incorporate these two features in that anti-competitive conduct with cross-border effects is to be disciplined at the regional level, and anti-competitive conduct that is confined in its effect to a particular member state is to be governed by national competition laws.

---

[2] Gal, Michal (2009), 'Regional Competition Law Agreements: An Important Step for Antitrust Enforcement', New York University Law and Economics Working Paper.

Perhaps more important is that the governance arrangements do not suggest a strong commitment to a timely implementation process for competition law and policy. Commitments undertaken at the regional level require the establishment of competition authorities, amendment of domestic legislation, and, absent a system for the binding effect of regional directives, possible recourse to developing constitutional jurisprudence to establish the primacy of regional competition law.

We now examine the governance arrangements in CARICOM under the RTC and the extent to which these foster the effective enforcement of competition policy, the role of the Community Commission and its relationship with other bodies and particular challenges for meeting some of the objectives of effective enforcement of competition law and policy.

Of the goals identified for effective competition policy in RTAs with developing countries, two can be identified as possibly necessary conditions, namely, the fostering of market integration through harmonization and the existence of policy flexibility for special and differential treatment. However, while these two objectives are often complementary, the governance arrangements in CARICOM do not necessarily avoid the possibility of conflict in giving effect to these objectives.

Market integration is one of the central objectives of competition policy under the RTC. Modelled on EU governance arrangements, the RTC involves both positive and negative integration, that is, the elimination of obstacles to the free movement of goods, services and factors of production and the adoption of common policies to ensure the effective operation of market forces.

The competition rules provided for in Chapter 8 of the RTC allow for minimal harmonization, setting minimum rules and standards for member states to implement in domestic legislation, but also allowing member states the flexibility to adopt more stringent ones.

Special and differential treatment is another goal pursued. The RTC recognizes that CARICOM states include countries at different stages of development, and provides for policy flexibility in accordance with the principle of special and differential treatment. Thus Article 1 refers to disadvantaged countries in the following terms:

(a) the Less Developed Countries within the meaning of Article 4; or
(b) Member States that may require special support measures of a transitional or temporary nature by reason of:
  (i) impairment of resources resulting from natural disasters; or
  (ii) the adverse impact of the operation of the CSME on their economies; or

(iii) temporary low levels of economic development; or
(iv) being a Highly-indebted Poor Country designated as such by the competent intergovernmental organization.

The less developed countries may also apply to the Council for Trade and Economic Development (COTED), as a temporary measure to promote industrial development, for suspension of Community origin treatment of eligible imports on the ground that the product is produced in one of their territories.

Further recognition and acceptance of the principle of special and differential treatment is observed in Article 49 of the RTC regarding removal of restrictions on the right of establishment, Article 51(2)(h) of the RTC with respect to the objectives of the Community industrial policy, and Article 52(2) of the RTC concerning a special regime for the implementation of the Community industrial policy that factors in the special needs of disadvantaged regions.

In the context of the enforcement of competition law, there is no express provision recognizing special and differential treatment for less developed countries in the application of the prohibitions against anti-competitive conduct. Nonetheless, there are provisions in the RTC that permit this flexibility.

In addition to the substantive rules, particular Community organs are enjoined to develop Community competition policy, and this has been supplemented with the establishment of the Caribbean Court of Justice (CCJ) to adjudicate on trade disputes in its original jurisdiction.

Instrumental in the decision-making process is the Community Commission, which is mandated to decide on competition issues that have cross-border effects. Its relationship with other CARICOM bodies in the development of competition policy and the adjudication of disputes is critical for effective enforcement in terms of harmonization and the recognition of special and differential treatment in the application of competition law and policy. The particular relationship with the governance organs within CARICOM is now explored.

3. CONFERENCE OF HEADS OF GOVERNMENT AND THE COUNCIL FOR TRADE AND ECONOMIC DEVELOPMENT (COTED)

The Conference of Heads of Government (CHG), composed of the heads of government of the member states, may be involved in the development of Community competition policy in accordance with Article 20 of the RTC. Article 20(1) of the RTC provides for cooperation among Community organs in the development of Community policy where the policy to be developed impacts on the spheres of competence of another Community organ.

The Community organs are referred to in Article 10 of the RTC as the CHG and the Community Council of Ministers (as the principal organs); and the subordinate organs include the Council for Finance and Planning, COTED, the Council for Foreign and Community Relations, and the Council for Human and Social Development.

In the relationship between the CHG and COTED, there is likely to be some impact on the latter through policy developed by the former that would require their cooperation in accordance with Article 20 of the RTC. This is so because Article 12(2) of the RTC stipulates that the CHG 'shall determine and provide policy direction for the Community', and Article 12(7) of the RTC provides that the CHG 'may issue policy directives of a general or special character to the other Organs and Bodies of the Community concerning the policies to be pursued for the achievement of the objectives of the Community and effect shall be given to such directives'.

4. RELATIONSHIP BETWEEN COTED AND THE COMMUNITY COMMISSION

4.1 Development of Competition Policy

Article 15 of the RTC provides that COTED is the body charged with the 'promotion of trade and economic development of the Community'. Pursuant to Article 152 of the RTC, COTED is charged with developing and establishing appropriate policies and rules of competition within the Community.

While COTED is charged with the development of competition policy in the Community, the Community Commission also plays an advisory role in the development of competition policy. For example, Article 173(2)(b) of the RTC requires the Community Commission to 'keep the Community Competition Policy under review and advise and make recommendations to COTED to enhance its effectiveness'.

5. COTED AND A NATIONAL INVESTIGATION AGENCY

The relationship between a national competition authority and COTED is indirect in the sense that COTED is charged with promoting trade and economic development in the Community. However, this broad mandate is likely to impact the operation of national competition authorities in terms of COTED's power to exclude particular sectors from the provisions relating to prohibited conduct under Article 177 of the RTC, which provisions are to be incorporated into the domestic law of CARICOM members.

In addition to this general relationship, there is the more specific relationship contemplated under Article 182 of the RTC whereby COTED is the body charged with developing and establishing appropriate policies and rules of competition within the Community that are to be adopted by national competition agencies. Pursuant to Article 182 of the RTC, COTED is charged with developing special competition rules for particular sectors. This broad mandate will doubtless translate into the development of competition rules that factor in other policy concerns for the development of CARICOM members, including the Community industrial policy.

This broad mandate is also apparently designed to ensure that common competition rules apply to particular sectors throughout the Community, thereby fostering harmonization of competition policy.

However, there is no provision for *directives* to be issued to a national competition authority from COTED when it recommends the adoption of particular competition policy or special rules for particular sectors. Arguably, this loophole may contribute to member states maintaining different rules for particular sectors, consistent with their development objective, and this will definitely affect the harmonization process.

6. COTED AND THE CARIBBEAN COURT OF JUSTICE (CCJ)

Decisions of COTED can be examined by the CCJ, although it is doubtful that this would apply to policy directives. Article 187(c) of the RTC permits suits to be brought against an organ of the Community on the ground that it has acted *ultra vires*. This power to review COTED's decisions is limited to situations where COTED has exercised its discretion.[3] Moreover, Article 211 of the RTC gives the CCJ jurisdiction to decide disputes between member states and the Community, which includes Community organs.

The exercise of discretion on purely political policy questions may not be justiciable, and it is, therefore, to be expected that disputes between member states and Community organs on political questions regarding development policy will remain largely unresolved, if not by conciliatory means at the level of the conference heads of government.

Undoubtedly, the absence of governance mechanisms for definitive resolution of policy disputes among member states provides flexibility for special and differential treatment in competition policy, but this goal may be achieved at the expense of harmonization, unless individual action by member states is constrained by general policy positions for which agreement has already been obtained by the CHG.

7. COMMUNITY COMMISSION AND THE CCJ

Article 175(12) of the RTC provides that 'a party that is aggrieved by a determination of the Commission under paragraph 4 of Article 174 in any matter may apply to the Court for a review of that determination'.

Paragraph 4 of Article 174 of the RTC refers to orders or directives that the Commission makes to remedy or penalize anti-competitive conduct referred to in Article 177 of the RTC. Pursuant to Article 174(4) of the RTC, the Commission 'shall ... order the termination or nullification ... of agreements, conduct, activities or decisions prohibited by Article 170'. The Commission may also direct the enterprise to cease and desist from anti-competitive business conduct and to take such steps as are necessary to overcome the effects of its abuse of dominance in the market or any other business conduct inconsistent with the principles of fair competition in Chapter 8 of the RTC. In addition, the Commission may order the payment of compensation to persons affected, and impose fines for breaches of the rules of competition.

Although Article 175(12) seems confined to orders or directives issued by the Commission for compliance with its findings, it is arguable that an

[3] See *Trinidad Cement Company Limited v. The Caribbean Community* [2009] CCJ 4 (OJ), para. 41.

aggrieved party may also challenge the particular findings as the basis on which the orders or directives were made.

Importantly, where the Commission determines that there is anti-competitive business conduct and requires a party to take the necessary action to remove the effects of that conduct, the party to whom the directive is given is to take the appropriate remedial course of action within 30 days of notification by the Commission. If the enterprise cannot comply with the Commission's order within the 30-day period and fails to inform the Commission, the Commission may apply to the CCJ for an order.

However, it is unclear whether there is any limitation to the specific order for which the Commission may apply to the CCJ. For example, Article 175(11) of the RTC does not stipulate whether the order to be applied for is limited to a declaration of breach of the competition provisions in the RTC or would encompass an order for compliance with a determination of the Commission.

It is noteworthy that if the CCJ issues an order for compliance with a determination of the Commission, this may not be achieved, because the existing governance mechanism does not *require* a decision of the CCJ to have direct effect and be enforceable within a CARICOM member and against a CARICOM national found to have breached the competition provisions of the RTC.

The Caribbean Court of Justice Act incorporated in several of the various CARICOM states provides for the compulsory jurisdiction of the CCJ to be given effect in CARICOM states, whether in the CCJ's original or appellate jurisdiction, but does not require decisions of the CCJ that are directed at a member state or a national of a member state to have direct enforcement in the domestic legal order of CARICOM members.

Further, in the event that an order of the CCJ includes an order for compliance with a determination of the Commission and the route chosen for enforcement of this order is by provisions in domestic legislation requiring decisions of the Commission to be binding in the domestic legal order of CARICOM members, compliance with the order may be frustrated by reluctance to incorporate such provisions.

Importantly, several CARICOM countries have passed legislation to give effect to the RTC provisions on competition law and policy, but this action by itself is insufficient to give effect to these provisions without the necessary promulgation or amendment to domestic legislation to incorporate specifically the provisions of the RTC.

This is because some provisions of the RTC are drafted in mandatory terms that would have an effect on the promulgation of the relevant law to give effect to the RTC, while other provisions, although drafted in mandatory terms, contain a permissive component in the language or may be directory, requiring a further legislative act. For example, Section 3 of the Caribbean Community Act (2004) of Antigua and Barbuda, provides that 'Subject to this Act, the Treaty, the text of which is set out in the Schedule, shall have the force of law'.

In this context, consider Article 170(1)(b) of the RTC.

> (b) the Member States shall:
> (i) take the necessary legislative measures to ensure consistency and compliance with the rules of competition and provide penalties for anti-competitive business conduct;
> (ii) provide for the dissemination of relevant information to facilitate consumer choice;
> (iii) establish and maintain institutional arrangements and administrative procedures to enforce competition laws; and
> (iv) take effective measures to ensure access by nationals of other Member States to competent enforcement authorities including the courts on an equitable, transparent and non-discriminatory basis.

Another example is Article 170(2), which provides: 'Every Member State shall establish and maintain a national competition authority for the purpose of facilitating the implementation of the rules of competition.'

Yet another example is that provided in Article 177 of the RTC, which states:

> 1. A Member State shall, within its jurisdiction, prohibit as being anti-competitive business conduct, the following:
> (a) agreements between enterprises, decisions by associations of enterprises, and concerted practices by enterprises which have as their object or effect the prevention, restriction or distortion of competition within the Community;
> (b) actions by which an enterprise abuses its dominant position within the Community; or
> (c) any other like conduct by enterprises whose object or effect is to frustrate the benefits expected from the establishment of the CSME.

These provisions are in mandatory terms but require some further action on the part of member states beyond the promulgation of the terms of the Treaty as an act of parliament. Because the language used is directory in nature the passage of an act to give effect to the Treaty cannot result in these provisions having direct legal effect in as much as further action is required.

By contrast, some provisions are drafted in mandatory terms that can take effect when the treaty is promulgated in domestic law. For example, the general exemption provision of Article 168 with respect to the scope of Chapter 8 of the RTC excludes negative clearance rulings and collective bargaining arrangements.

To ensure that Community competition law and policy is harmonized, Article 174(6) of the RTC provides that 'Member States shall enact legislation to ensure that determinations of the Commission are enforceable in their jurisdiction'. This provision establishes a positive obligation with respect to determinations by the Commission, albeit not with respect to the Commission's other powers, for example, powers exercisable pursuant to Article 174(2)(a) and 174(2)(b) of the RTC.

It is not clear whether *all* determinations of the Commission should be enforceable in CARICOM member states or only those relating to a dispute involving an enterprise incorporated in the particular member state.

The fact that not all determinations are included in this obligation, coupled with the requirement of further action by CARICOM members to implement the necessary enactments to give effect to decisions of the Commission, provides some modicum of flexibility for CARICOM members to pursue competition law and policy consistent with their particular development objectives.

8. COMMUNITY COMMISSION AND NATIONAL INVESTIGATION AUTHORITIES

Under Article 176(1) of the RTC, national competition agencies are enjoined to conduct a preliminary examination of conduct of a business enterprise within the CARICOM Single Market and Economy (CSME) on the request of the Commission, if the Commission is of the view that such conduct prejudices trade and prevents, restricts or distorts competition with the CSME.

This obligation under the RTC will often require the amendment of domestic law for effect to be given to it. In some jurisdictions, such as Jamaica, there is no provision in the competition legislation for investigations to be conducted at the request of an external body. Section 5 of the Jamaican Fair Competition Act (FCA) requires the Fair Trading Commission (FTC) to conduct investigations at the request of the relevant minister, and it is arguable that a request by the Commission for a preliminary examination of business conduct could be done through this medium.

This approach, however, leaves much discretion to members, while Article 176(1) of the RTC was not intended to provide such discretion but rather an obligation to conduct such preliminary examinations. Through such discretion national objectives can be pursued with flexible policy options at the expense of Community objectives for competition policy.

This is not to suggest that members have no discretion with respect to the conduct of an investigation. The discretion is, however, confined to jurisdictional disputes – thus, whether a national investigating authority or the Commission is to conduct an investigation, as opposed to a preliminary examination, where the Commission finds that further investigation is warranted, following its dissatisfaction with the outcome of a request for a preliminary examination of business conduct to be done by a national investigating authority.

Amendment of domestic legislation may also be required where the preliminary examination to be conducted involves companies whose conduct has an effect on a market other than that of the territory of the investigating authority. For example, Section 2(3) of the FCA of Jamaica states that: 'Every reference in this Act to the term "market" is a reference to a market in Jamaica for goods or services as well as other goods or services that, as a matter of fact and commercial common sense, are substitutable for them.'

Given that a preliminary examination requested by the Commission is in respect of conduct that has an effect within the CSME or affects the operation of the CSME, it is not inconceivable that a request for such an examination can be made regarding conduct whose effect is limited to the territory of the investigating authority, since the market of each CARICOM state is a part of the single market. But if the term 'cross-border effects' connotes conduct whose effect is not limited to a particular territory, it is unclear what the basis for a request for a preliminary examination would be when the conduct and its effect is confined to a particular member state.

It may be that the term 'cross-border effects' denotes, for example, anti-competitive conduct that has an effect outside of the member state where the conduct originates. If this is so, Community competition policy, to the extent that the promotion of this objective is largely within the mandate of the Commission, may not adequately address domestic anti-competitive conduct that frustrates market access.

In addition, the investigative function of the Commission may be affected due to the absence of competition laws and functioning competition authorities in some CARICOM member states. Article 174(2) of the RTC provides for the Commission to carry out its investigations in accordance with applicable national laws. This may require domestic legislation to compel nationals of CARICOM states against whom investigations are to be conducted to appear before the Commission to provide evidence, and it may require the Commission, whether by itself or in association with a national competition authority, to be able to conduct discovery and to require the production of documents to conduct its investigation.

However, many CARICOM states have not promulgated competition legislation, and while legislation may exist in some countries, there are but two fully functioning competition authorities in the region, that is, in Jamaica and Barbados.

This state of affairs has, by default, provided CARICOM members with manoeuvring space to fashion competition law and policy for their particular development objective. Although this would not necessarily be in keeping with satisfying the application of the 'special and differential' principle endorsed by developing countries in operationalizing competition law and policy, the absence of the required legislation, or substantial delays in its promulgation and in the establishment of functioning competition institutions to facilitate effective Community competition policy, provide incentives for the pursuit of development objectives tailored to national concerns.

This too will affect the process of harmonization, which is regarded as critical for Community competition policy.

9. CHALLENGES TO EFFECTIVE ENFORCEMENT OF COMPETITION POLICY IN CARICOM

The existing relationship between the governance organs within CARICOM suggests challenges for effective enforcement of competition policy. The smooth resolution of jurisdictional issues between competition and regulation and between the mandate of national investigation authorities and the Community Commission is not readily apparent.

Drawing a precise line for the operation of competition law and regulation is often difficult in practice, given the established rules of statutory interpretation: these do not readily favour a statutory construction that results in one ordinary legislation taking precedence over another in a similar category. Consequently, competition legislation may be drafted in general terms to cover particular activities, but challenges arise for the legislation to apply to such activities when the statute is construed.

Jurisdictional issues of this sort that have implications for enforcement of competition law may occur in the following situations:

- Another legislation authorizes conduct that is forbidden by the governing competition legislation.
- The governing competition legislation exempts conduct governed by another legislation.
- The governing competition legislation exempts a particular activity or conduct altogether.
- A particular sector is regulated by special legislation, with the oversight body having discretion to transfer the matter for determination under the governing competition legislation.
- One legislation governs particular conduct but is silent as to the application of the governing competition legislation regarding the same conduct.

9.1 Doctrine of Implied Repeal

In resolving these jurisdictional issues, resort is usually had to the doctrine of implied repeal. The doctrine of implied repeal holds that if conduct is governed by two pieces of legislation that are inconsistent, one must be held to have repealed the other. On the other hand, if the pieces of legislation are not inconsistent or can be applied harmoniously there is no implied repeal. However, regardless of the position taken, that is, whether there is an implied repeal or not, the result is an all or nothing approach as to the legislation to be applied. That is to say, one piece of legislation will apply to the conduct or person.

For example, in *FTC v. General Legal Council*,[4] the Court of Appeal of Jamaica held that the Legal Profession Act and the FCA could be applied harmoniously and that there was therefore no implied repeal of the Legal Profession Act by the FCA. Consequently, in the court's view, the Legal Profession Act, and not the FCA, applied to the dispute, thereby ousting the jurisdiction of the FTC.

The case concerned the relationship between earlier special and later general legislation in terms of their application to a person and the conduct of that person, that is, the General Legal Council and its conduct of prescribing fees for practicing attorneys. In this case the earlier special

---

4 *The General Legal Council v. The Fair Trading Commission*, Suit No. E 35 of 1995.

legislation governing both the person and conduct of the person took precedence over the later general legislation. There was no examination here of whether the pieces of legislation were fundamentally inconsistent such that one must be held to have repealed the other. This is perhaps unsurprising given that it is later legislation that in all likelihood would fit within that category. That is, an implied repeal can only be found in respect of later general or special legislation in its relationship to earlier special or general legislation.

9.2 Conduct Versus Classification of Conduct

No distinction is usually drawn between the conduct and the classification of the conduct in terms of *who* or which body should properly classify the conduct for purposes of determining which legislation applies. In other words, there is no requirement that the jurisdictional question be determined in terms of, or be conditioned on, which body is the proper body for classifying the particular conduct. Thus, a body authorized to set fees under a particular legislation is shielded from the FCA, even if its conduct could be classified as anti-competitive by another body and regardless of whether another body is given the authority to classify the conduct as anti-competitive. Therefore, an argument to the effect that a particular body has express authority under a particular provision to examine a specific conduct is not determinative of the jurisdictional issue.

What then determines which legislation applies? And what if later specific legislation makes reference to earlier general legislation, but there is no reference to the conduct sought to be governed by the earlier general legislation? Does the all-or-nothing approach apply? Should one make a distinction between the subject and the subject matter or conduct governed by the legislation to decide which legislation applies?

The general rules applied are that later special legislation takes precedence over earlier general legislation, and earlier special legislation takes precedence over later general legislation. Unless there is some specific reference in one piece of legislation to another piece of legislation and the extent to which one qualifies the other, these principles will be applied to determine which legislation should govern particular conduct.

The specific reference that is necessary is one that safeguards the jurisdiction of another body for conduct governed by special legislation. This can be done in the general legislation or in the special legislation, although the preference is for it to be done in the latter. One example of this is Section 73 of the 2000 Telecommunications Act of Jamaica.

Section 73 provides as follows:

> 73 (1) The provisions of the Fair Competition Act shall not affect an agreement between the Minister and a universal service provider in relation to the universal service obligation or any agreement approved by the Office after consultation with the Fair Trading Commission;
>
> (2) Except as provided in subsection (1) nothing in this Act shall be construed as affecting the right of any person to refer a matter to the Fair Trading Commission in accordance with the Fair Competition Act.

Notwithstanding this provision, the reference to the right of any person to refer a matter to the FTC is distinct from whether, in a particular case, the FCA would apply to the conduct in question from a jurisdictional standpoint.

In any event, the amendment process is generally a long one and expediency may recommend amendment through the general legislation as against each piece of legislation that governs a particular sector. It has been suggested, for example, that jurisdictional issues could be resolved in this way by words in the general act to the effect that the act applies to all other acts unless expressly exempted by the general act.

This recommendation is unsatisfactory for at least three reasons. First, it is unlikely that this approach will be embraced or be practical. Embracing this recommendation presupposes that there is a desire for competition law and policy to trump other values of governance. Second, governments, in particular those of developing countries, have not agreed at the multilateral level on the exact scope or coverage of competition law and policy in their domestic domain, as the failure to incorporate the WTO Singapore issues into a multilateral framework demonstrates. Third, many developing countries have only agreed to a minimalist approach for the operation of competition law and policy in the domestic domain. The General Agreement on Trade in Services (GATS), being the only WTO Agreement that expressly addresses competition law and policy, for example, requires domestic implementation of only abuse of dominance provisions and, particularly, in respect of a monopoly supplier of services doing business in sectors for which specific commitments are made at the multilateral level. Consequently, a monopoly supplier of a service may likely abuse its dominance in sectors in which it operates and for which no specific commitments are made at the multilateral level.

It seems unlikely that this minimalist and piecemeal perspective for the implementation of competition law and policy will change sooner rather than later, if, as suspected, competition law and policy is perceived to be lower on the agenda of the priorities of developing countries than other concerns and is therefore likely to be used as a negotiating strategy to obtain concessions on concerns that are higher priorities.

Finally, even if amendment of the general legislation in the manner suggested above were approved, it is doubtful that it would defeat the application of the implied repeal doctrine. This is so because some sector-specific legislation expressly authorizes conduct that may be otherwise deemed to be anti-competitive. In this situation, a conflict emerges between the general legislation and the special legislation that could only be resolved through application of the doctrine of implied repeal, since actual repeal cannot be found on the face of the general legislation, as regards the special legislation, without some particular reference to the special legislation within the general legislation.

This observation presumes that actual repeal and implied repeal require a reference to the specific legislation to be repealed. To be sure, existing case law does no more than sustain the application of the doctrine when the two statutes are necessarily inconsistent or there is some express reference to the previous legislation.

Notwithstanding the above, it is worth noting the prevailing exceptions to the application of the doctrine. It has been held, for example, that the doctrine does not apply to constitutional statutes or statutes bearing on fundamental rights. As Lord Steyn has observed extra-judicially:[5]

> What is the significance of classifying a right as constitutional? It is meaningful. It is a powerful indication that added value is attached to the protection of the right. It strengthens the normative force of such rights. It virtually rules out arguments that such rights can be impliedly repealed by subsequent legislation. Generally only an express repeal will suffice.

This doctrine was recently applied in *Thoburn v. Sunderland City Council*,[6] in which, in the United Kingdom Divisional Court, the issue arose as to whether the 1972 European Communities Act[7] (which gave the executive the power to amend primary legislation by Order in Council to be consistent

---

[5] The Rt Hon. Lord Steyn (2003), 'The Intractable Problem of the Interpretation of Legal Texts', **25** (1) *Sydney Law Review*, 5.

[6] *Thoburn and Others v. Sunderland City Council and Others* [2002] 3 WLR, 247.

[7] European Communities Act 1972 (UK), s. 2(2) and (4).

with any European Community Directive)[8] was impliedly repealed by the 1985 Weights and Measures Act,[9] which permitted the use of imperial and metric measurements in trade.

The appellants argued that by permitting the use of imperial measurements in trade, the Weights and Measures Act impliedly repealed the broad powers contained in the European Communities Act and that consequently the 1994 Units of Measurement Regulations[10] that purported to amend the Weights and Measures Act by forbidding the use of imperial measurements was *ultra vires*.

The Court found against the appellants, holding that the European Communities Act was a constitutional statute, and as such could not be impliedly repealed. In identifying which statutes may fit this classification, the Divisional Court proposes a test that denotes a constitutional statute as one that 'conditions the legal relationship between citizen and the state in some general, overarching manner, or enlarges or diminishes the scope of fundamental constitutional rights'.[11]

9.3 Resolving Jurisdictional Issues Under the Doctrine of Implied Repeal

As shown above, a later statute will not prevail over an earlier one if there is no indication that the legislature intended the later statute to have that preference. One way to resolve jurisdictional issues raised by the doctrine of implied repeal is to treat some statutes as 'constitutional statutes'. Under this doctrine a constitutional statute is one that: (a) conditions the legal relationship between citizen and state in some general, overarching manner; or (b) enlarges or diminishes the scope of fundamental constitutional rights.

As applied in *Thoburn*,[12] the European Communities Act was included under the first limb of the above test of the legislation and treated as a statute to which the doctrine of implied repeal would not apply. Recent attempts to

---

[8] In particular Directive 80/81/EEC was implicated because its aim was to harmonize the use in the European Community of units of measurement.

[9] Weights and Measures Act 1985 (UK), s. 1.

[10] The Units and Measures Regulations 1994 were adopted pursuant to s. 2(2) and (4) of the European Communities Act (UK) 1972 permitting secondary legislation to bring the UK into compliance with its obligations under EU law.

[11] *Thoburn v. Sunderland City Council* [2003] QB 151 (Div Ct.), per Lawson L.J., para. 62.

[12] *Thoburn and Others v. Sunderland City Council and Others* [2002] 3 WLR, 247.

treat treaties governing economic relations as constitutions or as giving rise to constitutional rights suggest some possibilities for the application of this doctrine if such treaties are incorporated in domestic legislation. However, this position is not yet recognized in local jurisprudence.

A related possibility is for the treatment of acts passed to give effect to treaties governing economic relations, which may be classified as legislation that 'conditions the legal relationship between citizen and the state in some general overarching manner',[13] as covered by the constitutional-statute criterion.

9.4 Judicial Review of Agency Determinations

Judicial review of agency determinations may also present challenges for enforcement of competition law. Judicial review proceedings are contemplated in national competition agency determinations in those CARICOM member states that have instituted competition laws. The law to be applied in a particular case may be difficult to discern if the dispute concerns a question that has not been addressed by the Community Commission. Where the matter has been addressed by the Community Commission but was not referred to it by the member state faced with a similar matter, the issue arises as to whether the jurisprudence developed there should be taken into account, in the absence of a domestic provision to give direct effect to such rulings. Article 174(6) of the RTC provides that member states 'shall enact legislation to ensure that determinations of the Commission are enforceable in their jurisdiction'. It is not clear whether this is to be done in such a way that all determinations should have direct effect or only those involving a particular member.

The Caribbean Court of Justice Original Jurisdiction Act of 2005 (CCJ Act) contemplates that these questions may be referred to the CCJ for a ruling that can then be enforced by an order from the CCJ. But the legislation affords much discretion to the judge in determining whether these questions ought to be referred at all, particularly if the position is taken that the local dispute does not involve cross-border issues that implicate the application of the provisions of the RTC. Section 7 of the CCJ Act of 2005 provides, for example, that:

> (1) Where a court or tribunal is seized of an issue whose resolution involves a question concerning the interpretation or application of the Treaty, the Court or

13 Lord Steyn, *supra* n. 5.

> tribunal concerned may, before delivery of its judgment in the matter in writing request the designated authority to refer the question to the Court for an advisory opinion to be given.

The discretion here is considerable, presumably covering situations ranging from one in which the court determines whether the interpretation or application of the RTC is in issue, to one in which, even if it is in issue, a determination can be made whether the resolution of the issue involves the application of the RTC.

10. CONCLUDING REMARKS

Regional competition law is often desirable as the optimal solution in the context of resource constraints where the pooling of resources in administrative design and enforcement are necessary to meet the goals of competition policy, particularly where cross-border intra- and inter-Community anti-competitive conduct is to be monitored and remedied.

Centralized enforcement seems more desirable to achieve this outcome, although policy flexibility warrants some modicum of decentralization to satisfy development objectives as determined by RTA members, and to address the monitoring and remedying of anti-competitive conduct that is limited to the territory of one RTA member.

Chief among the goals of Community competition policy in CARICOM are market integration through harmonization and the operationalization of special and differential treatment. The governance arrangements in CARICOM provide flexibility for achieving these two important goals but the flexibility provided exposes potential conflicts in meeting these objectives.

In addition, challenges for effective enforcement of Community competition policy in CARICOM threaten the integration process. The Community Commission is enjoined to investigate and adjudicate cross-border disputes, and in this regard the establishment of a centralized body can assist in achieving the goals of harmonization and special and differential treatment in the application of competition policy, bearing in mind the Community Commission's mandate in the development of Community competition policy.

However, the relationship between the Community Commission and other Community organs does not necessarily ensure that either goal can be met harmoniously, since policy flexibility that supports the one can militate against the achievement of the other.

This notwithstanding, regionalization of competition policy may suggest that the adoption of an international competition policy within a multilateral framework is more feasible with respect to common principles that are included in treaty arrangements and the corresponding domestic legal regime to give effect to treaty obligations.

10. The COMESA regional competition regulations

George K. Lipimile*

1. THE NEED FOR A REGIONAL COMPETITION POLICY

As a result of the much-supported regional economic integration process taking place in the Common Market for Eastern and Southern Africa (COMESA) region, it has become imperative for national competition authorities in the region to cooperate in their competition law enforcement work in order to deal effectively with restrictions on competition that have cross-border effects. Similarly, in order for COMESA to achieve success in the integration of its markets, there is a need to increase transparency and accountability of government actions, expand and deepen cooperation between competition authorities, and encourage greater soft harmonization and convergence of the different national legal systems.

Increased globalization has further meant that a higher percentage of competition cases now have significant regional and international components. As trade and investment liberalization reduces entry barriers, firms may have greater incentives to engage in anti-competitive practices and mergers, which would limit market access by other firms. Therefore, the need for increased regional cooperation can be achieved at different levels and in different forms. The regional competition law and policy is one such initiative.

---

* Mr George K. Lipimile is currently the Director and Chief Executive Officer of the newly established COMESA Competition Commission – a regional body charged with the enforcement of competition and consumer policy in 19 member states of the Common Market for Eastern and Southern Africa. He was, further, Senior Advisor on Competition and Consumer Policy to UNCTAD in Geneva. Prior to that, he established and was Executive Director of the Zambia Competition Commission.

It has also become necessary for businesses, politicians and economic policy makers to focus on the necessary adjustments to accommodate the changing economic environments in the region. The task of COMESA member states is to provide the right environment for the regional economic integration process. This has resulted in a range of economic reforms, from the creation of a common legislative framework to the mutual recognition of standards and qualifications. The COMESA Competition Regulations aim to firmly establish one of the foundation stones of the economic integration process in the region.

On the other hand, national economic developments arising partly from privatization, the dismantling of public-sector monopolies, the liberalization of foreign investment and trade, and the economic liberalization programmes, in general, have, at national and regional levels, led to a concentration of economic power among a few regional and national business operators. Most COMESA member states have continued to witness the transformation of what used to be the public-sector monopoly into a hardcore private-sector monopoly. This has raised concern at both national and regional levels, and, as a result, the need for a regional framework to address possible anti-competitive trends, including abuse of dominance and cartel behavior, has become increasingly urgent. For example, the COMESA region has witnessed single dominance of foreign firms in two or more member states. The Ilovo Sugar Company, an international sugar-producing conglomerate, has a single-dominant presence in Swaziland, Zimbabwe, Zambia and Uganda. The likelihood of abuse by such a company is very high. It is able, by its strong economic power and its presence through its holding company, to engage in various anti-competitive practices if not effectively monitored, and the national competition authorities in the region have recognized that such monitoring can only be effective at regional level.

The COMESA member states have fully recognized that the benefits of market integration can be achieved only in a dynamic competitive economic environment where new market barriers are not erected in place of those that have been dismantled. Concentrations of economic power that lead to market dominance and reduce or eliminate competition must be dealt with at the regional level. At the same time, and more importantly, legal certainty must be provided if enterprises are to be alive to the possibilities and respond to the challenges of regional economic integration. In this respect, the COMESA Competition Regulations are intended to establish conditions for free and effective competition in the common market and to ensure that anti-competitive practices do not create new barriers to trade or other forms of protectionism. The COMESA Competition Regulations set down minimum standards and allow enterprises to penetrate the common market and to establish themselves without barriers or restrictions, thereby facilitating intra-COMESA trade and cooperation.

Creating legislation for the regional competition regulations was inevitable. The few member states with national competition laws were quick to realize that such laws were not effective enough to deal with anti-competitive practices, which were manifested most at regional level. In considering policy and the effects of globalization, a key challenge faced by the national competition authorities stems from the recognition that the law is national but markets have continued to extend beyond national boundaries. For the COMESA member states, the question has been, if markets are broader than national boundaries, are national laws and their enforcement sufficient to deal with the new market problems of the region? Further, is it possible to rely upon national laws, yet at the same time work towards the development of a more seamless regional system that facilitates the workings of the national, regional and global markets? This dilemma in enforcement has been fully acknowledged by all the national competition authorities in the region, namely, Kenya, Zambia and Zimbabwe.

As mentioned earlier, it is incontestable that globalization of business activities has led to a large increase in competition cases with a regional or international dimension. The national competition authorities have already had to deal with cases involving regional anti-competitive activity, with the participating firms being located in two or three countries in the common market. A large proportion of merger/takeover investigations carried out by the respective competition authorities in the region have involved a foreign party or assets or information located abroad. The regional competition cases have begun to pose difficult challenges for competition law enforcement that can only be effectively solved through enhanced regional cooperation. Cooperation and transparency in procedures is also essential for business, which otherwise would be subject to excessive costs arising from parallel and poorly coordinated investigations. To address the problems being encountered by the national competition authorities, the solution lies in a regional approach to the competition cases with regional coverage.

Although multilateral trade liberalization and regional integration may provide significant welfare gains, there is still need for complementary regulatory and competition policies to ensure that the predicted benefits are not impaired by private anti-competitive practices. As national governments' restrictions on trade are progressively reduced, there is increased concern that the benefits of trade liberalization could be denied through anti-competitive business practices with market foreclosure effects. Anti-competitive practices are not only detrimental to the welfare of the country where they take place, but are a matter of legitimate concern to other trading partners too. For example, national players can organize themselves into import or market-sharing cartels in order to keep new competitors from abroad out of their market. Further, exclusive distribution practices can sometimes be a formidable obstacle to companies trying to gain a foothold in foreign markets. In such circumstances, the only appropriate and effective remedy lies in a policy of active competition-law enforcement at both the national and the regional level. Attempts to address such 'market access' cases through extraterritorial competition law enforcement can antagonize other countries. They can also prove ineffective because vital evidence is often located abroad. The regional competition regime offers the option to deal with cases of an extraterritorial nature.

The member states of COMESA have, in recent years, witnessed a change of attitude towards the role of governments in the globalization economy. In line with the liberalization of trade and investment restrictions and regulatory reforms, competition laws have been introduced or reinforced in countries at different levels of development. More than ten countries in COMESA have already enacted a competition law and at least four others are in the process of preparing competition legislation. Most of these competition laws came into effect in the last 15 years. These figures suggest growing regional consensus on the need for competition law as an integral part of the domestic reforms necessary for integration in the regional economy. These figures also show that competition law and policy is an issue of genuine interest to countries at all levels of development. Cooperation in the competition field should not therefore be limited to COMESA members.

Indeed, competition authorities in the sub-region have stressed the importance of enhancing regional coordination, including technical assistance, exchange of information and cooperation in enforcement. Over the years, more competition authorities have become operational in the region, and most of these countries enact laws that require or provide for different types of cooperation notifications. This has led to the business community expressing concerns relating to the unduly burdensome and costly notification requirements demanded by different competition authorities in the region relating to the same transaction. For example, in a case of a cross-border merger, the merging parties with international business operations potentially must determine whether notifications to all competition authorities in whose jurisdiction they operate are necessary or advisable.

Consequently, both the competition authorities in the region and the business community have called for the rationalization of all the competition notification systems in the region, but at the same time wish to ensure that the enforcers still possess the necessary tools to indentify and remedy anti-competitive transactions affecting the common market. The regional competition framework offers an institutional framework for such cooperation.

The majority of developing countries, in the absence of an effective regional competition policy, will find it difficult, especially where there are no national competition laws, to stop anti-competitive behavior by the local subsidiaries of merging multinationals in developed countries. These multinational corporations may behave competitively in Europe because of the effective competition rules, but may indulge in anti-competitive practices in developing countries. It is evident that firms can engage in, and tend to engage in, cross-border anti-competitive behavior with impunity, especially in countries that do not have domestic competition laws, and most of the member states in the common market are particularly vulnerable to the practices. The COMESA Competition Regulations offer member states without national competition laws an opportunity to assess any anti-competitive conduct through the COMESA route.

2. THE REGIONAL EXPERIENCES

The need for a regional competition regulation can be exemplified by the various competition cases that have been witnessed in the region. These cases have one thing in common: they are of a cross-border nature and affect at least two COMESA member states. The national competition authorities in the region considered that well-enforced regional competition regulation could resolve such cases in future to the benefit of all affected parties and that they would be more comprehensively tackled and resolved by such a regional regime.

Merger-control regulations for COMESA form part of Articles 16 and 18 of the Competition Regulations, which impose a cross-border condition. The rule applies only when the merger affects trade between member states. The cases dealt with by the competition authorities involving the carbonated soft drinks, tobacco and cement sectors were of a cross-border nature and therefore affected one or more member states of COMESA. This shows that the COMESA Competition Regulations are timely and, if effectively enforced, will be of great economic significance for the common market.

BOX 10.1 COCA-COLA COMPANY/CADBURY-SCHWEPPES MERGER

Introduction and Relevant Background

The Coca-Cola Company (TCCC) and Cadbury Schweppes (CS) plc signed an agreement for the purchase by TCCC of the CS commercial beverages brand and trademarks outside the United States, continental Western Europe and a few other countries. In Zambia, TCCC lodged a notification under Section 8 of the Act to acquire Cadbury Schweppes Zambia (CSZ) Limited. TCCC produces carbonated soft drinks in Zambia, while Cadbury Schweppes produced both carbonated and non-carbonated drinks, as well as clear beer (whisky black).

Major Findings

TCCC had a 92 percent market share in carbonated soft drinks in Zambia, while CSZ had 8 percent. Their products are almost perfect substitutes. Imports of competing products are eligible and are mainly done by Kazuma Enterprises on a niche-market basis, including Pepsi products from Namibia. The takeover of the Cadbury Schweppes brand in Zambia by TCCC effectively eliminated competition and any possible entry into the carbonated soft drinks market in Zambia, especially since ownership and/or authorized use of patents and know-how are key to substantial investments in Zambia and the Zambian operation had only been awarded a franchise to use the TCCC trademark and beverage brands.

The Zambian operation needed re-capitalization. The parties submitted that TCCC would infuse the operation with its expertise in the beverage sector and assist CSZ in achieving efficiencies. Third-party concerns were raised regarding the concentration of economic power in TCCC in Zambia as well as the future of Goldsport in Ndola, which is an SME with a TCCC franchise for secondary brands.

Commission Decision

There existed entry barriers in the carbonated soft drinks market in Zambia, even before the notification of this transaction. In Zambia, the transaction entailed elimination of a vigorous competitor by TCCC and consolidation of TCCC market power, as well as likely abuse of the same in relation to distributors and retailers. However, CSZ required re-capitalization. CSZ had already sold the brands to TCCC, and CSZ did not have the franchise to produce the brands. Closure of CSZ would have had worse effects on both the social and economic spheres in the country.

The transaction was authorized with conditions, which included the following:

- TCCC was to cease operation of any exclusive dealings and territorial restraint arrangements in Zambia.
- TCCC was not to fix prices or excessively advertise the recommended price.
- TCCC and cooperating bottlers in Zambia would continue to comply with the provisions of the Competition and Fair Trading Act.

In the COMESA regional context, the problem, and its consequences, of multiple merger notification would make it imperative that merger-control provisions should be incorporated into the regional competition law. The region has a number of practical examples supporting this view. For instance, the global Coca-Cola/Cadbury Schweppes merger was reviewed in the COMESA region by the competition authorities of Zambia and Zimbabwe. The merger was notified to, and reviewed by, the two competition authorities separately, even though its effect was regional in view of the almost completely free trade between COMESA member states. In the case of Zimbabwe, the merger was approved with certain conditions, which included partial divestiture and undertakings on the part of the merging parties to develop local beverage brands. In Zambia, as reported in the 1999 Annual Report of the Zambia Competition Commission, the merger was also conditionally approved but with different endeavors 'aimed at enhancing completion, including the obligation on the Coca-Cola Company to notify its exclusive dealing arrangements, restrictive territorial allocation agreements and stop price fixing arrangements'.[1]

It should however also be noted that while the merger affected other COMESA countries, such as Uganda, the absence of national competition legislation or merger-control provisions in those countries prevents it from being notified and reviewed by the affected countries. As such, the countries could not obtain countervailing concessions on the merger's consummation, as Zambia and Zimbabwe did.

The competition authorities of Zambia and Zimbabwe also separately reviewed the global Rothmans of Pall Mall/British American Tobacco merger. The Zimbabwean authority approved the transaction on conditions of both a structural (partial divestiture aimed at promoting new entry into the cigarette-making industry) and a behavioral nature (undertakings not to increase cigarette prices for a specific period of time). The Zambian authority unconditionally approved the merger since it was found that 'the concentration was likely to enhance competition as market offerings were likely to be enlarged in terms of brands'.[2]

BOX 10.2 ROTHMANS OF PALL MALL

In January 1999, British American Tobacco (BAT) plc of the United Kingdom announced that it had reached an agreement with the shareholders of Rothmans International, Compagnie Financière Richemont AG of Switzerland and the Rembrandt Group Limited of South Africa to merge their international tobacco businesses. Subsequent to the completion of the international merger between BAT and Rothmans International, Rothmans of Pall Mall (Zimbabwe) Limited in September 1999 applied to the Competition Commission under Section 35 of the Competition Act, 1996 for authorization to acquire the entire issue share capital of BAT Zimbabwe Limited.

The merging parties gave as one of the reasons to merge the declining market for cigarettes in Zimbabwe. It was presented that the Zimbabwean manufactured-cigarette market had declined to

1 The Annual Report 1999, Zambia Competition Commission, p. 27.

2 See Zambia Competition Commission Staff Paper, which can be accessed by request to the Commission (email: zcomp@zamtel.zm).

such an extent that it was no longer big enough for the continued viability of two manufacturers, as evidenced by the poor performance of BAT Zimbabwe Limited in its financial year that ended on 31 December 1998.

The case was evaluated as a horizontal merger as defined in Section 2 of the Competition Act. Through its investigations, the Commission noted that although the merger would result in the creation of a monopoly situation in the relevant market (i.e. the manufactured-cigarette market) it had other public-interest benefits. Section 32(5) of the Competition Act includes as such benefits the creation of greater economies of scale resulting in more efficient use of resources, the generation of foreign currency through exports, and the stabilization of product prices on the local market. The failing-firm defense put forward by the merging parties was also considered a strong point in this connection.

The Commission therefore authorized the merger with certain conditions aimed at alleviating the adverse effects of the monopoly situation created. The conditions related to the disposal of surplus cigarette-making equipment to third parties interested in entering the Zimbabwean cigarette-making industry and constant surveillance by the Competition Commission of future cigarette price increases, with price rises needing the Commission's authorization for as long as the monopoly situation created remains in existence.

Other notable examples include the acquisitions by Pretoria Portland Cement of South Africa and Lafarge of France of major cement companies in various COMESA member states in Southern Africa. Even though the acquisitions had the effect of drastically changing the structure of the whole regional cement market, individual countries reviewed them separately on national rather than on regional considerations.

BOX 10.3 THE TAKEOVER OF CEMENT PLANTS IN MALAWI, TANZANIA AND ZAMBIA BY LAFARGE OF FRANCE

This is the matter in which the Commonwealth Development Corporation (CDC) subsidiary, Pan African Cement Group (PAC), notified of its intention to take over the CDC interests in Chilanga Cement plc (Zambia), Portland Cement Company (Malawi) and Mbeya Cement Company (Tanzania). Further, an agreement was already signed by PAC/CDC to allow Lafarge of France take over the three PAC cement companies as the majority shareholder.

Lafarge was a relative newcomer to the sub-Saharan region, that is, Eastern and Southern Africa. As of 1997, the firm had five plants in Africa, located in Kenya and Cameroon. In 1998, Lafarge bought a plant in South Africa from Murray Roberts and the recent acquisition of Blue Circle Industries (BCI) in 2001 entrenched its market position. The takeover when concluded will enhance Lafarge's position in the region as shown below.The acquired BCI regional cement plants include:

	Capacity (MT)	Market Share
1. South Africa	2.3 million	30 percent
2. Kenya	250,000	
3. Uganda	120,000	
4. Zimbabwe	350,000	

This is in addition to the proposed acquisition of PAC/CDC's cement plants in the region:

	Capacity (MT)	Market share
1. Zambia	400,000	80 percent
2. Malawi	150,000	70 percent
3. Tanzania	250,000	22 percent

Lafarge has a cement plant in the Republic of South Africa (RSA) with a capacity of 2.3 million tons and it has an excess capacity of about 600,000 tons. Lafarge has had joint venture cement operations in Kenya, Nairobi and Mombasa. Lafarge does not export any cement to the Chilanga Cement markets. This scenario changes the market position of Lafarge when one takes into account the announcement that Lafarge has taken over the British BCI. This effectively means that Lafarge is present in Zimbabwe, Kenya and Uganda. Despite this, Lafarge's Facility in Zimbabwe cannot export into Zambia because its current production is all taken up by local demand. Its Uganda and Kenya plants are logistically unable to export into Zambia due to the prohibitive land-based transport costs. Its Indian ocean trading company, Cementia, could sell into Zambia through a Tanzanian port. This trading wing has eight ships and eight terminals to facilitate its operations. Lafarge is well positioned to take on Zambia from the north, south and east. This is fine, if it goes to enhance competition and not to eliminate it by buying off the potential competitor, Chilanga Cement.

A regional approach to the above transnational mergers could not only have avoided dissimilar outcomes on the same transactions but could have eliminated the threats and likelihood of plant relocations from one COMESA member state to another by the merging parties. A regional competition law with merger-control provisions would also ensure that the beneficial effects of merger-control provisions will accrue to all COMESA countries, and not only to those few countries with such legislation. It would further assist those countries with limited resources to embark on full and effective merger control at regional level.

The COMESA region is ripe for active involvement in merger control, given the advanced stage it has reached in integrating the economic activities of its member states, particularly in the area of trade cooperation. Cross-border business transactions, including investment and business concentrations and alliances, are now becoming the norm in the region, thereby justifying merger control at regional level. There is therefore a great need for merger-control provisions in any competition law that COMESA will adopt. The EU's 'one stop shop' approach to merger notification has a lot of merit and is justifiably suitable if adapted correctly to the COMESA region's particular needs and requirements.

Mergers that raise possible competition issues in more than one country have become commonplace in the region, as is the review of a single transaction by multiple competition authorities. These transactions move independently through the various procedural stages in individual national competition authorities, and the timing and processes often vary among the different authorities. This has raised the cost of doing business in the common market, and, therefore, requires firms to understand the procedures and analysis that each competition authority will employ in its review of any anti-competitive matter. Coordination of procedures alone, however, is not sufficient if national laws are not designed to address market-access issues that foreign firms may face. These problems can only be resolved if COMESA member states in the region enact sound competition principles and enforce them effectively.

3. NEED FOR CROSS-BORDER IMPACT

Article 55(1) of the COMESA Treaty,[3] which prohibits 'any agreement between undertakings or concerted practice which has as its objective or effect the prevention, restriction or distortion of competition within the Common Market', is identical to Article 101 of the Treaty on the Functioning of the European Union (TFEU) (ex Article 81(1) of the EC Treaty). It should be pointed out, however, that Article 55(1) does not specifically state that the offensive agreement must 'affect trade between Member States', as is the case with Article 101 TFEU.

Notwithstanding that omission, it is submitted that an effect on cross-border trade is an implicit prerequisite for application of this Article, in light of the wording of Article 16(1) of the Regulations. According to this provision, the Commission essentially can only intervene when there is an effect on trade between member states. The Regulations, more specifically Articles 16 and 18, and to some extent the Merger Control Regulation, do not apply unless the agreement or conduct 'may affect trade between Member States' and has as its object or effect the 'restriction or distortion of competition within the Common Market'. The concept of an agreement that may affect trade between member states provides a jurisdictional limit to the prohibition laid down in Articles 16 and 18. The criterion confines the scope of the application of Articles 16 and 18 to agreements having a minimum level of cross-border effect within the common market; hence the practices must appreciably affect trade between member states.

COMESA comprises 20 member states. Obviously, via a treaty, these states have voluntarily decided to take on certain obligations vis-à-vis each other. They have not given up their rights as sovereign nations. In order for COMESA to assert jurisdiction, therefore, the conduct in question must cross borders.

The above contention is buttressed by the Preamble to the Treaty itself, which, after listing the 20 member states that are party to it, declares them: 'Conscious of the overriding need to establish a Common Market for Eastern and Southern Africa … Having regard to *the principles of international law* governing relations between sovereign states, and the principles of liberty, fundamental freedoms and the rule of law' (emphasis added).[4]

---

3 The Treaty Establishing the Common Market for Eastern and Southern Africa. Available at: http://www.comesa.int.

4 http://www.comesa.int.

Additionally, Article 55(1) prohibits anti-competitive practices 'within the Common Market'. The common market is defined in Article 1 of the Treaty, and Article 1(2) states that the common market is only open to the 20 listed member states. In other words, the Treaty is concerned with activity between these member states, not with conduct solely within the borders of any one state.

That having been said, it must nonetheless be made clear that a broad interpretation must be given to the concept of 'conduct which affects trade between Member States'. Support for a broad interpretation comes from the handling of the same concept in the European treaties: any conduct that will trigger the intervention of the European Commission is something which might influence, directly or indirectly, the pattern of trade between Member States, for example prejudicing the aim of a single market in all the Member States. The European Commission has always tended to apply the provision in a liberal manner.

The fact that the Court's definition encompasses 'potential' impact as well as 'actual' and also considers what 'might' prejudice the aim of a single market shows the breadth of the Court's reach.

For COMESA to adopt a comparable approach, support may be found in Article 4 of its Treaty, specifically number 6(d), which states:

> In the field of economic and social development [the member states shall]: ...
>
> (d) adopt a regional policy that will look into all possible economic problems that Member States may face during the implementation of this Treaty and propose ways and means of redressing such problems in a manner that will satisfy the conditions of equitable and balanced development with the Common Market.

Additionally, Article 6(c), under the heading 'Fundamental Principles', states that:

> The Member States, in pursuit of the aims and objectives stated in Article 3 of this Treaty, and in conformity with the Treaty for the Establishment of the African Economic Community signed at Abuja, Nigeria on 3rd June 1991, agree to adhere to the following principles: ...
>
> (c) inter-State cooperation, harmonization of policies and integration of programmes among the Member States.

The creation of a cohesive single market is obviously an important objective of the member states. Regional integration is not only a 'specific undertaking' but also a 'fundamental principle'. Conduct that affects trade between member states is therefore a concept to be broadly defined in order to ensure the attainment of a true common market.

4. SUPREMACY OF THE COMESA COMPETITION REGULATIONS

There are provisions for cooperation between the Commission and the member states in the application and enforcement of the Regulations and other legal rules. These relate to both the applications of the law and practical cooperation. The concurrent jurisdiction of the Commission and national courts to apply the Regulations means that consistent application is required. Any inconsistency would offend against the principle of legal certainty, which is one of the fundamental principles of the Treaty.

Within the common market there are at least two legal orders: national legal orders comprising the respective bodies of legal rules within each of the COMESA member states, and the regional legal order comprising the body of legal rules created at COMESA level. The latter includes the COMESA Treaty and the secondary legislation of the common market, principally Regulations and Directives, all of which are of equal application within all member states. Under Article 5 of the Treaty, member states must shape their domestic legislation accordingly:

> Article 5: General Undertakings
>
> The Member States shall make every effort to plan and direct their development policies with a view to creating conditions favourable for the achievement of the aims of the Common Market and the implementation of the provisions of this Treaty and shall abstain from any measures likely to jeopardize the achievement of the aims of the Common Market or the implementation of the provisions of this Treaty.

Member states found to be in breach of the Regulations in combination with their duties under Article 5 of the Treaty are required to cooperate with the COMESA institutions in achieving the objectives of the Treaty, which include the institution of a system ensuring that competition is not distorted. Member states could be in breach of these duties if they enact legislation requiring or encouraging undertakings to act contrary to the COMESA Competition Regulations or reinforcing the effects of such conduct. The conclusion to be drawn from this is that the COMESA competition regulations constitute a new legal order of international law under which the member states have limited their sovereign rights, albeit within limited fields, with the subjects of the new order comprising not only member states but also their nationals.

Independent of the legislation of member states, the Competition Regulations not only impose obligations on individuals, but also intend to confer upon them rights that will become part of their legal heritage. These rights arise not only where they are expressly granted by the Treaty, but also by reason of the obligation that the Treaty imposes, in a clearly defined way, upon individuals as well as upon the member states to take steps to make the provisions of the Treaty an integral part of their legal systems and one that their courts are bound to apply.

The common-market legal system has precedence over national law, and a member state may not unilaterally nullify a provision of the Regulation by its own subsequent domestic legislative measure. The decisions of the COMESA Court of Justice on the interpretation of the provisions of the Treaty has precedence over decisions of national courts. For example, it may be that a particular agreement is permitted under domestic competition law but is forbidden under Parts 3 and 4 of the Regulations; in that case, the principle that the COMESA Treaty and Regulations have supremacy over domestic law means that Parts 3 and 4 will prevail over the domestic law and that the agreement will be forbidden. Conversely, an agreement that is permitted under Parts 3 and 4 of the Regulations cannot be prohibited under domestic competition laws.

Moreover, the Regulations, upon publication in the official gazette of the common market, are directly effective within national legal order, independent of any measure of reception or enactment to national law. This direct effect is full and uniform in all member states from the date of entry into force of the regulations and for so long as they continue to be in force. In accordance with Article 10(2) of the Treaty, the Regulations are binding on all the member states in their entirety. Consequently, national courts are expected to apply the regulations in their entirety and protect those rights that the Treaty confers, as well as to enforce obligations on the part of individuals and firms.

The question of whether the Regulations form part of national legal orders is resolved under Article 5(2)(b) of the Treaty, which confers upon the regulations of the Council the force of law and the necessary legal effect within all member states.

5. ENFORCEMENT INSTITUTIONS AND THEIR RESPECTIVE JURISDICTIONS

The COMESA Treaty establishes various organs of the common market, namely, the Council of Ministers, the COMESA Competition Commission, the Board of Commissioners and the COMESA Court of Justice. We shall briefly examine the role of each of these institutions in relation to the creation, application and enforcement of competition law and policy.

5.1 Council of Ministers

The Council of Ministers of the Common Market established by Article 7 of the Treaty is the supreme legislative body of COMESA and takes the major economic and political decisions pertaining to the common market. It consists of such ministers as may be designated by each member state. The Treaty, under Article 11, places a duty on the Council to adopt appropriate regulations and directives to give effect to the principles set out in the Competition Regulations.

5.2 COMESA Competition Commission

The COMESA Competition Commission is the executive arm established under Article 6 of the Regulations. It has broad responsibilities, which include the implementing of the decisions of the Council and the putting forward of opinions or recommendations on matters dealt with under the Regulations. The Commission has a central role in relation to competition; it is responsible for both the development of policy in relation to competition law and the application and enforcement of the Regulations. It also has powers and duties to enforce the consumer-protection provisions of the Regulations. Decisions and other public statements made by the Commission will be important in setting out general principles about the way in which it proposes to act.

The Commission as established under Article 6 enjoys an international legal personality. It has, in the territory of each member state, the legal capacity required for the performance of its functions under the Treaty and the power to acquire or dispose of movable and immovable property in accordance with the laws of each member state.

The Commission, under Article 7 of the Regulations, has been bestowed with the functions of applying the provisions of the Regulations with regard to trade between member states and is responsible for promoting competition within the common market. In carrying out its functions, the Commission may:

- monitor and investigate anti-competitive practices of undertakings within the common market;
- mediate disputes between member states concerning anti-competitive conduct;
- help member states promote national competition law and institutions;
- harmonize national laws with the regional Regulations;
- cooperate with and assist member states in the implementation of its decisions;
- provide support to member states in promoting and protecting consumer welfare.

Irrespective of whether an agreement or arrangement has been notified to the Commission or a complaint made, it is open to the Commission to launch its own investigation in relation to any agreement, practice or other activity that it may suspect infringes the competition rules. This general supervisory function of the Commission in competition matters demonstrates further why the competition rules are all-embracing and cannot be circumvented or ignored by member states.

Consequently, the Commission's powers of investigation have, due to its international character, taken into account the need for observing the principles of natural justice. The provisions of the Regulations must be applied in accordance with the general principles common to the member states. These include principles of proportionality, equality and non-discrimination, legitimate expectation, legal certainty and the right to a fair hearing. Fundamental human rights as derived from the constitutional traditions of the member states, and as set out in the African Union Charter for the Protection of Human Rights and Peoples' Rights, must be taken into account when the Regulations are implemented. The Regulations further provide for remedies and penalties for persons who contravene or fail to comply with any provisions of the Competition Regulations and pursuant rules.

5.3 Board of Commissioners

The third important enforcement institution is the Board of Commissioners, which was established under Article 12 of the Regulations. The composition and appointment of the Board reflects the regional character of COMESA. The members of the Board are drawn from the member states of COMESA. The Council appoints them on the recommendation of the Secretary General. The functions of the Board include the determination on any conduct and adjudication on any matter provided for under the Regulations. The Board is also to hear appeals or review any decision of the Commission that may, in terms of the Regulations, be referred to it. It may also delegate any of its functions to another COMESA agency established to coordinate and regulate a specific sector.

5.4 The COMESA Court of Justice

The COMESA Court of Justice was created under Article 19 of the Treaty. Its major function is to ensure adherence to law in the interpretation and application of the provisions of the Treaty. This includes conducting judicial review of acts of COMESA institutions, which include any disputes arising out of the application of the Regulations by the Commission. Member states, legal persons and natural persons have *locus standi* before the Court. Referrals to the Court may be made by the Secretary General of COMESA, any person who is resident in a member state, and the member states themselves, for a ruling on whether the act, regulation, directive or decision is *ultra vires* or unlawful or an infringement of the provisions of the Treaty.

The COMESA Court of Justice can receive appeals against the decisions of the Board. The judgment of the Court is binding in matters of law in all member states. The Court has seven judges and jurisdiction to hear all cases brought by individuals and undertakings against measures of the Commission. Actions against the Commission in competition cases must generally be taken to the Court. The Court has unlimited jurisdiction to review the decisions of the Commission, imposing penalties for infringements.

The Court hears appeals from the Board on points of law in relation to competition cases. It also hears positions on points of law from the national courts of the member states, actions brought by member states or undertakings against the Commission and actions brought by the Commission against states (infraction proceedings).

6. REMEDIES BEFORE MEMBER STATES' DOMESTIC COURTS

Since the Regulations apply directly in member states, private parties may file complaints to initiate infringement procedures under the Regulations. This is more so given the fact that the Regulations create rights and obligations between individuals as well as between individuals and member state governments.

Private persons and firms can invoke Articles 18 and 19 of the Regulations in two procedural situations before national courts:

- as a defense in a civil action involving a prohibited agreement or as part of an action for an injunction; or
- when damage has been incurred as a result of an infringement of the Competition Regulations.

In private actions, national courts have jurisdiction to determine whether the Regulations have been violated. They are able to assess a case involving the Regulations, although they must consider legally binding acts by the Commission: for example, the Commission can exempt certain categories of agreements under Article 16(4) of the Regulations. In this context, the consistency of the COMESA Competition Regulations throughout the common market is guaranteed by Article 30 of the Treaty, which empowers and, in certain circumstances, requires national courts to refer a case to the COMESA Court of Justice for preliminary ruling on questions of interpretation on the legality of the act or regarding a decision made under the Regulations.

It is important to note that the system allows national courts to concurrently apply the Regulations and the national law. Article 29 of the Treaty provides that, except where the jurisdiction is conferred on the Court by or under the Treaty, disputes to which the common market is a party must not on that ground alone be excluded from the jurisdiction of national courts. For example, although only the Commission can grant an exemption pursuant to Article 16(4) of the Regulations, the national courts may be empowered to enjoin any party from infringing Article 16 of the Regulations. It will therefore be necessary for the national courts to decide whether, in any particular case, the agreement does so clearly infringe Article 16 that exemption is very unlikely to be granted by the Commission, even if it has been notified to the Commission, or whether there is no infringement of Article 16 of the Regulations and therefore the question of an exemption under Article 16(4) does not come into play.

Invariably an agreement that is the subject of legal proceedings under the Regulations before the national court will also be the subject of consideration before the Commission. In this situation, national courts have the option either to adjudicate upon the dispute or to suspend the proceedings pending determination by the Commission. Similarly, when it is clear that the Regulations apply, and there is no possibility that the Commission will grant an exemption under Article 16(4), the national court may proceed to rule on the matter. However, if the situation is unclear, the national court will most probably not issue a final decision, but stay proceedings or adopt interim measures and seek assistance from the Commission or the COMESA Court of Justice.

Member states are further employed in the execution of judgments that impose a pecuniary obligation. In such a case, the rules of civil procedure in force in the member state in which execution is to take place govern the process.

It is envisaged that the Commission should actively encourage private parties to seek remedies before national courts and that it has a duty to give advisory opinions regarding questions of law that arise from the provisions of the Treaty and that affect the common market.

7. MECHANISM FOR COOPERATION IN THE APPLICATION AND ENFORCEMENT OF COMPETITION REGULATIONS

The Regulations provide a mechanism for cooperation for the operation of regional and national competition laws. Under Article Seven of the Regulations, the functions of the Commission include:

- to cooperate with competition authorities in Member States;
- to cooperate and assist Member States in the implementation of its decisions;
- to facilitate the exchange of relevant information and expertise;
- to provide support to Member States in promoting and protecting consumer welfare;
- to enter into such arrangements as will enhance its ability to monitor and investigate the impact of conduct outside the Common Market but

which nevertheless has, or may have, an impact on trade between Member States;
- to cooperate with other agencies that may be established or recognized by COMESA to monitor and regulate any specific sector.

It is important to note that the COMESA Competition Authority commenced its operations in February 2011 with the appointment of the Board of Commissioners and the Director, and that there are still very few member states with operational national competition authorities. Consequently, we shall base our analysis on the existing provisions of the Regulations, knowing very well that once the Commission becomes operational, it will develop further rules or directives as necessary for the efficient performance and implementation of the Regulations.

As stated earlier, under Article 5 of the Treaty the member states have a general duty to make every effort to implement the provisions of the Treaty and to abstain from taking any measure likely to jeopardize their implementation. One such provision is Article 55 of the Treaty, discussed above in section 3, which calls for the implementation of competition law and policy. This obligation in the Treaty is further enhanced by Article 5 of the Competition Regulations, which requires the member states, first, to take all appropriate measures to ensure fulfillment of the obligations arising out of the Regulations, and, second, to abstain from taking any measure that could jeopardize the attainment of the objectives of the Regulations.

Further, the member states have made it a specific undertaking, under Article 4 of the Treaty, to eliminate rigidities in the structures of production and manufacturing in the fields of industry and energy so as to provide goods and services that are of high quality and are competitive in the common market.

The mechanism for cooperation deals with the application and enforcement of the Competition Regulations under Parts 3, 4 and 5 of the Regulations. As stated above, these operate against the legal background of the supremacy of the Treaty or the Regulations over national competition laws, the direct application of the Treaty and the duty of sincere cooperation contained in Article 5 of the Treaty.

The Commission, pursuant to Article 7 of the Regulations, has the power to issue notices and guidelines to provide guidance for business and indicate the Commission's view on certain matters relating to the application of the Regulations, for example exemptions under Article 16(4) of the Regulations. The Commission has quite recently issued guidelines for the application of Article 16(4), setting out the way in which the Regulations will apply to such agreements, and also a more general guide for businesses and for the national authorities on the application of the exemption provision.

In a regional competition regime, it is important that there are practical mechanisms to ensure the appropriate enforcement of the Regulations at national level and that the operation of national law does not conflict with operation of the Regulations in cases where jurisdiction may be overlapping.

The Regulations, and the Rules issued pursuant to Article 39 of the Regulations, contain various provisions to ensure cooperation at national level with the Commission's investigation and enforcement powers. Under Rules 43 and 44, before the Commission undertakes an on-site investigation, it must inform the competent authority of the member state in whose territory the investigation is to be carried out. Officials from the competent authority may assist the Commission with investigations, and where the investigation is opposed by the parties concerned, the member state must give the necessary assistance to the Commission officials to enable them to carry out their investigations. The officials from the competent national competition authority will be expected to accompany the Commission officials to an on-site investigation.

Further, decisions of the Commission that impose penalties for infringement of the Competition Regulations are enforceable in accordance with the COMESA Treaty. Enforcement is governed by the rules of civil procedure in the member state where the enforcement is carried out. In the case of member states with common-law systems, this may require the Commission to cause a decision to be registered with the High Court as a result of which it will have the same effect as if it were a judgment or order given or made by that Court on the date of registration.

To this end, national competition laws may be required to revise, amend or enact appropriate provisions with the aim of realigning their law with the requirement of the Regulations.

For the implementation of certain provisions of the Regulations, the Commission may require the cooperation of the national competition authority. For instance, under the Merger Control Regulation, a member state, having attained knowledge of merger notification submitted to the Commission, may request the Commission to refer the merger for consideration under the member state's national competition law if the member state is convinced that the merger, if carried out, is likely to disproportionately reduce competition to a material extent in the member state or any part of the member state.

Further, for all merger enquiries, all relevant member states are required to be notified and to submit written representations to the Commission. Member states may not apply their own national competition laws to concentrations with a regional dimension, except in certain limited circumstances. Conversely, the Commission may not use the Merger Regulations to investigate concentrations without a regional dimension, except in certain limited circumstances.

The Commission may refer mergers with a regional dimension back to a member state to take action under national legislation if there is a competition problem in a distinct market within the member state. Member states may take action in relation to a merger that falls under the exclusive competence of the Commission in order to protect 'legitimate interests'. The Merger Regulation may recognize the exclusions under Article 4 of the Competition Regulations as such legitimate interests. The Commission may further use the Merger Regulation to investigate concentrations without a regional dimension at the request of a member state. However, the general rule is that if a merger meets the tests for assessment by the Commission, the national competition authority will not investigate. As noted above, in such cases the Commission has exclusive competence, subject to certain limited exceptions.

It is important to note that the approval of the Competition Regulations by the Council makes them, in accordance with Article 10 of the Treaty, binding upon each member state to which they are addressed as to the result to be achieved but not as to the means of achieving it. The entry into force of regulations is provided for under Article 12 of the Treaty, which stipulates that regulations must be published in the official gazette of the common market and that they enter into force on the date of their publication or on such later date as may be specified in those regulations.

POSTSCRIPT

The COMESA Competition Commission is now fully established and its office premises are based in Lilongwe, Malawi. The Board of Commissioners was appointed in 2006 and the Chief Executive Officer to run the affairs of the Commission was appointed in 2011. The Commission has since commenced conducting advocacy and awareness programs in the Member States. The full commencement of the operations of the Commission is currently awaiting the completion of the drafting of the enforcement rules, procedures and the notification forms. The Commission is scheduled to start receiving and dealing with cases by August 2012.

PART IV

The development dimension of regional integration and competition policy

11. Economic integration and competition law in developing countries

Josef Drexl

1. INTRODUCTION

Developing countries may have a variety of reasons for introducing competition law in the framework of regional integration systems. Sometimes regional competition law simply comes as part of a more comprehensive package on economic integration. In this regard, the very successful European competition law model seems to work as the most convincing argument for agreeing on a regional competition policy. Hence, developing countries seem to 'cut and paste' the European integration model by liberalizing trade within the region and protecting such trade against cross-border restraints of competition. The EU itself tends actively to export its model, such as in the framework of the recent Economic Partnership Agreement with the CARIFORUM States (EU-CARIFORUM EPA).[1] This agreement obliges the Caribbean states to have a CARICOM Competition Commission,[2] which was consequently established in Paramaribo, the capital city of Suriname.[3]

---

[1] Economic Partnership Agreement between the CARIFORUM States, of the one part, and the European Community and its Member States, of the other part, [2003] OJ L 289/I, p. 3. See also Stewart, T., 'Regional Integration in the Caribbean: The Role of Competition Policy', in this volume, Ch. 8. For an evaluation of this policy, see also Bakhoum, M. (2010), 'Commerce International, Politique de Concurrence et Accords de Partenariat Economique: Réflexions sur les Enjeux et Perspectives d'un Triptyque', *Revue Africaine sur le Commerce et le Développement*, (2), 3, at 5 et seq.

[2] See Article 125 No. 1 EU-CARIFORUM EPA. More importantly, the establishment of a common competition commission is mandated by Article 171 of the Revised Treaty of Chaguaramas, which constitutes the founding treaty of CARICOM. See Revised Treaty of Chaguaramas establishing the Caribbean Community

The EU may well perceive regional competition laws in developing countries as an important tool in the framework of promoting sustainable development rather than solely as part of a self-interested commercial policy. Yet it is not so clear whether regional competition law works the same way and may produce the same benefits in a region of developing countries. This chapter will therefore focus on the traditional goal of regional competition law as it is known from the European model, namely economic integration. The question is: how can regional competition policy be constructed as a tool of regional integration, specifically from the perspective of the needs and benefits of developing countries? In answering this question, this chapter aims to avoid the automatic 'cut and paste' approach when looking at enhancing more targeted regional competition policies. Thereby, it also aims to provide additional insights that can help both the developing countries and the EU when these parties negotiate and design competition policies in the framework of their trade policies.

In the following, this chapter will first discuss the goal of economic integration with regard to competition law in a more abstract way (at section 2, below). It will then turn to the changing role of economic integration in times of economic globalization (at section 3, below). Once this chapter has produced a clearer picture of the role of regional competition policy in a development context, some ideas will be expressed on the types of countries that should join such a system (at section 4, below). Then, the analysis will turn both to the specific advantages of having a regional competition policy (at section 5, below) and the particular challenge of promoting a competition culture locally (at section 6, below). Finally, this chapter will explore

---

including the CARICOM Single Market and Economy of 2001, http://www.caricom.org/jsp/community/revised_treaty-text.pdf (accessed 10 October 2011). Hence, it seems that the EPA simply reformulated what the CARICOM states had planned as part of their own policy. However, the EPA obliges the Bahamas, a Member of CARICOM since 1983, also to accept the jurisdiction of the CARICOM Competition Commission despite its resistance to signing the Revised Treaty of Chaguaramas and, thereby, joining the CARICOM Single Market and Economy (CSME). This case demonstrates that the external competition policy of the EU may even lead to a reshaping of regional integration systems. Today, the Dominican Republic remains the only CARIFORUM state that has not become a member of CARICOM. Article 125, No. 1 EU-CARIFORUM EPA takes this into account by allowing the Dominican Republic to have its own competition agency, the *Comisión Nacional de Defensa de la Competencia*. On the competition policy in the Caribbean region see also Stewart, this volume, Ch. 8.

[3] See the Commission's website at: http://www.caricom.org/jsp/community/competition_commission.jsp (accessed 10 October 2011).

the relationship between 'economic' integration and other forms of integration, namely legal and social integration (at section 7, below), before drawing some final conclusions (at section 8, below).

2. THE GOALS OF REGIONAL ECONOMIC INTEGRATION

Especially in the context of a treaty establishing a common market or an economic union, economic integration may be formulated as a proper and immediate legal goal.[4] However, economic integration as such does not explain why states decide to integrate. Integration is not an end in itself. Rather, it is expected to serve further purposes, in particular of an economic and/or political nature. Accordingly, in the context of regional integration systems, competition law aims at promoting economic integration as an immediate goal;[5] and with economic integration countries pursue further economic and political goals. From this it is to be concluded that competition law as a tool of economic integration indirectly serves other economic and political goals that will be identified in the following sections.

---

4 See, e.g., Article 3(1)(1) EU Treaty, which provides as follows: 'The Union shall establish an internal market …'.

5 This chapter will not delve into the question of whether, in the light of the particular goal of integration, a supranational competition law is to be applied differently than a national competition law or whether the goal of economic integration coincides with the otherwise endorsed goals of competition law, i.e. economic efficiency and consumer welfare. The European Commission seems to be in favour at least of coherence of these goals. See DG Competition discussion paper on the application of Article 82 of the Treaty to exclusionary practices (2005), http://ec.europa.eu/competition/antitrust/art82/discpaper2005.pdf (accessed 10 October 2011), para. 4 ('Effective competition brings benefits to consumers, such as low prices, high quality products, a wide selection of goods and services, and innovation. Competition and market integration serve these ends since the creation and preservation of an open single market promotes an efficient allocation of resources throughout the Community for the benefit of consumers'). Yet some economists consider economic integration, as a goal of competition law, a political rather than an economic, efficiency-oriented, goal. See Motta, M. (2004), *Competition Policy – Theory and Practice*, p. 23. Cf. also Drexl, J. (2010), 'Competition Law as Part of the European Constitution', in A. von Bogdandy and J. Bast (eds), *Principles of European Constitutional Law*, 2nd edn, Oxford: Hart Publishing and Verlag C.H. Beck, p. 659, at 696 et seq. (defending integration as an 'economic' objective of competition law, which, however, does not always coincide with the goals advocated by industrial economics).

2.1 The Economic Goals of Regional Economic Integration

It is clear from the outset that countries first and foremost agree on economic integration because of the economic effects and benefits that flow from economic integration. As regards the functional relationship between regional competition policy and economic integration, it is helpful to distinguish between immediate and more indirect effects and purposes.

The *immediate* objective of regional competition policy is to protect the larger common market of the participating countries against restraints of competition initiated by private market actors. Accordingly, EU competition law only applies to restraints that affect trade between the member states. In this perspective, regional competition law is intrinsically tied to the free movement principles. If countries agree to liberalize cross-border trade by abolishing state-initiated barriers to trade, it will not be acceptable that undertakings restore similar barriers to trade based on restraints of competition. This may also be the reason why, at the end of the 1990s, the European Community took the – albeit unsuccessful – initiative to complement the free-trade regime of the WTO with a WTO competition law.[6]

The question, however, remains whether this trade-liberalization logic of regional competition law can also justify regional competition policies in developing countries. Doubts arise from the fact that the potential of cross-border trade is rather limited between developing countries. Developing countries mostly export natural resources and agricultural products to the developed world and are importers of fabricated products from the developed world. A nice description of this phenomenon is given by the chapter on the Caribbean region (CARICOM) in this volume.[7] The major export products from the Caribbean states are fruits and tourism services for the consumer markets mostly in North America and Europe. Consequently, intra-Community trade remains very limited, with petroleum from Trinidad and Tobago as the major product traded among the CARICOM member states, and will have very little potential to grow in the future. The situation may certainly be somewhat different in regions that include land-locked states that depend on transit of goods for their imports and exports from and

---

6 This European initiative finally failed when the developing countries refused to start negotiations on any of the so-called Singapore issues, including competition policy, at the 2003 Cancún Ministerial Conference. See Drexl, J. (2004), 'International Competition Policy after Cancún: Placing a Singapore Issue on the WTO Development Agenda', *World Competition*, **27**, 419.

7 See Stewart, this volume, Ch. 8.

to the outside world or integration systems that include emerging economies with considerable industrial production.[8] Although practical experience shows that in certain instances and for certain products developing countries have to deal with cross-border restraints of competition involving neighbouring countries,[9] enhancement of cross-border trade provides a

---

[8] This is especially the case for ASEAN, which, however, has so far made only very limited steps towards the implementation of a common competition policy. See Thanadsillapakul, L., 'The Harmonization of ASEAN: Competition Laws and Policy from an Economic Integration Perspective', in this volume, Ch. 1. It also seems that there is considerable intra-community trade among the states that are contracting parties to the Central American Free Trade Agreement (CAFTA). According to the recently initialled Association Agreement between the EU and Central America, the Member States of the so-called Guatemala Protocol 2007, which was concluded in the framework of the General Treaty on Central American Economic Integration (Tratado General de Integración Económica Centroamericana) will establish a common Central American Competition Body. See Article 277(2)(b) of the EU-Central America Association Agreement, initialled on 22 March 2011, but at the time of writing not signed, available at: http://trade.ec.europa.eu/doclib/press/index.cfm?id=689 (accessed 20 April 2012). The situation is very complex in Africa, where external trade with other African countries can vary considerably between countries. According to some statistics, 32.92 per cent of Kenyan exports went to other African countries in the period 2004–2006, while the figure for Chad was 0.01 per cent. See statistics provided by Nkendah, R. (2010), 'Renforcement de l'Intégration Régionale pour une Relance des Economies Africaines', *Revue Africaine sur le Commerce et le Développement*, (2), 14, at 17.

[9] A very prominent example is provided by the so-called Tanzanian beer case. In this case, South African Breweries (SAB) bought Tanzania Breweries as the incumbent beer provider in Tanzania. After Tanzania Breweries/SAB was challenged by intensive competition from East African Breweries from Kenya and both companies entered into a cross-border price war, they finally ended the war by closing down production facilities and agreeing to make the competitor the sole distributor of their own brand in the other country. Thereby, both companies managed to maintain their dominant position in the respective countries. Neither the Kenyan nor the Tanzanian competition agencies seemed powerful enough to act against the agreement. The situation only changed when the British multinational Diageo acquired the majority of shares in East African Breweries and did not want to continue the deal with SAB. It was only recently that the Tanzanian Fair Competition Commission started to act against unilateral restraints by Tanzania Breweries/SAB in the Tanzanian market, which had potential foreclosure effects on Serengeti Breweries, a Tanzanian subsidiary of East African Brewery. See *Serengeti Breweries Limited v. Tanazania Breweries Limited, Decision of the Commission*, Complaint No 2 of 2009, available at: http://www.competition.or.tz/fcc_files/public/sbl_vs_tbl_final_ruling_-_2010.pdf (accessed 10 October 2011). On this case, see in more detail Drexl, J. (2011), 'Perspectives européennes sur la politique

much less convincing justification for having regional competition laws in developing countries than in the developed world.

These considerations also have to be taken into account with regard to the more indirect economic benefits that flow from economic integration. Economic integration and competition law as such are expected to enhance economic growth, economic development and consumer welfare. These are, however, general benefits that can be expected from any, also national, competition law.[10] The question therefore remains whether these goals are better promoted by a regional or a purely national competition policy or a specific combination of both. In general, it may be concluded that the limited scope of the economic benefits accruing from regional integration of developing countries presents a much weaker case for regional competition policies.

2.2 The Political Goals of Regional Economic Integration

European economic integration cannot be fully understood or explained without taking into account the political dimension of the integration process. In the 1950s, when the process of integration started, the driving idea was predominantly to guarantee peace between the former war enemies. Creating political stability in countries that had just converted from right-wing dictatorships to democratic regimes, namely in the case of Greece, Spain and Portugal, and, finally, the 'reunification' of Europe by accepting economically weak, former socialist countries of the East, explain the later rounds of enlargement.

---

de la concurrence dans l'espace OHADA', *Revue International de Droit Economique*, 281, at 286–88.

[10] See also Gerber, D. (2010), *Global Competition: Law, Markets, and Globalization*, Oxford: Oxford University Press, p. 258, who explains the economic benefits of having competition laws in African countries as follows: 'The potential benefits of competition law are particularly significant for Africa, and thus there are potentially strong incentives for competition law development. In addition to the generic benefits of reducing prices, enhancing consumer choice and providing a more flexible and efficient economy, competition law in Africa can help address the fundamental issue of economic diversification. By most accounts the most significant problem facing many African countries is the lack of diversity in their economies. The colonially-imposed and state-controlled economic model has proven difficult to change, but without such structural changes the countries of Africa will be left exposed to the vagaries of world markets that have periodically devastated their economies.'

In contrast, regional integration in Africa, Latin America, the Caribbean and Asia are to a much lesser degree driven by political considerations. In some cases, at least, the member states of regional integration systems share a common cultural background or language. This is true in particular of the West African Economic and Monetary Union (WAEMU), which – with one exception (Guinea-Bissau) – assembles the French-speaking countries of the region. However, even sharing the same language and culture does not necessarily provide a sufficiently strong glue for a regional integration system to work, as is demonstrated by the Andean Community, whose functioning has constantly been encumbered by conflicts between some member states. In the Caribbean Community (CARICOM), the common use of English[11] and a common colonial history of the majority of the member states is no guarantee that the Community will work. CARICOM does not only have to cope with the 'island mentalities' of several different states; for example the Bahamas is a case where a member state may feel a greater, even cultural, closeness to the United States than to other CARICOM countries. Finally, in the case of the Common Market for Eastern and Southern Africa (COMESA), there is now a territorially extremely extended integration system with a supranational competition policy that is composed of a group of politically and culturally highly diverse states.[12] What can generally be seen in the case of the African regional integration system is that these systems are very open to accepting countries with great instability and clear lack of democratic background. Thus, one may well doubt how a regional competition system can work that includes countries such as Libya (prior to the most recent political changes in 2011), Sudan, the Democratic Republic of Congo, Zimbabwe and Swaziland. From a political perspective, the best one can say about such economic integration is that it may enhance stability in states where there is no economic and political stability.

Hence, also in the light of political goals, regional integration in the developing world presents a much weaker case than in Europe. In general terms, it is to be concluded that the traditional rationale for having regional economic integration does not necessarily entail a sufficient need for regional competition laws in developing countries. In addition, it is clear that economic and political benefits similar to those known from European

---

[11] The two exceptions are Haiti and Suriname with French and Dutch as their respective official languages.

[12] See Lipimile, G., 'The COMESA Regional Competition Regulations', in this volume, Ch. 10.

integration cannot and should not be expected of regional integration in developing countries. The same applies to the potential economic benefits that may accrue from regional competition law as far as its effects on the economic integration of the member states are concerned.

3. ECONOMIC INTEGRATION REDEFINED IN TIMES OF GLOBALIZATION

Against the background of the results of the preceding analysis, the conclusion is not necessarily that developing countries should not enter into regional integration systems and should not establish regional competition systems. Rather, it is important to redefine the role of regional economic integration in the light of the economic transition that has been taking place in recent years in the developing countries.

Economic development in the developing countries, including the rapid spread of integration systems, is very much driven by economic globalization. As has already been pointed out,[13] developing countries may economically depend much more on trade with countries outside of their region than do developed countries. The process of globalization has convinced most of the developing countries that they can only develop if they liberalize their domestic markets by opening them up to international trade and foreign investment. As part of that process, it is not only important that they protect their domestic markets against restraints of competition initiated by local firms, it is also important to create effective institutions that address specific issues of outbound restraints of competition law that affect trade with third states and control the conduct of firms coming from outside the region, including big multinational firms that enter the domestic market and create competition problems.[14] Regional competition policies may well be the better tool to address such issues.

Hence, the role of economic integration may have to be redefined in times of globalization. Whereas, traditionally, economic integration has mostly been justified by the economic benefits that accrue from intensifying intra-regional trade, regional integration may nowadays seem much more important as a response to economic globalization. This is a conclusion that

---

[13] At section 2.1, above.

[14] In general, on the role of competition law as a tool to protect developing countries against restraints of competition in times of globalization, see Bakhoum, *supra* n. 1, at 4.

has some validity in the case of the European Union, too. From the very beginning, the implementation of a common commercial policy was an integral part of the European integration model. European integration has never been exclusively inward-looking; it always had an external dimension. Along these lines, European competition law has always been applied 'extraterritorially' to conduct initiated from outside that affected competition in the internal market.[15] What is changing, however, is that the importance of the external dimension of European integration is rapidly increasing.

Still, in comparison to the situation in the EU, it has to be concluded that, as a matter of degree, the role of regional integration in *integrating developing countries in the world economy*, and the benefits accruing from it, are much more important than what can be gained from integration of the individual economies of the participating countries. Accordingly, the goals of regional competition policy should predominantly be defined in the light of *international economic integration*, which does not exclude the beneficial effects of regional competition policy with regard to intra-regional integration where there is potential for economic growth and welfare by intensifying intra-regional trade.

In the following, the analysis will therefore turn to the question of how to design regional competition policies in the light of the particular goal of promoting international economic integration of developing countries, by concentrating on two questions: first, which countries should join a regional integration system (at section 4, below) and, second, which particular advantages can be expected from regional integration in the light of the goal of enabling developing countries to draw maximum benefits from economic globalization (at section 5, below).

4. WHICH COUNTRIES SHOULD INTEGRATE?

The question of which countries should integrate in the framework of a given integration system is extremely difficult to answer. This is so because the answer obviously depends on the level of integration pursued. A free-trade agreement that solely consists in the abolition of tariffs for goods

---

[15] The most striking examples are presented by merger control cases. In one instance, EU merger control law was applied to the merger of two South African firms with potential anti-competitive effects on the internal EU market. See Case T-102/96 *Gencor v. Commission* [1997] ECR II-879 (decision by the Court of First Instance confirming the prohibition of the merger between Gencor and Lonrho).

produced in the member states is obviously very different from a customs, economic and monetary union. As a rule of thumb, the more intensive the economic integration is, the more similar the level of economic development of the participating parties should be. As can currently be witnessed in the euro zone of the EU, with the debt crisis in Greece, a monetary union works better with countries of comparable economic strength and countries that respect the same rules on financial stability.

Along the same lines, the question of which countries should participate can only be answered with regard to the specific policy field. This means that integration with regard to the establishment of a monetary union will lead to different considerations than integration with regard to competition policy. Hence, in the following, the analysis will concentrate on competition policy considerations alone, although it is clear that regional integration systems, in the developing world as well as elsewhere, are not limited to competition policy. Based on the results of the analysis so far, a number of conclusions can be drawn concerning the countries that should participate in a regional trade agreement as far as competition policy is concerned.

First, implementation of a common competition policy does not require a similar level of economic development of the participating countries. The core rules of competition law do not significantly depend on the level of economic development of the individual countries. Hence, agreement on a cartel prohibition and a prohibition of abuse of market dominance can easily be reached even among states at different stages of economic development. What matters more is the concrete application of these rules to individual cases. In identifying the countries that should participate in a regional integration system, it is therefore more important to look at the trade flows and the direction of economic activity that may be harmed by anti-competitive behaviour or that may cause competition problems. This is why, for instance, it is very important, from a competition policy perspective, that South Africa participate in currently emerging integration systems in Africa such as the Southern African Development Community (SADC). South Africa is an important, sometimes the most important, trading partner of other African countries, and in particular in its Southern African neighbourhood, so that economic integration with South Africa would actually produce significant welfare gains. From a competition perspective it is more important to prevent South African firms from restraining cross-border trade and monopolizing the markets of other, especially neighbouring, countries.[16] Many of these South African firms gained market-dominant positions in that country prior to the introduction of a domestic competition law thanks to the former apartheid regime, whereas now they have to face effective enforcement action in South Africa.

Second, it can be noticed that in some of the emerging regional integration systems an imbalance is created by the participation of one dominant player. While the predominantly francophone WAEMU lacks such a dominant player – Senegal may currently be considered the economically strongest country, but does not have a predominantly large population or economy – the creation of a competition policy within the Economic Community of West African States (ECOWAS) in the same region points to the participation of Nigeria as the regional economic powerhouse. The problem is not the participation of the big kid on the block as such. Rather, economic arguments, as just explained, advocate such participation. The current ECOWAS debate demonstrates that problems arise more from the imbalance of bargaining power among the countries at the stage of designing regional competition policies. Countries such as Nigeria may be tempted to fight for exemptions in favour of sectors in which they claim to hold a particular 'national interest', such as the oil industry, although it is exactly in these sectors that the other countries should be most concerned that market dominance will be extended to their markets.[17]

Third, sometimes participation or non-participation of individual countries in regional integration systems does not seem to follow any logic. While in terms of geography alone, regrouping the East African states of Kenya, Uganda, Tanzania, Burundi and Rwanda into an economic integration system makes obvious sense, the culturally, politically and geographically very diverse and extended composition of the member states of COMESA seems almost coincidental.[18] In particular, one may wonder why Tanzania, which is surrounded by COMESA states, quit the organization in 2000. The major reason for this was that Tanzania did not want to be a member of two overlapping economic integration systems, namely

---

[16] An example is provided by the involvement of South African Breweries in the Tanzanian beer case mentioned at n. 9, above.

[17] See also Ngom, M., 'Regional Integration and Competition Policy in the Economic Community of West African States (ECOWAS) Region', in this volume, Ch. 6.

[18] COMESA currently includes Burundi, Comoros, the Democratic Republic of Congo, Djibouti, Egypt, Eritrea, Ethiopia, Kenya, Libya, Madagascar, Malawi, Mauritius, Rwanda, Seychelles, Sudan, Swaziland, Uganda, Zambia and Zimbabwe.

COMESA and the East African Community (EAC).[19] As regards competition policy, nothing is wrong with such a geography. Rather, having an organization such as COMESA may be helpful in stabilizing a larger region. Countries may join such an organization with a competition policy at a politically favourable time, and thereafter may stay within the organization, thereby keeping a competition policy even when the political wind has changed again.

5. BENEFITS FROM REGIONAL COMPETITION POLICIES IN AN ECONOMICALLY GLOBALIZED WORLD

Regional competition policy may help developing countries to optimally benefit from economic globalization in two regards.

First, regional competition agencies may be more powerful and more effective institutions than national agencies in enforcing the law against the anti-competitive behaviour of multinational firms.[20] While such firms may easily convince decision-makers in the developing countries to abstain from intervention by threatening to withdraw all economic activity from that country, such a strategy is less likely when this firm has to withdraw from a larger region composed of several states.

Second, regional competition agencies may also act against national governments that would otherwise try to maintain state-imposed barriers to entry to the detriment of their own domestic economy and local consumers. Developing countries are often transition countries that not many years ago were still characterized by central planning and state-controlled economies. As a legacy of this time, the economy of these countries may still feature strong state-owned incumbents. Given its higher degree of independence from local economic interests,[21] a regional competition policy may be much

---

19 Similarly, the SADC countries Lesotho (1997), Mozambique (1997), Namibia (2004) and Angola (2007) also quit COMESA.

20 In the same vein Gal, M. (2009), 'Antitrust in a Globalized Economy: The Unique Enforcement Challenges Faced by Small and Developing Jurisdictions', *Fordham Int'l L.J.*, **33** (1), at 3; id. (2010), 'Regional Competition Law Agreements: An Important Step for Antitrust Enforcement', *U. Toronto L.J.*, **60**, 239, at 244 et seq.

21 In general, on the role of independence in the effectiveness of competition law, cf. Tay-Cheng Ma (2010), 'Competition Authority Independence, Antitrust Effectiveness, and Institutions', *Int'l Rev. L. & Econ.*, **30**, 226.

better placed to address the anti-competitive conduct of such state-owned enterprises, making it more likely that foreign firms will invest in these countries. This in turn would make formerly state-controlled industries, such as in the telecommunication sector, more efficient, not only in the interest of consumers but also in the interest of economic development of other sectors that depend on the efficient provision of goods and services by such firms.[22] In this vein, it is usually regional competition law alone that can offer an effective means to combat national subsidies for domestic firms, which protect the national industry against competitive pressure from abroad and thereby reduce the efficiency and, hence, the international competitiveness of exactly these domestic firms.

6. THE CHALLENGE OF PROMOTING COMPETITION CULTURE LOCALLY

However, regional competition policy does not come without a price that has to be paid on a local level. While regional competition policy is better placed than national competition policies to secure economic benefits from globalization, regional competition policy is less well equipped to establish a competition culture on the ground.

Problems arise in a variety of ways: first, a competition culture will only emerge if the citizens of the member states recognize the benefits of competition policy. However, in the framework of a regional integration system with centralized competition law enforcement, decisions are taken by a geographically remote and often unknown entity. This is even more so with regard to young regional integration systems that, unlike the European Union, are not considered by the citizens to play a major role in their daily lives.

Second, in integration systems where supranational competition laws are not complemented by domestic competition systems with proper laws and enforcement agencies, the national legislature and the administration will be much less dedicated to respecting competition principles in drafting and applying other laws that have an impact on the economy. Competition policy, after all, is not limited to competition law alone but, as a 'horizontal'

---

[22] Cf. also Gal (2010), *supra* n. 20, at 249 (arguing in favour of regional competition law as a tool to open up markets in order to make domestic firms more efficient).

policy, should be taken into account in all other fields of economic legislation and regulation.

Third, regional competition policy is not well equipped to protect competition effectively against restraints of competition of a purely local scope. Only if there is such effective local enforcement will domestic entrepreneurs learn about competition law and internalize the competition principle as part of their mindset as business people. Similarly, only if local enforcement is guaranteed will citizens recognize the benefits accruing to them from competition, and support competition law politically. Hence, especially much centralized enforcement of competition law in larger geographical regions, such as in WAEMU,[23] may fail to promote a local culture of competition.

In the light of these problems, developing countries should when drafting regional competition policies be most concerned about appropriately defining the scope of application of the regional competition law and the degree of centralization of enforcement power. Regional competition policies need immediate application, including direct legal effect. However, centralization of the standards of competition law should not exclude decentralization of enforcement.

In general, the EU provides a good example of how well a supranational competition law can promote a competition culture locally. European competition law still today only applies to restraints that affect trade between the member states, and not to local restraints. Since EU law neither obliges the member states to have domestic competition laws nor to harmonize their national law, a much more viable culture of competition developed in such member states, above all in Germany, where domestic competition policies were introduced at an early point in time. It may also be said that local awareness and the effectiveness of national competition

---

[23] See the critical analysis of the centralization of enforcement power within WAEMU by Bakhoum, M. (2007), *L'articulation du droit communautaire et des droits nationaux de la concurrence dans l'Union Economique et Monétaire Ouest Africaine (UEMOA)*, Berne and Brussels: Staempfli Edition and Bruylant; id. (2006), 'Delimitation and Exercise of Competence Between the West African Economic and Monetary Union and its Member States in Competition Policy', *World Competition*, **29**, 653; Weick, D.P. (2010), 'Competition Law and Policy in Senegal: A Cautionary Tale for Regional Integration?', *World Competition*, **33**, 521, at 526–30 and 531–4.

agencies have considerably increased due to the adoption of Implementation Regulation 1/2003, which confers the power to enforce European competition law on the competition agencies and the courts of the member states.[24]

Regional integration systems in developing countries may push aside national competition law and national enforcement beyond the EU-style scope of domestic effects for a number of reasons. For instance, WAEMU competition law also applies to purely national cases and confers all decision-making power to the supranational agency, thereby preventing the member states from developing their own systems. This principle stems not only from a lack of national legislation but also from a prevalent doubt that national legislatures and national enforcement bodies – including the courts – would have enough expertise to draft and apply national competition laws appropriately and accurately.[25] In the light of the need, among other things, to promote a competition culture locally, this principle may go way too far. A better balance can be achieved by the approach of 'downloading' regional competition laws as domestic competition law, an approach found in the competition law of the Andean Community.[26] According to this system, the regional competition law only applies to restraints that affect intra-Community trade. This may considerably reduce the number of relevant cases to be dealt with by the supranational agency, since cross-border cases will be rare in a Community with little intra-Community trade. However, in the Andean Community, member states that have not yet adopted national competition law are under an obligation to provide for the application of this law as national law by local authorities. Thereby, the law of the Andean Community guarantees that there is domestic competition law applicable to

---

[24] See Articles 5 and 6 Council Regulation (EC) No. 1/2003 of 16 December 2002 on the implementation of the rules on competition laid down in Articles 81 and 82 of the Treaty, [2003] O.J. L 1, p. 1.

[25] It has to be noted that centralization of legislation in economic matters has a long tradition in the francophone African countries. In these countries, many economic laws are adopted as uniform and directly applicable laws of OHADA (Organisation pour l'Harmonisation en Afrique du Droit des Affaires; Organization for the Harmonization of Business Law in Africa). See the organization's website: http://www.ohada.org/ (accessed 10 October 2011). For a comparison of the legislative approach of the EU and OHADA with a view to assessing the usefulness of OHADA for the development of competition law in Africa see Drexl, *supra* n. 9.

[26] See also Cortázar, J., 'Andean Competition Law: Looking for the Private Sector, or the Quest for the Missing Link in Antitrust', in this volume, Ch. 7.

purely domestic cases and, finally, that domestic enforcement may gradually contribute to the emergence of a local competition culture. What is needed, however, is trust in the local authorities to have sufficient expertise at their disposal and to apply the law correctly.

7. OTHER TYPES OF INTEGRATION

Economic integration is not the only form of integration that matters when developing countries design regional competition policies. Other forms of integration to be considered are legal integration and social integration.

7.1 Legal Integration

'Legal integration' is a term usually used to mean harmonization or unification of national laws within the framework of a regional integration system. In many fields of economic regulation, recognition of the principles of free movement will not suffice as a means of economic integration, but there will also be a need for identical or at least similar legal rules that apply to purely internal cases. Such uniformity or harmonization eliminates distortions of competition arising from different legal standards in the individual countries. This explains why, in 1986, the member states of the former European Economic Community agreed to create a decision-making mechanism to enhance legal integration by harmonization with a view to establishing an 'internal market'.

However, the situation in the field of competition law is quite different. The functioning of common and internal markets does not so much depend on having identical rules of national competition law. In competition law in general, the wording of the legal rules matters less than the institutional design of the enforcement system, which has a crucial impact on a country's willingness to enforce the law, and, thereby, to protect competition effectively. Hence, in competition law, enforcement plays a much more important role than in other fields of economic regulation.

These particularities may explain why existing regional competition policies do not simply rely on uniform domestic laws or legal harmonization. They rather present a broad variety of approaches and combinations of legal integration and rules on supranational and national enforcement of different degrees of integration. These approaches range from: mere obligations of the member states to introduce domestic competition law, as is the case with ASEAN;[27] the creation of uniform competition rules that only apply to restraints of competition affecting cross-border trade with centralized enforcement; the 'downloading' approach of the Andean Community, which guarantees that all member states have laws that protect competition against domestic restraints;[28] to full legal centralization combined with almost complete centralization of enforcement, in the case of WAEMU.[29] What is most surprising is that, with regard to the choices regional integration systems make, the question of which approaches are economically needed to achieve the desired results is hardly ever asked.

From the analysis in this chapter, the following principles can be formulated:

(1) At least with regard to restraints of competition that affect cross-border trade, the creation of uniform competition rules is clearly advisable. In addition, these rules should in principle be applied by a central regional authority, as decentralization of enforcement power to national authorities, like in the EU under Regulation 1/2003,[30] may endanger uniform enforcement standards.
(2) There are also arguments to make the regional law applicable to domestic restraints of competition. This is most important with regard to large, multinational firms coming from outside the region that may monopolize domestic markets in individual member states. However, in most instances, when only domestic markets are monopolized by firms, this will create barriers to entry to the domestic market and typically lead to the application of the regional competition law anyway.
(3) Regional competition law should not deprive national competition authorities of decision-making power, as has happened within WAEMU, since such deprivation will considerably reduce the willingness of local authorities to investigate and enforce the law, thus

---

[27] See, in more detail, Abad, A.A., 'Competition Law and Policy in the Framework of ASEAN', in this volume, Ch. 2; Thanadsillapakul, L., 'The Harmonization of ASEAN: Competition Laws and Policy from an Economic Integration Perspective', in this volume, Ch. 1.

[28] See Cortázar, *supra* n. 26.

[29] This effect was clarified by a decision of the WAEMU Court of Justice in its Advisory Opinion 3/2000/CJ/UEMOA (27 June 2000), available at: www.ohada.com/imprim_juris.php?article_juris=32 (accessed 10 October 2011).

[30] See *supra* n. 24.

hampering the evolution of a local competition culture.[31] On the other hand, it may make sense to establish forms of cooperation between the regional authority and the national competition agencies with regard to investigating and enforcing the supranational law. Such cooperation will enhance the expertise of the domestic competition agencies and promote the likelihood that cases of a regional dimension, especially in a large geographic community, are actually identified and investigated.

(4) Unlike in the EU, regional integration systems in the developing world should also be concerned about the quality of substantive law in the member states. If the regional competition law only applies to restraints that affect cross-border trade, there will be no guarantee that individual states effectively protect competition against local restraints. In many instances, being part of a regional competition system may even serve national governments as an excuse for not introducing national competition laws. There are three main options for how regional competition systems can deal with the issue: first, the scope of application of the regional competition law could be extended to purely domestic restraints of competition (the WAEMU approach). Second, the regional law could oblige the member states to introduce harmonized standards of national competition law (the harmonization approach). Third, the regional competition law could be made applicable as a default rule, namely for the case that the individual member states do not adopt national competition laws autonomously (the Andean 'downloading' approach). According to the analysis presented in this chapter, a combination of the second and third approaches seems advisable. In principle, the third approach should be preferred to the first approach. Allowing member states to develop their own competition laws and policies will enhance their responsibility for competition, and has the further benefit that the states will be more likely to design their other rules on economic regulation in a more competition-oriented manner. Such domestic responsibility will be more conducive to the development of a national competition culture than full legal centralization under the first approach. However, regional law should introduce some degree

---

[31] See Weick, *supra* n. 23, at 522 (reporting that after the advisory decision of the UEMOA Court of Justice that clarified this very vast scope of application, Senegal's Competition Commission ceased enforcement action for violation of the Senegalese competition law).

of harmonization with regard to guaranteeing a minimum of substantive standards, in particular by acting against broad exemptions in favour of certain industries. This seems most important in overcoming economic pressure and rent-seeking by both local undertakings and multinational firms from abroad. However, there may also be cases in which the first (WAEMU) approach would seem to be preferable. Full centralization makes sense in regions where resources are too scarce for having national competition laws.[32] This is especially true for micro-states in developing countries. The best case for full harmonization is therefore found in those regions that only consist of micro-states, such as the Organization of Eastern Caribbean States (OECS).[33]

7.2 Social Integration

Furthermore, it is important not to forget that competition also plays a particular and important role with regard to social integration in developing countries. In developed jurisdictions, the standard argument in favour of competition law is that it promotes consumer welfare. While 'consumer welfare' can be used either as a criterion for measuring efficiency or in the sense of promoting real consumer interests, in developing countries it is important to identify the positive social effects more broadly.

First of all, an economy based on the competition principle will distribute wealth differently than an economy that allows firms to exploit others based on cartels and monopoly pricing. Competition law is therefore a crucial element of a policy that is designed to alleviate poverty. Competition agencies in developing countries can set their enforcement priorities in order to fight those restraints first that affect the poorest members of their

---

[32] On a regional competition policy as one of the means to address the problem of scarce resources in the enforcement of competition law, see Gal, M. (2010), 'When the Going Gets Tight: Institutional Solutions When Antitrust Enforcement Resources are Scarce', *Loyola U. Chicago L.J.*, **41**, 417, 430 et seq.

[33] According to a Draft Treaty for revising the existing OECS Treaty, the OECS Member States are also envisaging the creation of regulatory and competition authorities. See Article 4.2 Draft of the New Treaty of the Organization of the Eastern Caribbean States, available at: http://www.gov.gd/egov/docs/other/OECS_draft_new_treaty.pdf (accessed 10 October 2011).

society.[34] In general, competition law can be helpful as an element of a national policy against poverty.[35]

Yet there is also another reason why competition policy seems more important in the developing countries than in developed ones. Developing countries are in particular characterized by a large informal sector. Most or a large part of the population does not work in the framework of stable employment relationships. Hence, many individuals depend on their personal economic initiative to make a daily living. Becoming small entrepreneurs is often the only chance to escape from poverty. Many kinds of policies, such as the promotion of micro-credits, but also competition policy, may be helpful to promote entrepreneurship of individuals. Competition law can especially protect small businesses against dependence on and abuse of superior market power by larger firms. Competition law, in this regard, can be applied as a policy to enable individuals to take an active role in the economic life of developing countries. A good example of that dimension of competition law is provided by South African competition law, which pursues the broader participation of formerly disadvantaged ethnicities in economic life as one of its goals.[36]

---

[34] A good example is provided by the enforcement action taken by the South African Competition Agency against a bread cartel. See Knowler, W. (2010), 'Bread Cartel Saga Ends', *IOL News*, 8 February, available at: http://www.iol.co.za/news/south-africa/bread-cartel-saga-ends-1.472815 (accessed 10 October 2011). The South African Competition Tribunal in this case finally imposed a fine of R195 million (€20.5 million) on Pioneer Foods, which was the highest fine ever imposed on a cartelist in South Africa. Yet the Competition Commission appealed the case to the Competition Appeals Court with the objective of obtaining a fine of R1.5 billion (10% of Pioneer's annual turnover). Later, the case was settled with a fine of R500 million. On the terms of the settlement see Mncube, L. (2011), 'The Pioneer Foods Settlement Agreement: Restoring Competition in Bread and Flour Markets', *Competition News – Official Newsletter of the Competition Commission of South Africa*, (40), 4.

[35] See, in general, the contributions in Qaqaya, H. and G. Lipimile (eds) (2008), *The Effects of Anti-competitive Business Practices on Developing Countries and their Development Prospects*, New York and Geneva: UNCTAD, United Nations, and more particularly: Kaira, T. (2008), 'The Role of Competition Law and Policy in Alleviating Poverty: The Case of Zambia', ibid., p. 133; Fox, E.M. (2008), 'Antitrust, Economic Development and Poverty: The Other Path', ibid., p 179; Wilson, J. (2008), 'Competition Policy and Poverty Alleviation: The Case of Pakistan', ibid., p. 207.

[36] See Article 2(f) of the South African Competition Act, which reads as follows: 'The purpose of this Act is to promote and maintain competition in the

Concerning these two arguments, the term 'social integration' is not specifically used with regard to regional integration policy. Indeed, the social benefits accruing from competition policy, especially in favour of the poor in developing countries, may be pursued through national, regional and international competition policies.[37] However, there is a particular aspect of 'social integration' that relates especially to regional integration. Regional integration systems are typically composed by states with a somewhat different economic power and different social conditions. While competition law in regional integration systems is usually considered as a tool for guaranteeing market access to firms, it also protects the poorest members of society against cross-border cartels and small local businesses against the abuse of market dominance of larger firms.

8. CONCLUSION

As a result of the foregoing analysis, it is possible to identify three major reasons why regional competition laws may produce benefits for developing countries in particular.

First, while regional competition policy in the developed world, such as within the EU, is mostly expected to enhance economic growth through intra-community economic integration, regional competition policies involving the participation of developing countries should mostly be used as a tool to enhance the integration of the developing countries in the world economy.

Second, regional competition policies should also be used as a tool to enhance national competition policies and the emergence of competition culture in the member states. In particular, regional competition policies can protect national governments against rent-seeking and political pressure exercised by domestic or foreign firms, national bias and corruption.

Republic in order … (f) to promote a greater spread of ownership, in particular to increase the ownership stakes of historically disadvantaged persons.'

[37] See Drexl, J. (2009), 'Le droit de la concurrence international, menace ou gardien des droits de l'homme?', in Boy, L., J.B. Racine and F. Siiriainen (eds), *Droit économique et droits de l'homme*, Brussels: Larcier, p. 817 (arguing that the goal of a future international competition regime should consist in enabling equal changes of persons and firms from all countries, in particular developing countries, to pursue their economic interests in a globalized market).

Third, regional competition policy and regional integration is also an important element of a policy for the economic empowerment of individuals.

12. Regionalization, development and competition law: exploring the political dimension

David J. Gerber

1. INTRODUCTION

In discussions of the regionalization of competition law, the political dimension often leads a shadowy existence. Regionalization tends to be presented with a hint of a halo around it. States are presented as acting for a shared policy objective intended to benefit all, and political issues often sit uncomfortably with that image. This is particularly true when regionalization involves 'developing countries'. Here there is often a further level of 'common good' discourse. Regionalization is here portrayed not only as a communal experience and goal, but also as one designed to reduce poverty and aid economic development. Where regionalization involves competition law, an additional veil often lies across the discussions. Competition law is about economics, it is said, and it serves the economic gains of the participating countries. This tends to distance the enterprise from any political factors. Each of these forms of discussion emphasizes safe, sanitized language and imagery.

Yet few would actually argue that the political dimension is not central to the process of regionalization. A key issue, then, is how to view, analyse and discuss the political dimension that everyone knows exists, but that many find awkward or unpleasant to talk about. Finding a language for discussing the political dimension thus takes on a central role.

In this chapter, some of the elements and factors that may be relevant to such an effort are sketched. The focus is on the regionalization of competition law in so-called developing countries, but the analysis is intended to be applicable to the regionalization of competition law in other contexts as well. Moreover, although the focus here is on the 'political' dimension in the regionalization of competition law, in my view a similar analytical approach can be usefully applied to other dimensions of the regionalization process as well.

With its origins in a symposium on the regionalization of competition law in developing countries, this chapter refers primarily to issues raised at the symposium and to regionalization contexts discussed there.[1] It also goes beyond that material, however, and sketches some tools that can be used in analysing it.

Three basic objectives shape the chapter. One is to outline some conceptual tools that may be useful in analysing this new set of issues. In my experience, these issues are typically discussed in very loose terms that tend to obscure rather than to enhance insights into the dynamics of regionalization. A second goal is to locate political elements at two key points in the regionalization picture – that is the impetus for regionalization and the process of competition law implementation. The third is to assess some of the consequences of this process.

The investigation revolves around two principal themes. One is the centrality of the political dimension in the process of regionalizing competition law, perhaps especially in the context of developing countries. Although seldom addressed in more than a perfunctory way, it is critical to understanding the regionalization phenomenon as well as generating insightful analysis of its implications. The other is the intertwining of economic language and political dynamics. Discussions of this issue tend to focus on its economic dimension, but the political dimension is typically, perhaps always, interwoven with the economic dimension, and it is this relationship that must be at the centre of effective analysis.

The chapter first identifies what I mean by the 'political dimension' and sketches a way of analysing it that I believe has analytical value. It then looks at the political dimension in two contexts involving the regionalization of competition law, and asks how the impetus to regionalize competition law is shaped and how this then affects the implementation of competition law. Finally some implications of this analysis are identified.

Before I examine these issues, however, it is necessary to clarify some issues of scope. First, the chapter uses the term 'regionalization', but it is important to recognize that the term is highly contingent. The dynamics of a specific instance of regionalization depend on many factors – for example, the number of countries involved in the process, their geographical location, the wealth and economic and social characteristics of the participants, as

---

[1] Many of these issues are also included in the symposium volume of which this chapter is a part.

well as the economic and power relationships within the group, and so on. The term is used here in an abstract and general sense, but it is important to keep these factors in mind. The original symposium focused on regionalization in the context of economic development, with many participants from Africa, and thus these experiences were naturally in the forefront of the contributors' thinking about the subject, even when they are not specifically addressed. Second, the term 'competition law' refers to laws whose function is to combat restraints on competition. In some countries, notably the United States, the term 'antitrust law' is used to refer to this type of law. Note also that the term 'competition law' is used more broadly in some legal systems, where it may refer to 'unfair competition law', that is, law designed to protect competitors from unfair conduct by other competitors. Third, my concern here is with regionalization in the so-called developing world. In particular, I do not include here issues of regionalization in Europe.[2]

2. IDENTIFYING THE POLITICAL DIMENSION

As noted above, one objective of this chapter is to develop ways of analysing the regionalization of law, in particular the regionalization of competition law in developing countries. The loose language typically used to refer to this process tends to obscure the value of analysing its components carefully. In my view, this is an obstacle to effective analysis and decision making, and thus I provide here the lines of analysis that I use for this chapter.

The analysis starts from the basic proposition that regionalization is a *process* – a set of interactions over time among an identifiable set of participants. Although obvious at one level, this process perspective is seldom given much attention, and few focus on it in analysing the phenomenon with which this chapter is concerned. However, this process perspective is central to this analysis.

Using this starting point, I need to specify the scope and contents of the process. Here I am concerned with a specific process, that is, the process of

---

[2] Many of the issues and problems faced by developing countries in their efforts to regionalize competition law were also faced by European countries in the process of European integration. Some of those problems remain, but the process of European integration has altered them, often fundamentally. Moreover, developing countries often face additional problems in this area that Europeans have not faced. A comparative analysis of these issues could be very valuable, but it is beyond the scope of this chapter.

regionalizing competition law. The process consists then of the interactions over time related to development of a competition law that is applicable throughout a geographical region. It is thus defined geographically by reference to a region. It is also defined by reference to its content. It refers to interactions that relate, *inter alia*, to the creation and operation of a *competition law system* – its norms, its institutions and its procedures.

Penetrating further into the process, the chapter asks what its basic elements are. This question leads to a focus on decisions as the components of the process.[3] Viewed together, the decisions taken in relation to the regionalizing competition law *constitute the process*. The term 'decision' can be misleading, because in discussions of law it is typically used to refer to formal decisions such as those of courts or administrative authorities. Here, however, the concept is broader. I use 'decision' to refer to any decision by any actor that is part of the process of developing competition law. It includes, therefore, formal decisions of institutions, for example the enactment of a national statue permitting the government to transfer some of its authority to regional institutions. It may also include, however, many other decisions, for example decisions by actors (decision makers and those they influence) in one set of institutions to talk with actors in another state about the regionalization process.

Decisions are, however, products. They are always shaped by a variety of factors, and it is these factors that thus provide access to understanding decisions and permit analysis of their significance in relation to the regionalization process. They must, therefore, also be taken into account in analysing the process. The actual decision is just a kind of temporary stopping point at which decisional influences interact.

These decisional influences take a variety of forms. In some contexts, they relate to a text, for example an agreement that creates obligations on a regional level. Institutions that are involved with the regionalization process – whether national, regional or supra-regional – represent a second category of influence. Communities – status relationships, contacts, networks, etc. – provide a third form of decisional influence. For example, where a group of economic officials or scholars or business leaders perceives the value of competition law, the relationships within the group can be an important form of support for competition law development. Shared perceptions of the potential harms from regionalizing competition law may also, of course,

---

[3] For fuller discussion of this perspective, see Gerber, D.J. (1998), 'System Dynamics: Toward a Language of Comparative Law', 46 *American Journal of Comparative Law* 719–37.

create or support opposition to such a project. Finally, patterns of thought – values, perceptions, etc. – represent another form of influence that may or may not be tied to the other forms of influence just noted, that is, institutions, communities and texts.

The term 'political' is often used very loosely in discussions of regionalization (and in legal discussions involving international issues generally). It is important, therefore, to specify how the term is used here. For our purposes, the term 'political' refers to decisions that are associated with the acquisition, maintenance or exercise of political authority. This definition includes factors that are normally considered political, such as efforts to maintain power in a particular political system, but it also includes the use of that power in an international context. For example, when officials of the United States government seek to influence a foreign government in decisions about competition law, this is also a political influence, because they represent the political institution that is the US government.

The concept of 'association with' is used here to describe the boundaries of the inquiry – that is, it identifies the kinds of influences that will be considered as 'political'. I use the term 'association' in a relatively broad sense, but for our purposes the lack of precision regarding its borders does not create significant problems. Its function is to identify those factors that influence decisions related to competition law, and these factors can vary along numerous lines. The decisions may themselves be based on or authorized by political authority, but they may also be influenced by factors such as the personal or institutional interests of the decision makers or by cognitive factors such as the perception of competition law's potential value. The fact that the boundaries of the category are not always clear does not, therefore, diminish the value of the term. In any event, this focus on decisions and decisional influences enables a more precise analysis of the political dimension.

Influences on these decisions can come from three basic levels. One is national. National institutions or groups will necessarily be important influences on decisions by national authorities. Regional institutions or groups are a second level of influence. In most of the developing world, these institutions and groups remain relatively weak, and they are seldom well supported. This is not always the case, however, and regionalization as a project typically reflects an interest in further developing them. Finally, influences may derive from outside the region. They can be called 'supra-regional' influences; for example, international institutions may have such influence, and foreign governments often play such a role.

This analysis is briefly applied to two key elements of the process of regionalization of competition law. One includes decisions related to the formal regionalization of competition law – that is, the impetus to locate competition law at the regional level. This represents a formal transfer of authority for competition law issues to the regional level. It says nothing about how that authority is used. The other element of the process relates, then, to the actual implementation of competition on a regional level. In each case, I examine the location of the decisions, the sources of influences on those decisions and the forms of influence. Thus it is shown that the influences are aligned very differently in these two domains.

3. THE IMPETUS TO LOCATE COMPETITION LAW AT THE REGIONAL LEVEL

The central question in the regionalization of competition law is whether to do it, so the analysis above is first applied to this set of decisions. The decisions involved are identified as well as the types of influences to which they may be subjected. The analysis suggests that the potential for significant support of competition law regionalization among developing countries may be quite high, and examples of this kind of support can increasingly be found in developing countries, most notably in Africa.[4] It is important to remember that many such countries do not have national competition laws or, if they have them, they are minimally enforced.[5]

Regionalization can take many forms, but for the purposes of this analysis, I use the term to refer to *formal decisions* to locate competition law norms at the regional level and to rest primary responsibility for enforcement at the regional level. These are the elements that appear to be commonly assumed in discussions of the regionalization of competition law.

The decision to regionalize competition law is the prerogative of national decision makers – that is, it is located on the national level. At least in the developing world, states have generally not ceded the power to regional

---

[4] Numerous contributions in this volume document this support in Africa. *See*, e.g., Lipimile, G.K., 'The COMESA Regional Competition Regulations', in this volume, Ch. 10.

[5] The leading analysis of competition law issues in small market economies is Gal, M. (2003), *Competition Policy for Small Market Economies*, Cambridge, MA: Harvard University Press. For discussion of experience with these issues see Gerber, D.J. (2010), *Global Competition: Law, Markets and Globalization*, Oxford: Oxford University Press, pp. 236–58.

organizations to make such decisions on their own authority. The task then is to identify influences on national decision makers to transfer political authority to regional institutions to this extent and for these purposes. Although the decisions are located at the national level, influences on those decisions may come from national, regional or global levels.

3.1 Domestic (National-level) Influences

On the domestic level, the influences revolve around the fact that political decision makers typically focus their attention on achieving and/or maintaining domestic support for themselves and their actions. In other words, the decisions are political in the sense used here – that is, they relate to the acquisition and maintenance of political authority. The question then is whether regionalization of competition law is perceived as a significant benefit by national-level decision makers and, if so, to what extent. To the extent that it is perceived to bring greater benefits than costs, this represents an incentive to regionalize. Of course, there are disincentives to regionalize when the benefits do not outweigh the costs. 'Benefit' here refers not only to perceived benefits to the 'common good', but also to personal benefits. These may take many forms – from straightforward payments to public officials to more subtle benefits related to the power, status or resources of the decision makers.

I distinguish here between two forms of influence. For the purposes of this argument, 'process factors' include those that are related to participation in the process of locating competition law at the regional level. Here the issue is not what benefits or harms are produced by the process, but rather what benefits or harms are produced by participating in it. In contrast, 'product factors' include those related to the results or consequences of the process – that is, what the process produces. This chapter identifies some of those that were most prominent at the symposium and in the subsequent discussions of these issues.

3.1.1 Process factors

Process factors can provide significant incentives for developing countries to regionalize competition law. Here the focus is, as noted, on the benefits and costs of creating and participating in the process of regionalizing competition law.

3.1.1.1 Incentives Among the more prominent incentives is the desire to shift cost and responsibility from the national level to the regional level. A national competition-law system is likely to be expensive for a small country, especially if it actually intends to implement the law. Developing countries, by definition, are thin on public resources, at least those devoted to public benefit. Moreover, they are often small. They typically, therefore, do not have significant resources to support competition law. There is an attraction, therefore, in merely shifting responsibility for competition law to the regional level.[6]

This shift is also likely to have a related benefit – it can deflect national-level resistance to competition law from national officials and politicians to regional-level institutions and decision makers. Competition law inevitably creates resistance from many business leaders, who fear that it will limit their potential range of competitive strategies and impose compliance costs. This is especially likely when competition law is new and its potential benefits are difficult to perceive. This is typically the case in developing countries. When, however, business decision makers perceive the potential benefits of competition law, these perceived benefits can counterbalance such concerns. This may be the case, for example, when they have recognized and understood the potential of competition law to support economic growth in the country or when they have recognized that it might help to protect them against larger and more technologically advanced 'western' firms.

Another incentive to regionalize competition law relates to pressures from foreign or international sources. When competition laws may impact a foreign firm, that firm and its representatives are likely to resist the application of these laws by putting pressure on the competition authorities and others in government. This can be a cost to domestic officials (although it can also be a source of remuneration for them). If the responsibility for enforcement is transferred to the regional level, such pressures will be diffused and tend to be less of a burden on national officials and politicians.

A regionalized competition law can also be expected to have a stronger voice internationally than the voice of a single, developing country, especially if the country is small or has limited economic leverage. In the context of globalization, therefore, there may be significant incentives for

---

6 For in-depth analysis of these issues, *see* Bakhoum, M. (2007), *L'articulation du droit communautaire et des droits nationaux de le concurrence dans l'Union Economique et Monétaire Ouest Africaine (UEMOA)*, Bruylant: Stämpfli, Berne. A shorter English version is in Bakhoum, M. (2006), 'Delimitation and Exercise of Competence Between West African Economic and Monetary Union (WAEMU) and its Member States in Competition Policy', **29** *World Competition* 674.

such countries to regionalize in order to strengthen their collective voice, thereby also enhancing the status and possibly the geopolitical power of the countries in the region.[7]

The regionalization of competition law may also create incentives related to influence and power relationships within the region. It may allow some countries to extend their power and influence. Larger, more economically or politically powerful countries tend to have correspondingly more influence within regional organizations. The regionalization of competition law can be used as a means of extending countries' reach throughout the region through influencing the rules for competition in the area. The capacity to extend influence in this type of context depends, of course, on specific situations of regionalization, but the examples of the West African Economic and Monetary Union (WAEMU) and the Central African Economic and Monetary Community (CEMAC) indicate the potential role of these issues.[8]

3.1.1.2 Disincentives Disincentives related to the process of regionalization often centre on the loss of control over a state's markets. Competition law seeks to establish the parameters of competitive conduct in a market; control of the rules of competition at the national level can have significant value for many in the country, among both government officials and businesses. When competition law is regionalized, domestic capacity to influence these rules of competition is shifted to the regional level. This reduces the influence not only of national governments, but also of those who are able to influence domestic decisions at the national level but may have less influence on regional decision makers. In such situations, the only way to influence the rules of competitive conduct in one's own market is to influence decisions at the regional level, and this may be far more difficult and costly than influencing decisions in a domestic system.

A related issue involves the potential 'interference' of regional institutions within domestic economic and possibly political life. Where the

---

7 These issues are important, e.g., in efforts in the Caribbean to develop regional competition law. For discussion, *see* the contribution by Stewart, T., 'Regional Integration in the Caribbean: The Role of Competition Policy', in this volume, Ch 8.

8 For discussion, *see*, e.g., Boy, L. and L. Boumsong, comments on the competition law of CEMAC, workshop on 'Regional Integration and Competition Law in Developing Countries', unedited. Also, Bakhoum, M. and J. Molestina, 'Institutional Coherence and Effectiveness of a Regional Competition Policy: The Case of the West African Economic and Monetary Union (WAEMU)', in this volume, Ch 5.

rules for competition are set and enforced by regional institutions, a state and its stakeholders not only lose control, but they also run an increased risk of interference with domestic business. In a regional context in which there is a lack of trust among members, each may also fear that 'regional decisions' are in fact being influenced by their economic and/or political competitors.

Finally, the lack of perceived equality among members in the regionalization process can be a significant disincentive to regionalization. The benefits and costs of a competition law regime are often difficult to assess, much less effectively apportion among members. 'Why should we pay for protection of their market?' might well be a response to many situations. At the very least, there is significant potential for conflict and uncertainty in the apportionment of costs and the evaluation of benefits.

3.1.2 Product factors

Product factors are those that relate to what regionalization is expected to produce – that is, the economic or other results that can be expected from it. Here the assumption is that competition law will produce positive results. Expectations of such results can be significant factors in a state's decision to agree to regionalizing competition law. These expectations are, however, necessarily vague and uncertain. The history of regionalizing competition law in developing countries has yet to demonstrate clear product results, and expectations of product are, therefore, based on assumptions and even aspirations.

One 'product' is an expected increase in the effectiveness of competition law. Support for regionalizing competition law generally assumes that competition law at the regional level is likely to be more effective than domestic-level competition law in combating restrains on competition. One basis for expecting such an increase in effectiveness is that regionalization allows the pooling of resources, especially financial and knowledge resources. Decision makers in developing countries are typically aware that the lack of resources hampers the effectiveness of the laws they promulgate, and thus this resource enhancement is likely to be a paramount objective. In addition, regionalization can be expected to increase effectiveness by reducing opportunities for foreign firms to avoid competition law constraints by playing one country off against others in the region. In this scenario, dominant firms can often expect to get a better deal in relation to competition law in one country in the region by threatening to move their operations to a neighbouring country. This was apparently an impetus for regionalization in southern Africa.[9]

In addition to increased *effectiveness* of competition law, it is often assumed that competition law at the regional level will be more *efficient* – that is, it will not only be more effective than national-level competition laws, but its costs will be lower in relation to its product. For example, in a region of small, developing countries such as West Africa, regionalization can be expected to reduce costs and increase efficiency in the elaboration and implementation of competition law.

Given that these expectations are based on little more than assumptions, however, those who make different assumptions are likely to arrive at different expectations. For many, there is little reason to suppose that competition law will be more effective at the regional level than it is at the national level or that it will be less costly in relation to the benefits it produces. Others are more optimistic about this prospect.

3.2 Regional-level Influences

Regional-level influences on domestic decisions to regionalize competition law are likely to be limited, except in those relatively rare situations in which regional institutions have been set up without including competition law and those institutions have achieved significant status and credibility throughout the region. In such situations, regional institutions are likely to encourage competition law to be added to the capacities and tools available to the regional organization. Where a regional organization is established, its goals are typically to increase economic integration and/or improve intra-regional trade. Competition law is often portrayed as a tool for supporting these goals, and this is likely to lead regional institutions to seek to transfer it to the regional level.

In the more common situation, the regionalization of competition law is presented as part of the general 'package' of issues attending the question of whether to establish a regional organization. Here the issue is whether to include competition law in the regionalization package, and decisional influences at the regional level will thus derive from non-institutional sources. For example, perceptions of the value of including competition law in a regionalization package may be shared across a region, thus providing a

---

[9] See, e.g., the contribution of Mamhare, G., 'Southern African Development Community (SADC) Regional Competition Policy', in this volume, Ch. 3.

means for mutual reinforcement of support for including competition law as part of the general plans for regionalization.

3.3 Extra-regional Influences

Governments in countries outside the region also influence national-level decisions regarding the regionalization of competition law. Competition law can significantly impact the incentives to invest in a region and the costs of doing business there. As a consequence, countries whose businesses might be involved in transactions or operations in the region have an interest in whether competition law will be regionalized. For example, a foreign government may wish to have greater uniformity of competition law in the region or it may wish to have competition issues centralized at the regional level so there are fewer key decision makers. This reduces the number of officials with whom it may have to negotiate, and it may increase the capacity of the foreign government to influence them. Extra-regional government officials may also be interested for a different set of reasons. Officials may, for example, wish to spread their own influence, and the influence of their own institutions, by exporting their own version of competition law to an entire region.[10] The US, the European Union, Japan and other countries have made significant efforts to influence competition law development for reasons including these. In general, these countries have encouraged competition law, but they have, of course, encouraged their own forms of competition law.[11]

Extra-regional businesses may perceive similar benefits in regionalization. Creating greater uniformity in the rules applicable in an area and reducing the number of decision makers enforcing them can be a significant factor in assessing the profitability of investment and transactions in the area. Reducing disparities in the legal framework applicable within the region in and of itself reduces planning and compliance costs and increases predictability in planning. Moreover, it reduces the number of institutions and decision makers that may impact business decisions. This becomes especially clear when payments and favours to competition officials may be required in order to secure favourable decisions.

International organizations also represent extra-regional influences, and they tend to push in the same direction as the capital-exporting countries

---

[10] For discussion of such efforts by the US and EU, *see*, e.g., Gerber, D. supra note 5, at 236–58.

[11] For discussion of US efforts along these lines, *see*, e.g., ibid. at 156–7.

mentioned above. The International Competition Network (ICN) is a virtual organization that encourages discussions among competition law officials (and, in practice, others such as practitioners and even professors).[12] One of its goals is to establish 'best practices' in competition law that many countries will follow. Standardizing competition law at the regional level tends to foster this agenda. Given that in practice the organization tends to be strongly influenced by officials from the US and Europe, it also tends to favour competition law practices that follow the general outlines of competition law in those legal systems.

Two other organizations play important roles in this context.[13] The Organisation for Economic Cooperation and Development (OECD) is an organization of member governments that have achieved specified levels of economic development. It represents a kind of club for the 'developed countries', and thus membership represents status on the global level, which in turn creates incentives for countries to become and remain members. The OECD has generally encouraged competition law development and harmonization among its members, and in recent years it has paid increasing attention to encouraging and harmonizing competition law in non-member countries. The United Nations Conference on Trade and Development (UNCTAD) has long encouraged and supported competition law development in developing countries, and in recent years it has supported efforts to regionalize competition law. Both institutions thus support decisions to regionalize competition law.

This brief look at decisional influences relating to the regionalization of competition law reveals significant incentives to regionalize competition law and limited disincentives. This formal first step can have many consequences. It is obviously a necessary first step towards creating a regional competition law that is actually effective and influential. Moreover, it can support the general effort to increase regional integration. Nevertheless, until and unless there is implementation, its impact will be limited. When

---

12 For analysis of the ICN and its roles, *see* Fox, E.M. (2009), 'Antitrust and the Virtues of a Virtual Network', **43** *Intl Lawyer* 151–74.

13 The World Trade Organization does not directly deal with competition law, but it generally encourages market-based reforms for developing countries. There have been efforts to include competition law in the WTO, and many believe that these issues will eventually be included in some form in the WTO. For discussion of previous efforts to include competition law in the WTO, especially its relationship to economic development, *see* Drexl, J. (2004), 'International Competition Policy After Cancún: Placing a Singapore Issue on the WTO Development Agenda', **27** *World Competition* 419–57.

we look at costs and incentives at the implementation stage, however, the incentives actually to implement competition law may be far more limited.

4. IMPLEMENTING REGIONAL COMPETITION LAWS

The last section looked at the impetus to regionalize competition law. Here, some of the factors that relate to *implementing* competition law on a regional level are examined. The issue of whether and to what extent competition norms will actually have effect and whether the procedures put in place will actually be utilized is historically and theoretically different from the decision to establish formal regionalization of competition law. In particular, analysis of the political dimension reveals far less support for implementation at the regional level than it did for formal regionalization. Here again, the political elements tend to be underemphasized in many discussions of the subject, despite the obvious and fundamental point that competition law requires political support for its implementation.

Notice that the issue here is 'implementation' – the decisions taken to achieve the objectives of the law. This is normally equated with 'enforcement', and I will follow that practice in this chapter – that is, *focusing only on implementation through enforcement*. There are other tools for achieving the objectives of competition law, however, and a fuller analysis would examine them as well. In particular, education has been critical in the development of competition law in most countries and areas. Competition law is not an area of law that is easily understood. Especially when decision makers and political stakeholders have limited experience with the process of economic competition itself, and/or have limited confidence in state institutions, history suggests that education may be a critically important form of implementation.[14]

Recall also that for the purposes of this chapter it is assumed that enforcement occurs primarily at the regional level. There are a variety of ways of sharing enforcement responsibility with national-level authorities. In Europe, for example, primary enforcement of regional competition law was transferred to national-level authorities in 2004, although the principles

---

[14] For discussion of the role of education in developing competition law in Germany, *see* Gerber, D.J. (2001), *Law and Competition in Twentieth Century Europe: Protecting Prometheus*, Oxford: Oxford University Press, pp. 270–96.

and practices of enforcement remain closely controlled by Brussels.[15] In any event, space limitations preclude an investigation of these varieties here.

4.1 National-level Influences

Domestic political influences on regional-level decisions are subject to many variables. My objective here is merely to identify some of the factors that experience has shown to be relevant, or that decisional analysis predicts are likely to be relevant. I look here at the groups that may influence regional-level decision making and at some of the factors that shape that influence. It is worth emphasizing that regional-level institutions can be expected to be highly responsive to national-level pressures, perhaps especially in developing countries.

National-level influence on regional implementation decisions can be expected from four main sources. One is the government officials and institutions charged with competition law issues. This refers primarily to officials of the national competition law authority where one exists, but there are typically others in the government who have responsibility for competition issues, whether or not a competition authority actually exists. When competition law is regionalized, these national-level institutions and responsibilities are likely to remain. These officials are likely to know and interact with regional-level officials and to seek influence with them. For national officials, regional implementation can be expected to represent significant cross-cutting incentives. On the one hand, competition law officials, whether for personal or policy reasons, have incentives to increase their power and influence, and regional implementation may run counter to those objectives. On the other hand, as noted above, effective implementation at the regional level may increase the effectiveness of competition law norms and thereby foster their institutional objectives.

A second category includes other government officials who can be expected to have significant interest in implementation at the regional level. For example, the ministry of commerce is likely to put pressure on the regional authority not to harm the interests of its nationals or businesses. At the same time, the ministry presumably also has incentives to support the goals that regionalization presents. These officials thus also have cross-cutting incentives that may inhibit strong support for regional implementation efforts.

---

[15] For discussion, *see* Gerber, D.J., *supra* note 5, at 187–204.

National business leaders represent a third group who are likely to have significant incentives to influence competition law enforcement at the regional level. In general, businesses resist competition law enforcement, especially when it affects their own interests. Where enforcement is national, such leaders can often bring significant pressure to bear on national officials not to harm their interests. Where enforcement is regional, their interest in deterring it remains, but now they have the additional concern that some other group or government within the region may have greater influence on regional enforcement than they have and will use it to their own advantage. This is likely to lead to even greater scepticism and resistance to enforcement.

Finally, domestic professional groups may be particularly concerned with implementation. Lawyers, accountants and others are likely to have predominantly or exclusively domestic clients, and part of their value to their clients typically rests on their connections to local officials. Where implementation decisions are taken at the regional level, these national-level contacts diminish in value. This may be offset by other factors such as an increase in enforcement activity, but that effect is hard to predict, whereas the potential loss of influence by moving implementation to the regional level is obvious.

In each of these cases, therefore, national-level political influences are likely to impede enforcement at the regional level.

4.2 Regional-level Influences

Regional-level influences obviously become greater and more diverse when competition law becomes part of a regional organization. The regional institutions themselves and the interests associated with them now become sources of influence. In principle, these institutions can be expected to foster and support implementation of competition law at the regional level. Regional-level enforcement can enhance the effectiveness of other regional policies such as trade liberalization, and it can thereby strengthen regional institutions.

There are also, however, numerous disincentives for regional officials to engage in significant competition law enforcement. First, competition law is now part of the budget. The costs of implementation are now to be paid at the regional level, so that budgetary considerations become a factor, and, given the potential cost of significant enforcement, this factor can be significant. This is not only, or even primarily, a financial issue. Apportioning these costs among member states is often a highly sensitive political issue, especially in the early stages of regional integration, when the regional institutions are not well established and/or have not yet generated significant trust in their decisions.

Second, enforcement necessarily also engenders conflicts at the regional level. Questions such as 'who is enforcing against whom and for whose benefit?' are brought to the fore. Third, regional institutions are typically trade-promoting institutions. Their primary objective is to reduce barriers to trade between the countries of the region. While competition law supports this objective, its enforcement can increase conflicts and tensions within the regional bloc and make progress in trade negotiations more difficult. Experience confirms the influence of these types of factors.[16] There is little evidence as yet that regional organizations have paid great attention to enforcement of competition law.

4.3 The Extra-regional Level

Finally, the line-up of decisional influences at the extra-regional level changes, and again these influences tend to provide far less support for enforcement at the regional level than they do for formal regionalization of competition law.

International institutions generally have less influence on competition law enforcement than on the formal regionalization decision itself – that is, there is often significantly more attention paid to the establishment of a competition law system than to what it actually does. The ICN, for example, is not in a position to provide significant support for enforcement efforts. It is a voluntary organization that itself has no officials and no means of even monitoring enforcement efforts. This does not mean that it ignores enforcement issues. It does discuss enforcement issues and policies, and it seeks 'best practices' in these areas. These can be helpful as reference points for local administrators in convincing others that the practices should be followed at the regional level, but this type of influence is indirect and somewhat conjectural, depending, for example, on domestic views of the ICN mechanisms themselves. The ICN also has few incentives to do more

---

[16] For discussion of experience in this context in West Africa, *see*, e.g., Bakhoum, *supra* note 5, and the contributions of Bakhoum/Molestina and M. Ngom in this volume, Chs 5 and 6. For analysis of the reasons for lack of implementation in the Andean Pact context, *see* the contribution by Cortázar, J., 'Andean Competition Law: Looking for the Private Sector, or the Quest for the Missing Link in Antitrust', in this volume, Ch. 7.

than recommend best practices. It registers institutional successes when policies are formally adopted, but as a virtual organization its concerns cannot be expected to go far beyond that.

The OECD's efforts with regard to competition law enforcement have concentrated on its member states. Here enforcement issues are investigated, and the organization does support enforcement efforts. As noted, however, its members do not include developing countries. Its efforts in relation to such non-member states have generally focused on encouraging the introduction of competition law and on the analytical issues involved in establishing a competition law, but the organization has limited incentives to try to deal with implementation issues among member states, and it has limited leverage to encourage non-member states to follow its enforcement-level suggestions.

UNCTAD is the organization that has been most concerned with competition law enforcement in developing countries, and it has supported regional integration efforts in important ways. The UNCTAD staff travels widely in developing countries to monitor and develop enforcement efforts, and it regularly employs independent experts to investigate these issues. Especially in recent years, its activities at this level have been energetic and influential. Nevertheless, the organization has limited leverage in encouraging enforcement. It does not control access to significant amounts of resources or to status, and it does not have a well-developed means of prodding domestic or regional institutions to enforce competition law provisions.

The analysis in this section suggests that support for enforcement at the regional level may be limited, at least initially. It requires both support for competition law as a normative component of economic life and support for regional institutions. Yet in the context of developing countries, these requirements are not likely to be easily met. Competition law is seldom well known in developing countries, and experience suggests that significant time may be necessary for it to be widely understood and supported. Similarly, experience in the context of European integration and elsewhere suggests that support for regional institutions is likely to develop slowly at best. As a result, at least in the early stages of regionalization, support for competition law enforcement at the regional level is likely to face significant obstacles.

5. CONCLUDING COMMENTS

This review of the political dimension in the regionalization of competition law in developing countries reveals two very different vectors of incentives and decisional influences. On the one hand, decisional influences relating to political authority tend to support formal regionalization. There are many incentives formally to regionalize competition law, and the costs of formal regionalization tend to be limited. On the other hand, however, political factors provide far less support for implementation of competition law at the regional level. There the costs are higher and the political benefits more limited.

This analysis has many implications for plans to regionalize competition law in developing countries. Among the most important is the awareness that there is likely to be a very significant gap between the formal establishment of competition law as part of a regionalization effort and the actual enforcement of that law. Officials, politicians and other decision makers have conflicting incentives that are likely to lead them to talk about regionalization as a positive step, but to act in ways that are inconsistent with significant enforcement. I refer to this as bi-level conduct – one form of discourse and action that is directed towards global and regional communities, but decisions about enforcement that focus on local needs and political relationships.

A second implication is that competition policy at the regional level should take these cross-cutting influences into account. This suggests, for example, that expectations for immediate enforcement efforts should be low. As we have seen, there are many obstacles to achieving significant enforcement. A longer-term perspective on regionalization fits far better with the incentive structure. In such a perspective other forms of implementation such as education may take centre stage initially, and actual enforcement may be viewed as a longer-term objective for which education provides the foundation.

Our analysis has pointed both to the importance of analysing the political dimension of regionalizing competition law and to some of the difficulties in addressing these issues. There are many reasons for the frequent reluctance to talk about the political dimension and to focus discussion instead on the economic aspects of such regionalization. One is that the political dimension is often perceived to be in tension with the basic goals and justifications of regionalization. At another level, however, the discussion is hampered by the lack of a language in which the political dimension can be analysed and discussed effectively.

This chapter sketches the outlines of such a language – that is, a language that effectively analyses the political dimension in the regionalization of competition law. It has two key components. One is an emphasis on the value of a 'systemic' perspective that identifies interactions and influences between national institutions, interests and perspectives, on the one hand, and regional interests and objectives, on the other hand. Globalization dynamics are also integrated into this regional analysis. The other key component is the use of the concept of 'decisions' as a means of analysing the interplay among these system-based elements and systemic relationships.

13. Competition, development and regional integration: in search of a competition law fit for developing countries

Eleanor M. Fox*

1. INTRODUCTION

This chapter addresses the development dimension of competition policies in regional trade areas. In the context of regional collaboration, what character and design of competition law and policy will best enhance development? The question evokes a more generic one: In general, what competition law and policy will best enhance development?

I approach these questions by looking first at the daunting economic challenges of developing countries, the fit of competition policy and law to help address the challenges, and the choices available to developing countries as they choose a competition law perspective. I then review the benefits and costs of the regional context.

The chapter argues that developing countries must develop their own brand of competition law, resisting pressures to copy 'international standards' without regard to fit; and it makes suggestions as to how to find common ground on rules and standards that developing countries and regions can call their own.

* The author thanks Michal Gal, Simon Roberts and D. Daniel Sokol for their most helpful comments. She thanks the Filomen D'Agostino and Max E. Greenberg Foundation for research support.

2. DEVELOPMENT: WHAT IS NEEDED FOR DEVELOPMENT AND WHERE DOES COMPETITION FIT?

2.1 The Plight of Developing Countries

The developing countries, and especially the poorest, are infamously plagued by poverty, malnutrition, deficits in education, lack of jobs and poor institutions and governance. They are threatened by rising food prices in the world and by stunted growth. Globalization and trade liberalization have lifted millions of people above the poverty line, but millions remain impoverished and the poorest have in large measure seen no relief. Opportunities for trade into newly opened markets have been quickly filled by the more advantaged developing countries, leaving others shut out.[1]

Development – which includes education and opportunity and all other aspects of human dignity and welfare – is the top economic priority of these countries. Yet development is elusive. It is often said that all economic policies, including competition, must be designed in aid of development.

2.2 What is Needed for Development?

Developing countries need sustained and inclusive growth and development.[2] The need for sustained and inclusive growth may be divided into two parts. The first part is social policy. It is the more commonly referenced set of policies, and is the principal subject of the Millennium Development Goals.[3] These goals and vehicles require money – from governments and other sources of aid. They principally include: effective and inclusive education, healthful and sufficient food and clean water, health care and medicines, infrastructure including schools, housing, roads and transportation systems, and good governance to assure effective delivery of all of the above.[4]

---

[1] See Collier, P. (2007), *The Bottom Billion: Why the Poorest Countries are Failing and What Can Be Done About It*, Oxford: Oxford University Press.

[2] See Commission on Growth and Development, Spence, M. (chair) (2008), *The Growth Report: Strategies for Sustained Growth and Inclusive Development*, Washington DC: World Bank, available at: http://cgd.s3.amazonaws.com/GrowthReportComplete.pdf (hereafter 'Spence Report').

[3] See http://www.un.org/millenniumgoals/

[4] This first part is interdependent with the second part (competition and markets), for competition is an important tool for reducing prices and creating better

The second part is empowerment of the people to participate in the economy of the community, and perhaps beyond, implying open markets free of artificial restraints; opportunity and mobility of the people as participatory and creative economic actors; and, reciprocally, access of the people as buyers and consumers to goods and services at a price near cost. This second part is about markets, and it is the subject of this chapter: facilitating markets for the good of the people, and prohibiting practices and transactions that create and abuse power and hamper creativity. Thus, whereas the first tranche is about direct monetary contributions to social welfare, the second tranche is about (1) competition *policy*, which entails tearing down government barriers to entry, growth and mobility and preventing new barriers, privileges and cronyism from emerging; and (2) competition *law*, which entails prohibiting restraints by powerful and abusive market actors, private and public.

Where does competition policy/law fall on the list of tasks and policies needed for development? Competition *policy* – concentrated on opening markets, removing impediments and constructing a market environment conducive to participation – stands side by side with the critical goals (such as health and education) that need funds.[5] Competition policy empowers people to do what they can do for themselves.

3. WHAT KIND OF COMPETITION POLICY AND LAW IS NEEDED FOR DEVELOPMENT?

Helpful analyses have been written at an over-arching level on the appropriate design of antitrust for development, highlighting, for example, the importance of an independent competition authority, trustworthy institutions, judicial review and an advocacy role for the authority.[6] Little has

quality in the delivery of the services, for example, building schools and delivering health care. I am grateful to M. Gal for this observation.

[5] See, e.g., for the debate on whether economic growth does or does not tend to bypass the poorest, Lamont, J. (2010), 'High Growth Fails to Feed India's Hungry', *Financial Times*, 22 December 2010, available at: http://www.ft.com, contrasting J. Bhagwati's perspective with A. Sen's perspective.

[6] See, e.g., Kovacic, W. (2006), 'Institutional Foundations for Economic Legal Reform in Transition Economies: The Case of Competition Policy and Antitrust Enforcement', *Chi.-Kent L. Rev.*, **77**, 265; UNCTAD Secretariat (2010), 'The Role of Competition Policy in Promoting Economic Development: The Appropriate Design and Effectiveness of Competition Law and Policy', note submitted as part of

been written at the grass-roots level; namely, on the choice of a perspective or center of gravity around which the substantive principles of competition law are formed. This center of gravity or heart of the substantive-law system is typically constructed from a set of presumptions that become embedded in the law and normally are not transparent. This section is designed to make the premises transparent and thereby to provide a more open window to developing countries to make their choices.

3.1 The Washington Consensus Model

Over time, different answers have been given to the question: What kind of policy and law is needed for development? In the 1990s, the prescription was the Washington Consensus: remove government barriers and distortions – licensing, trade barriers, subsidies – and just let markets work. This was the prescription derived from John Williamson's book of 1990 designed for South America.[7] In a generalized form, it became the prevailing international prescription;[8] and it failed.[9] It failed because it presumed that markets were strong and would overpower (catch and punish) private actors that tried to exploit buyers and sellers and exclude meritorious but powerless rivals.[10]

The philosophic base of the Washington Consensus coincides with a conservative/libertarian philosophy that distrusts government intervention of almost every sort, especially 'handouts'. Its supporters pejoratively characterized government intervention as socialism or protectionism, and demonized it as undermining meritocracy. The Washington Consensus

---

the package for the Sixth United Nations Conference to Review All Aspects of the Set of Multilaterally Agreed Equitable Principles and Rules for the Control of Restrictive Business Practices, Geneva, 30 August 2010, TD/RBP/CONF.7/3.

7 Williamson, J. (1990), *The Progress of Policy Reform in Latin America*, Institute for International Economics. The concept was generalized, far beyond its meaning in context, to represent neo-conservatism.

8 The International Monetary Fund and the World Bank imposed Washington Consensus policies on developing countries as conditions of receiving aid. See Stiglitz, J. (2002), *Globalization and its Discontents*, New York: W.W. Norton.

9 See Rodrik, D. (2006), 'Goodbye Washington Consensus, Hello Washington Confusion? A Review of the World Bank's Economic Growth in the 1990s: Learning from a Decade of Reform', *J. of Economic Literature*, **44**, 973.

10 See, e.g., Stiglitz, *supra* n. 8; Peña, J. (2008), 'Competition Policies in Latin America', in Marsden, P. (ed.), *Handbook of Research in Trans-Atlantic Antitrust*, Cheltenham, UK and Northampton, MA, USA: Edward Elgar, Ch. 28, pp. 732–58, at p. 732.

argued for policies focused on increasing aggregate efficiency (aggregate wealth for the world). It assumed that markets 'let alone' (business freedom) would increase aggregate efficiency. It opposed policies that took account of distributional concerns and individual vulnerabilities, assuming that regard for these values undermines efficiency. The Washington Consensus policy and its assumptions became mirrored in competition policy and law, and reflected especially in US antitrust law, as explained below.

The Washington Consensus programs for development were immediately challenged by skeptics as founded on unrealistic assumptions and uncontextualized models, and on grounds that they tended to play into the hand of the rich, skilled and well-positioned, and to marginalize the poor, unskilled and powerless.[11] Not until the new millennium, however, did the challenges gain traction.

3.2 The Spence Growth Report

By the end of the 1990s the flaws in the Washington Consensus were well recognized, and the International Monetary Fund and the World Bank, among others, began to modify their recommendations to better match the context of the countries they served. Still, however, many economists ignored distributional concerns and continued to assert that inclusion of those concerns in market policies – as opposed to measures such as direct payments to the needy – would undermine efficiency.

In or around 2008 two important events marked a turning of the tide. One was the financial crisis, which prompted Alan Greenspan, veteran chairman of the US Federal Reserve Board and steward of the anti-regulatory policies that helped to trigger the crisis, to admit that there was 'a flaw in the model'.[12] The United States had placed too much trust in unregulated markets, based on the belief that markets work best when left alone, even when there are few leading players in the market and they are well situated to extract huge profits by playing with risk and leverage and flexing their power in an exploitative manner. The second marker was The Spence (World Bank) Growth Report.[13] The Spence Growth Commission, chaired by Nobel Laureate Michael Spence and comprised of experts principally

---

[11] See, e.g., Rodrik, *supra* n. 9; Stiglitz, *supra* n. 8.

[12] See Dealbook (2008) 'Greenspan, Snow and Cox on the Hill', 28 October, available at: http://dealbook.nytimes.com/2008/10/23/greenspan-snow-and-cox-on-the-hill/

[13] See Spence Report, *supra* n. 2.

from developing countries, worked for two years on grass-roots research, and, in 2008, issued its Report. The Report identified the characteristics necessary and important for growth designed to lift the peoples of developing countries out of poverty. It concluded that not only does growth critically matter, but *inclusive* growth critically matters. Distribution counts. And distribution of wealth[14] and, more important for our purposes, of opportunity and the chance for mobility, were deeply skewed.

3.3 How Developed-country Antitrust Tends to Fit the Washington Consensus, and Why Competition Policy for Development Must Be Tailored to the 'Spence Consensus'[15]

More than 100 nations and the European Union have adopted antitrust laws. A large portion of practices and transactions with anti-competitive consequences are cross-border or global. Yet there is virtually no international law of antitrust.[16] Understandably, there is a search for consensus principles, so as to avoid conflict and produce a more understandable, less confusing playing field for transborder business.[17] Several international fora have developed to facilitate the emergence of international standards. Prime among them is the International Competition Network (ICN), a

---

[14] Randerson, J. (2008) 'World's Richest 1% own 40% of All Wealth, UN Report Discovers', *The Guardian*, 6 December, available at: http://www.guardian.co.uk/money/2006/dec/06/business.internationalnews. Ten percent of adults own 85 percent of the world's assets. Half the world's adults own 1 percent of global wealth.

[15] By the time of the Spence Report there had developed a more responsive post-Washington Consensus. Moreover, the several commissioners who contributed to the Spence Report also had a range of views. I am exercising poetic license in drawing the dichotomy so sharply.

[16] An exception is the GATS Telecommunications Agreement and Annex, which prohibit abuse of dominance and require member states to prohibit their major suppliers from engaging in anti-competitive acts. See Fox, E. (2006), 'The WTO's First Antitrust Case – *Mexican Telecoms*: a Sleeping Victory for Trade and Competition', *Int'l Econ. L.*, **9**, 271. Other provisions of WTO agreements bear on competition and indeed almost all are pro-competitive since they bar or ratchet down state restraints of trade.

[17] See Almunia, J., Vice President of the European Commission responsible for Competition Policy (2010), 'Converging Paths in Unilateral Conduct', ICN Unilateral Conduct Workshop, Brussels, 3 December, available at: http://europa.eu/rapid/pressReleasesAction.do?reference=SPEECH/10/722&FORMAT=HTML&aged=EN&guiLanguage=en

virtual network of 117 antitrust authorities as of May 2011 – comprising almost all of the antitrust authorities of the world.[18]

Formation of international standards is a positive development and serves a useful purpose. But if the international standards that emerge (albeit only as soft law) are the developed-country standards, and if optimal standards for developing countries differ from those of developed countries, the convergence project may have negative effects as well. What is good for America is not necessarily good for (for example) sub-Saharan Africa.[19]

The 'international standards' that evolve tend to be those of the United States and the European Union. United States antitrust law corresponds with the premises underlying the Washington Consensus. For example, the US Supreme Court has repeatedly declared that predatory pricing rarely occurs and is even more rarely successful.[20] On that premise, combined with the aim to give consumers the benefit of low prices and the fear that courts will protect inefficient firms, the US Supreme Court has formulated a rule of law[21] that makes it nearly impossible for a plaintiff to win a predatory pricing case.[22] Similarly, the Court has all but abolished the antitrust duty of a dominant firm to supply a scarce input[23] or to refrain from price-squeezing an intermediate buyer who is also a competitor.[24] The Court fears that duties of dominant firms (which it pejoratively calls 'sharing duties') will undermine the dominant firms' incentives to invest and invent, and it virtually never examines the extent to which dominant

---

18 See http://www.internationalcompetitionnetwork.org/ – China, however, is not a member.

19 See Fox, E. (2009), 'Linked-In: Antitrust and the Virtues of a Virtual Network', *Int'l Lawyer*, **43**, 151. For a skeptical view of the benefits of competition law in some developing countries, see Rodriguez, A.E. and A. Menon (2010), *The Limits of Competition Policy: The Shortcomings of Antitrust in Developing and Reforming Economies*, The Netherlands: Wolters Kluwer.

20 *Brooke Group Ltd.* v *Brown & Williamson Tobacco Corp.*, 509 U.S. 209 (1993); *Weyerhaeuser Co.* v *Ross-Simmons Hardware Lumber Co.*, 549 U.S. 312 (2007).

21 *Brooke Group*, *supra* n. 9.

22 See, e.g., *United States* v *AMR Corp.*, 335 F.3d 1109 (10th Cir. 2003).

23 This is especially so when sector regulation exists. See *Verizon Communications Inc.* v *Law Offices of Curtis* v *Trinko, LLP*, 540 U.S. 398 (2004).

24 See *Pacific Bell Telephone Co.* v *linkLine Communications, Inc.*, 129 Sup. Ct. 617 (2009). See also *Leegin Creative Leather Products, Inc.* v *PSKS, Inc.*, 551 U.S. 877 (2007), and *Illinois Tool Works Inc.* v *Independent Ink, Inc.*, 547 U.S. 28 (2006), in which the Court said in effect: We now know that resale price maintenance and tying have many good purposes, and we should not be quick to condemn them.

firms' exercise of leverage will undermine powerless rivals' incentives to invest and invent. In societies long dominated by state-owned firms and their privileged successors, however, in which capital markets work poorly, barriers to entry are high, problems of capture are great, and social ties breed collusion and discourage detection, dominant firm predation and exclusion are rampant and harmful.[25] They are major forces in keeping markets closed and uncompetitive. In developing countries, the costs of antitrust non-intervention in many circumstances are likely to be higher than the costs of intervention.[26]

Moreover, in economies long marked by lack of mobility, by caste and by other types of stratifying discrimination, the imperative of including powerless firms on the economic pathways is urgent. The economists' argument that distributional values are irrelevant does not resonate. Accordingly, the American law of monopolization is increasingly irrelevant to developing countries, even though it is often insightful and should be read and understood.

These observations signify that developing-country antitrust should aspire to fit the Spence Consensus, not the Washington Consensus.[27]

3.4 Choices for Developing-country Competition Law

Developing countries face the important task of deciding on the substantive rules and standards appropriate to their economies and stage of development. To be sure, they have different contexts and different stages of development from one another, but they share sufficient characteristics to

---

[25] See Khemani, R.S. (2007), 'Competition Policy and Promotion of Investment, Economic Growth and Poverty Alleviation in Least Developed Countries', *FIAS Occasional Papers* No. 19, available at: http://www.ifc.org/ifcext/fias.nsf/Content/FIAS_OccasionalPapers. See also Fox, E. and A. Mateus (2011), Introduction to Volume II, in Fox, E. and A. Mateus (eds), *Economic Development: The Critical Role of Competition Law and Policy*, Cheltenham, UK and Northampton, MA, USA: Edward Elgar; Sokol, D.D. (2008), 'Order without (Enforceable) Law: Why Countries Enter into Non-Enforceable Competition Policy Chapters in Free Trade Agreements', *Chicago-Kent L. Rev.*, **83**, 231.

[26] See Lewis, D. (2009), 'Chilling Competition', in Hawk, B. (ed), *2008 Fordham Competition Law Institute*, Huntington, NY: Juris Publishing, Ch. 17, at p. 419.

[27] See Fox, E. (2007), 'Economic Development, Poverty and Antitrust: The Other Path', festschrift for Lawrence Sullivan, *Southwestern J. of Law & Trade in Americas*, **13**, 211, for metrics for formulating principles consistent with inclusive, mobility-enhancing development.

make contemplation of a substantive model or anchor useful. Common and defining characteristics include scarce human and financial capital, sluggish markets, especially sluggish capital markets, highly concentrated markets, high barriers to entry and expansion, pervasive state or parastatal ownership and privileged privatized business, an extensive informal economy, pervasive corruption and often a marginalized majority shut out of participation in the economic life of the community.[28]

If poor developing countries may need rules and standards different – at least in important respects – from developed countries, what should those rules and standards be? Is it feasible to develop an alternate track? Is it worth, or not worth, the costs of diversion from a more or less single perspective for the world? For simplicity and with over-generalization, I list six choices for competition law models in general. They are suggested merely as touchstones for a perspective; none is either a black box or a silver bullet; indeed, a single jurisdiction might draw ideas from all.

1. The first model is the US model: antitrust as a tool for, and only for, efficiency (including consumer welfare in itself or as a proxy), with the strong presumption that business freedom – of even dominant firms – produces efficiency.[29] This model demands minimal antitrust law except for law against cartels (which it prohibits).
2. Model 2 would adopt the general principles motivating the US model but modify the rules and standards to adjust to market realities of the large mass of developing countries. Thus, whereas US law describes predation as hardly ever tried and even more rarely successful, and bases its predation rule on these assumptions, developing countries would take stock of the relevant conditions in their countries. They might decide (for example) that a rule that tends to destroy and deter the only promising challengers in a monopolized market is more important than a rule that protects dominant firms' freedom to engage in low-price sharp-shooting;[30] or contrariwise they may prefer to protect the low prices for consumers, however transient. In all events,

---

[28] Ibid. See also Khemani, *supra* n. 25.

[29] This model dictates no antitrust enforcement unless the plaintiff proves that the challenged conduct limits output, subject to some shortcuts and proxies. See Fox, E. (2008), 'The Efficiency Paradox', in Pitofsky, R. (ed.), *How the Chicago School Overshot the Mark: The Effect of Conservative Economic Analysis on U.S. Antitrust*, New York: Oxford University Press, p. 77.

[30] See Stelzer, I., 'Some Practical Thoughts About Entry', in Pitofsky, *supra* n. 29, p. 24.

they would adjust the descriptions of markets, behavior and probable effects to the reality of their markets.

3. Model 3 is EU competition law and adjacent law, including not only the special regard for openness and access but also the suspicious stance toward competition-restricting state action and rules against discrimination in state procurement.
4. Model 4 would combine the law of certain developing countries that have already developed a compass. This basket of laws would prominently include South African case law, which is the most developed body of developing-country competition case law and which reflects the jurists' struggle to integrate feasible enforcement in view of scarce resources of the authority, well-endowed adversaries, and historically privileged dominant firms with the need to formulate and apply sound principles that promote competition and do not handicap efficiency.[31] The decisions of the South African Competition Tribunal, a number of which have been overturned by the appellate court on technical and interpretive grounds, are especially worthy of study by nations trying to construct a model sympathetic to inclusive development in a nation with an exclusionary, privileged, statist heritage.[32] This model would include the EU focus on openness and access as a means to produce and sustain efficient, dynamic markets. It would also combine aspects of EU law that limit abuses by the state and state-privileged firms. It could include the effort to create markets where they are blocked by corruption, privilege and statism.
5. Model 5 would explicitly introduce the value of fairness to local market actors. It would reflect wariness of the deep pockets and leverage of powerful multinational corporations. The model might

---

[31] I am not considering here South Africa's special regard for the long discriminated against majority in the years of apartheid; but if a jurisdiction chooses to accept into its antitrust law a value of equity for its own historically disadvantaged population, it is likely to find much merit in South Africa's methodology for integrating this concern. For a summary of South Africa's case law and practice, see Competition Commission and Competition Tribunal of South Africa (2009), *Ten Years of Enforcement by the South African Competition Authorities: Unleashing Rivalry (1999–2009)*, available at: http://www.comptrib.co.za/assets/Uploads/Reports/unleashing-rivalry.pdf, especially pp. 37–69.

[32] See, e.g., *Harmony Gold Mining Company Ltd.* v *Mittal Steel South Africa Ltd.*, Case No. 13/Cr/Feb04, p. 46, rev'd, *Mittal Steel South Africa Limited & Others* v *Harmony Gold Mining Company Limited, Durban Roodepoort Deep Limited*, Case No. 70/CAC/Apr07 (29 May 2009), p. 27.

conflate notions of competition and unfair competition, recognizing how the economies of many developing countries have been shaped by colonizing and imperial powers that have reserved to themselves a path for exploitation and exclusion.[33]

6. As a sixth alternative, each nation could invent its own model in view of its own needs, taking into account the values and methodologies especially of 3, 4 and 5 above.

Choosing a platform for developing-country competition law demands attention to the place of 'efficiency' in anchoring a competition law system. A vital characteristic of competition is its tendency to incentivize firms to be productive and creatively efficient. According to recent non-cartel US antitrust jurisprudence, laissez-faire antitrust (reluctance to intervene) is likely to produce these outcomes. This is one perspective. It is not necessarily true,[34] nor the best rule of thumb to achieve more robust markets in evolving economies. Some policy makers and scholars argue that concern for preserving the *process* of competition, openness of markets, access to markets and rivalry is more likely to lead to efficient outcomes than is US laissez-faire, even for developed economies.[35]

The indeterminacy as to how to reach efficiency, combined with the fact that the US model is based on market conditions quite different from those in developing countries, suggests that parts of the US jurisprudence may not fit the needs of developing countries. Accordingly, developing countries may be reluctant to adopt the US model (choice one) without refinement.

The second choice would adjust for market realities of developing countries (or a critical mass of them) while preserving the fundamental perspective of trust in the market wherever feasible. This adjustment, at least, should be made. Still, the second choice is founded on the same perspective about markets as in choice one, with antitrust as an instrument

---

[33] See Stewart, T., 'Regional Integration in the Caribbean: The Role of Competition Policy', in this volume, Ch. 8.

[34] See Rubinfeld, D., 'On the Foundations of Antitrust Law and Economics', in Pitofsky, *supra* n. 29, p. 51; Fox, E., *supra* n. 29, p. 77.

[35] See Stelzer, *supra* n. 30, p. 24. Stelzer writes: 'I have always believed that the free market system can be defended in the long run only if it provides fair and open opportunity to all comers, that its principal virtue is its contribution to social mobility, and that anti-competitive practices by dominant firms, and abuses created by … the ability of managers to pursue their own rather than their shareholder-owners' enrichment … are the greatest threat to the capitalist free market system.'

only to prohibit inefficient transactions, and with inefficiency narrowly defined. This is one view; it is the narrowest possible view of antitrust law.

The third choice would follow the EU model. EU law is positioned on a platform that is different from that of US law. Whereas US law looks first and essentially to whether the dominant firm's conduct (or merger, joint venture or agreement) will lessen output and raise price – thereby creating inefficiency, EU law looks centrally (also) to whether the market actors are 'sealing off the market' and frustrating access and entry. Moreover, EU law adds a valuable perspective on state acts and is more likely to catch state and hybrid obstacles to competition.[36]

The fourth choice – based on the case law of South Africa and perhaps that of other young, small and developing jurisdictions combined with EU attentiveness to openness and access and to anti-competitive blockage by the state – offers a different perspective. South African case law, especially as articulated by the Tribunal (which is sometimes reversed by the appeals court), is specifically tailored to the goal of inclusive development. This choice would shift burdens of proof on certain critical but minimal showings – of dominance, of discrimination, of excessive pricing. It would do so regarding conduct for which the US law provides no remedy at all or else requires sophisticated economic analysis that only mature authorities with large teams of economists and lawyers can handle. The jurisprudence has built-in checks to try to assure that the enforcement is efficient and serves the people. It has a good fit with the goal of legitimacy. Of all outstanding coherent bodies of competition law, the case law of the South African Tribunal may have the best fit with the Spence principle of efficient inclusive development.[37]

The fifth choice, again, alters the baseline, especially as compared with models 1 and 2 but even 3 and 4. It focuses on equity for and participation of

---

[36] A part of EU law's effectiveness is attributable to its internal 'trade' law, which complements its competition law, and part to its regional character. Even if EU trade and competition law cannot easily be adapted to national competition law, the EU model suggests goals that can be achieved by regional cooperation and integration.

[37] The fact that the Tribunal has been reversed not infrequently by the Appeal Court is not material to the inquiry of this article. The reversals are usually based on legalistic interpretations of words of the statute and do not necessarily illuminate what a good law would be. Nonetheless, the Appeal Court judgments also contain wisdom and bear study. Indeed the interplay between the Tribunal decisions and the Appeal Court judgments sharply focuses the issues and values at stake.

the people.[38] It extends antitrust beyond helping markets work efficiently. This model may appeal to jurisdictions in which local populations have been systematically excluded from doing what they can do best – as in Taimoon Stewart's examples of the tourism industry in the Caribbean, wherein exclusive contracts by the big hotel/leisure/travel chains shut out local independent hotels, drivers and others, even while competition among the chains themselves might assure a competitive product to consumer/travelers. Some existing bilateral competition agreements already support entrepreneurial opportunities of the developing partner to the agreement, as is the case in the partnership agreement between the European Union and CARIFORUM (the Caribbean countries and the Dominican Republic) with respect to tourism.[39] However, at least to the extent that antitrust rights for small and indigenous businesses would undermine benefits to consumer/buyers, the competition-and-equity paradigm falls outside of the realm of most contemporary versions of antitrust in developed countries.

I have noted a possible sixth choice: Each nation invents its own wheel. The idea is, however, daunting. In a world of a growing mass of international standards and perhaps some 50 or more idiosyncratic deviations, no alternative to the dominant developed world standard can be expected to gain traction as a recognized alternative. Whatever the choice of model, the choice should not be constraining. Indeed, it is more a choice of baseline. It is a platform or perspective; a coherent organizing point around which context-tailored competition law and policy is formed. Developing countries could benefit from a coherent perspective adopted by a critical mass, especially in a world in which 'international standards' are growing, all authorities of the world are being asked to sign on, and authorities in small and developing countries might signal their acceptance – they want to be counted as playing by international standards – without introspection as to what is best for them.[40]

---

[38] Note that some competition-law systems introduce certain fairness concerns by way of a provision against abuse of a superior bargaining position, as in Japan, and some contain a parallel competence for unfair acts, as in Zambia.

[39] Stewart, *supra* n. 33.

[40] See, for a discussion of the influence of the power of nations in setting international standards, Buthe, T. and W. Mattli (2010), 'Standards for Global Markets: Domestic and International Institutions for Setting International Product Standards', in Enderline, H., S. Walti and M. Zurn (eds), *Handbook on Multi-level Governance*, Cheltenham, UK and Northampton, MA, USA: Edward Elgar, Ch. 30, at p. 471 ('[Our analysis] suggests theoretically, and … has shown empirically, that power matters in international technical standardization and is unevenly distributed

Now, a caveat: this is an experiment. The experimental question is: what is the best competition-law perspective for developing countries, looking from the inside out? It is possible that, at the end of the exercise, one will conclude that divergences from the 'international standard'[41] are not worth the candle; there are costs of divergences and there are benefits to playing by international rules, such as attracting investment and garnering 'legitimacy'. Perhaps developing countries will conclude that building their own most appropriate law is not an enterprise worth the investment[42] or a battle worth the fight. But an informed decision cannot be made if the experimental question is never asked.

4. REGIONAL AGREEMENTS AND COMPETITION POLICY

Regional agreements come in many different configurations, from loose cooperation agreements to customs unions with centralized competition policy; thus, from loose to tight integration. Regional agreements can solve six problems of developing and small economies with regard to the effectiveness of their competition systems. The first is economies of scale in enforcement. Each economy may be too small to finance and staff a competition authority on its own. The second is leverage. Each alone may lack the strength to resist, or enforce law against, anti-competitive measures and acts launched from abroad. Together, but not alone, they might be able to induce developed countries (for example) to obtain and share critical documents, and perhaps even convince developed countries to prohibit their own firms' export cartels targeted at the developing countries.[43] Third is voice. Each alone may lack the voice to assert and maintain rules and

---

internationally'). See further, for a discussion of the problem of transplants, Gal, M. (2007), 'The "Cut and Paste" of Article 82 of the EU Treaty in Israel: Conditions for a Successful Transplant', *Eur. J. of Law Reform*, **9**, 467.

[41] There will never be complete convergence; there is not one set of international rules; but there are decided efforts towards convergence and the guiding lights of those efforts do not include what is good for economic development.

[42] Developing countries exploring the suggested territory may meet the resistance of aid agencies and mature competition authorities exhorting the importance of complying with best practices. See Sokol, D. (2010), 'Antitrust, Institutions, and Merger Control', *Geo. Mason L. Rev.*, **17**, 1055, 1098.

[43] See BNA (2011), 'Cartelization: Professor's Critique of Hostile Bid Triggers Discussion of Export Cartels', *Bureau of National Affairs Antitrust & Trade Reg. Report*, 99, 339.

standards tailored to their needs for development. Fourth is information and vision. A regional authority or watchdog may be better positioned to detect and fit together the pieces of the puzzle of restraints that transcend borders,[44] and to take a view from the top that accounts for all harms and benefits. The vision from the top may also enable more focused and more powerful advocacy to tear down regional border barriers. Fifth, as in the European Union, an economic community can surmount parochialism by its own member states, prohibiting state measures that impose negative externalities on their neighbors and prohibiting states from discriminating in favor of 'their own'. Sixth, as exemplified by the European Union, an effective remedy may need to be region-wide.

Regional entities can become nodes in the larger network of the antitrust family. If it is desired, these larger units might eventually provide stepping stones to broader regional frameworks or possibly even to a global one.[45]

But regional agreements also pose challenges. First, the regional agreements normally are framed as trade agreements, negotiated and operated by trade officials of nations that wish to gain the advantage of regional free trade by tearing down internal state trade barriers. Competition law is often an afterthought or adjunct, and competition may be sacrificed when it conflicts with nationalistic interests, such as competition-restraining anti-dumping laws. So it was with the North American Free Trade Agreement (NAFTA). NAFTA includes a competition chapter, implementation of which was a required subject of negotiations according to the Agreement itself.[46] No significant implementation occurred. NAFTA mandated a report on the competition chapter and its possibilities, but a report was not

---

[44] Frédéric Jenny has presented dramatic evidence of the cartel-like market-division arrangements of the major African brewers. See Jenny, F. (2009), 'Competition Enforcement in Testing Times: Beyond the National Level', in *Competition Principles Under Threat*, IDRC Pre-ICN Forum on Competition and Development, Zurich, Switzerland, 2 June 2009 (slides), available at web.idrc.ca/uploads/user-S/12447523741Frederic_Jenny.ppt

[45] See, for the benefits (as well as costs) of regionalism, Gal, M. and I.F. Wassmer, 'Regional Agreements of Developing Jurisdictions: Unleashing the Potential', this volume, Ch14, and Lipimile, G., 'The COMESA Regional Competition Regulations', in this volume, Ch. 10; Gal, M. (2010), 'Regional Competition Law Agreements: An Important Step for Antitrust Enforcement', *U. Toronto L.J.* **60**, 239.

[46] NAFTA (1994), Chapter 15. Article 1504 requires the formation of a Working Group on Trade and Competition, which was charged with reporting to the Commission within five years. For progressive possibilities for implementation, see the Report of the Task Force of the ABA Section of Antitrust Law on the

submitted. The competition chapter has had little significance,[47] even though the antitrust authorities of the three parties meet and cooperate bilaterally and trilaterally on issues less charged than seamless antitrust.[48] Consequently, there is no US–Canada–Mexico transnational competition law or policy. When Mexico and its telecoms companies imposed anti-competitive restraints harming AT&T, the United States complained to the World Trade Organization under the WTO Telecommunications Annex to the General Agreement on Trade in Services (GATS), not under NAFTA (and it won).[49]

Second, to the extent that a regional arrangement is an agreement for a community-wide competition law, and especially one with centralized enforcement, all of the problems that undermine successful national enforcement, other than lack of economies of scale, recur. Financial resources are still scarce and possibly inadequate. Each member nation must contribute its share of the costs. Most have been slow payers and some are non-payers; most do not regard the obligation as a priority. Personal talent is required to lead the supranational system in all of its phases – advocacy, investigation, prosecution, decision-making, appeals – and top-trained talent is likely to be scarce. The member nations might prefer to use their scarce resources at home rather than share them. For regional communities, sound, reliable, efficient, non-corrupt institutions must be built, and this too is an enormous challenge. Accountability may be even more difficult to achieve than at national level because the actors are farther removed from the grass-roots. Resolve to stand up to vested interests remains an enormous challenge, although when the private interests do not transcend borders, the problem may be better addressed at regional level. The regional collaboration can and should involve mechanisms to check national parochial interests, as the European Union so successfully does. But whether the member nations of a regional agreement will be bold and wise enough to pool their sovereignty to this extent for the greater good, as in the EU, or whether they will prefer to retain their own nationalistic advantages, is an open question.

Competition Dimension of NAFTA, Eleanor Fox, chair (ABA Antitrust Section 1994), available at: http://www.antitrustinstitute.org/files/430b.pdf

47 See Sokol, *supra* n. 25, analysing all free trade agreements in the western hemisphere and finding that none has a binding competition law provision.

48 Bilateral cooperation agreements, of which there are many, are designed for cooperation, not for common cross-border enforcement.

49 See Fox, *supra* n. 16.

Yet another problem arises if the member states must give up their own competition law enforcement – even for domestic harms. If they must defer to and await enforcement by the supranational authority, as they must in francophone West Africa,[50] local problems might go unaddressed. Even if member states must give up only the right to cross-border enforcement, a gap will arise if the supranational body is not ready, able and willing to enforce the law. In fact experience shows that competition law in the context of regional agreement is seldom robust and effective.[51] There is the danger that nations may rely on the prospect of region-wide enforcement but effective regional enforcement may not materialize for many years to come.

In sum, by definition, regional agreements that tear down artificial barriers, realize economies of scale and check nationalistic tendencies tend to enhance competition and development. Accordingly, competition law on the regional level holds much promise.[52] The expectation and promise of effective regional competition law may be greater than its delivery in the near term. But for the longer term, the project is vital.

5. CONCLUSION

Competition *policy* is highly important for efficient, inclusive development. Competition *law* has precisely the same potential, for at its best it frees up markets and creates pathways for mobility, participation and innovation. Regional competition law has great promise, because it could overcome the atomization and border-barrier problems. Regionalization of competition law also poses many challenges so that, even while jurisdictions are working to make it happen, the benefits are slow in materializing. Nations, therefore, understandably try to safeguard their own enforcement powers.

---

50 See Bakhoum, M. and J. Molestina, 'Institutional Coherence and Effectiveness of a Regional Competition Policy: The Case of the West African Economic and Monetary Union (WAEMU)', in this volume, Ch. 5.

51 The Australia-New Zealand shared law on abuse of dominance is a notable exception but a special case. Australia and New Zealand may go further; policymakers are considering the possibility of one antitrust authority for Australia and New Zealand. Meanwhile, Australia and New Zealand's Closer Economic Relations Trade Agreement continues to make progress towards greater integration. See Department of Foreign Affairs and Trade, Memorandum of Understanding Between the Government of New Zealand and the Government of Australia on Coordination of Business Law (2009), available at: http://www.dfat.gov.au/fta/anzcerta/memorandum_of_understanding_business_law.html.

52 See Gal, *supra* n. 45; Lipimile, *supra* n. 45.

What competition law should regional groupings adopt? This paper proposes that developing countries need to develop a perspective of their own. It proposes that certain competition-law principles of South Africa and other developing countries, informed by EU law, may comprise the best available anchor, on grounds that this set of laws best incorporates the Spence principle of efficient inclusive development while also incorporating important insights of the revised Washington Consensus; and it does so in a way that respects the problem of seriously limited resources. Regional antitrust of developing nations presents an excellent opportunity and a potential showcase for 'Spence antitrust'.

Finally, we revert to the experiment. It remains to be considered whether antitrust best tailored to the needs of development is worth deviations from 'international standards'.[53] The question has to be answered in light of the facts, and it can be answered only after developing countries construct antitrust that is the best for them.

---

[53] This may turn out to be a moot question, either because best-development rules are so close to industrialized-country rules as not to make a difference, or because of the indeterminacy of international standards, which may be revealed as a range into which developing country antitrust fits quite well, or because the exercise has opened minds to a better appreciation of (for example) the value of mobility and contestability as pathways to efficiency and competitiveness for all nations (see *supra* n. 35), and convergence towards rules and standards that incorporate these guideposts occurs.

14. Regional agreements of developing jurisdictions: unleashing the potential

Michal S. Gal and Inbal Faibish Wassmer*

1. INTRODUCTION

Regional competition agreements (RCAs) hold great potential for overcoming the major enforcement problems of developing jurisdictions. Indeed, it is no coincidence that the past two decades have seen an unprecedented upsurge in the number and scope of such agreements, especially in the developing world. Such agreements include, *inter alia*, in the Americas: MERCOSUR (the Southern Common Market); in the Caribbean: CARICOM (the Caribbean Community); in Africa: COMESA (the Common Market for Eastern and Southern Africa), WAEMU (the West African Economic and Monetary Union), ECOWAS (the Economic Community of West African States), SEACF (the Southern and Eastern Africa Competition Forum), CEMAC (the Economic and Monetary Community of Central Africa), SACU (the Southern African Customs Union), EAC (the East African Community) and SADC (the Southern African Development Community); and in Asia: ASEAN (the Association of South East Asian Nations). Most of these agreements are not specific to competition law, but involve other issues as well, mostly trade. In some, competition-law issues play a central role[1] while in others competition law serves only as a

* We thank Mor Bakhoum, Alberto Heimler and Tamar Indig for most helpful comments and the German-Israeli Foundation for their financial support.

[1] See, e.g., COMESA (2008), *Aide Memoire: Trade Capacity Building: Strengthening the COMESA Trade Region through a Culture of Competition.*

supplement or a scaffolding to other goals.[2] Many try to imitate the most (if not the only) successful regional competition regime in the world, the EU.

Yet as the experiences analysed throughout this book clearly demonstrate, the accumulated experience of almost all of these newly sprung RCAs is that thus far they have not significantly enhanced competition law enforcement in their regions, or have encountered serious difficulties in doing so. This empirical finding applies regardless of the region and the special characteristics of the jurisdictions within it. This creates a paradox: Why do so many countries invest in adopting such agreements in the first place, if the obstacles to their successful operation are high?

This chapter attempts to offer some answers to this paradox by analysing the obstacles that stand in the way of realizing the potential benefits of RCAs. Our purpose is to identify and analyse at least some of the variables that affect their adoption and operation in the real world. The fact that such obstacles are observed across RCAs strengthens the need to study the roots of such obstacles. Such an analysis can hopefully provide better tools to understand and predict when an RCA is likely to succeed or to fail, and what can be done to increase its chances of success. To do so, we combine the empirical observations on how RCAs operate in practice with theoretical analysis. The analysis builds, *inter alia*, on studies of the collective-action problem, including studies of successful collaborations in environments that face relatively similar obstacles to a successful joint collaboration. Such an analysis can also assist us in determining whether the current failure is mainly rooted in the regional aspect of the RCAs or rather in the fact that they involve competition law, the application of which would have encountered serious difficulties in the relevant jurisdictions regardless. Should it be the latter, time might be an important factor in determining the course of such RCAs. Also, as elaborated below, the regional aspect might strengthen rather than weaken the process of adopting and applying a competition law, *inter alia* by strengthening competition-advocacy efforts in member states.

---

[2] For an overview of competition law provisions in regional agreements see, e.g., Brusick, P. et al. (eds) (2005), *Competition Provisions in Regional Trade Agreements: How to Assure Development Gains*, Geneva: UNCTAD, available at: http://www.unctad.org/en/docs/ditcclp20051_en.pdf; Sokol, D. (2007), 'Order without (Enforceable) Law: Why Countries Enter into Non-Enforceable Competition Policy Chapters in Free Trade Agreements', *Chicago-Kent L. Rev*, **83**, 231; Dabbah, M. (2010), *International Competition Law*, Cambridge: Cambridge University Press, Ch. 7.

Accordingly, the rest of the chapter is divided into three parts. The first explores the potential benefits that can accrue from a successful RCA. The second, which is the heart of the chapter, analyses some of the obstacles to realizing such benefits that emerge from the case studies of the different RCAs, and places them in a wider theoretical context. The third part offers some potential solutions for overcoming such problems.

2. POTENTIAL BENEFITS OF RCAs

RCAs hold an important potential for overcoming some of the most significant problems that plague competition law enforcement in small and in developing jurisdictions. Since this claim is explored in length elsewhere, here we provide a broad-brush analysis.[3] Yet more real-world examples are integrated in the analysis below.

It should be noted from the outset that the benefits of RCAs are determined, *inter alia*, by the modalities of cooperation on which they are based. RCAs share two basic features, which are also reflected in their name: members are generally located within the same region and cooperate on competition-law issues.[4] Yet the level of cooperation and the goal the agreement seeks to achieve differ significantly among RCAs. The most cooperative models focus on joint competition enforcement and education through a regional joint competition-law authority (RJCA), whether in parallel (e.g. CARICOM) or not (e.g. WAEMU) to national competition-law authorities in the member states. Such agreements hold the greatest potential to create benefits for their members. Other models adopt lower degrees of cooperation, from the joint creation of a competition culture to information sharing and enforcement by national competition authorities (e.g. MERCUSOR). Obviously, the lower the level of cooperation, the lower the potential benefits, but possibly also the lower the obstacles to its adoption and enforcement. For example, the SADC agreement, which concentrates almost solely on educational efforts, does not enjoy the benefits of joint enforcement but it is relatively easy to implement. The analysis below concentrates mainly on RJCAs, which hold the strongest potential to create benefits from cooperation.

---

3 Gal, M. (2010), 'Regional Competition Law Agreements: An Important Step for Antitrust Enforcement', *University of Toronto Law Journal*, **60**, 239.

4 Competition law need not be the only area on which states cooperate. Indeed, as noted above, many RCAs are parts of wider agreements on trade.

2.1 Reducing Enforcement Resource Constraints

Possibly the main enforcement obstacle faced by developing and by small jurisdictions involves enforcement resource constraints – both financial and human.[5] RJCAs can significantly reduce such constraints by enabling jurisdictions to pool together scarce resources to reach economies of scale in enforcement activities (investigations, enforcement), as well as in competition advocacy and training.

In some situations RJCAs may provide the only viable solution for enforcement, given severe resource constraints. The Organization of Eastern Caribbean States (OECS) provides such an example: it is comprised of developing micro-economies, such as Montserrat with a population of about 5,000 and St Kitts with a population of about 40,000. Each alone cannot justify an investment in a competition law. Yet by pooling their resources they are able to create a joint competition authority that deals with competition-law issues that affect them.

2.2 Reducing Enforcement Capability Constraints

Even when no significant enforcement resource constraints exist, countries might still be constrained in their capability to enforce their laws in practice, especially with regard to multinational issues.

We identify five main obstacles. First, *evidence gathering* might be problematic if evidence is located elsewhere. Accordingly, information sharing is generally an integral part of RCAs. Second, small jurisdictions often cannot *create a credible threat* to prohibit the conduct of a foreign firm, given power asymmetries. If the foreign firm's gains from trade within it are limited, were the small jurisdiction to place significant restrictions on the foreign firm, it might choose to exit the jurisdiction. Interestingly, this problem sometimes also plagues large, developing jurisdictions as well, in specific product markets that do not carry high profits or when they are completely reliant on foreign firms to supply their markets.[6] By increasing

---

[5] Gal, M. (2009), 'Antitrust in a Globalized Economy: The Unique Challenges of Small and Developing Economies', *Fordham International Law Journal*, **33**, 1; Gal, M. (2010), 'When the Going Gets Tight: Institutional Solutions When Antitrust Enforcement Resources are Scarce', *Loyola University Chicago Law Journal*, **41**, 411.

[6] For example, the Chairperson of the Competition Commission of India has indicated the problems that country experiences in creating a credible threat to prohibit a possible cartel in the international potash market without international

leverage through the aggregation of consumers across member states and through creating a critical mass, RJCAs increase the ability to create a credible threat. It is noteworthy, however, that to achieve this goal member states might also need to overcome 'divide and conquer' strategies of international entities, which attempt to create different motivations for different member states.

This can be exemplified by tour operators in CARICOM countries. Foreign tour operators have taken over the tour markets in many Caribbean states, based on exclusive dealing and tying arrangements that block entry of others into the market, thereby significantly limiting the ability of the local residents to benefit from the industry. Given the multiple Caribbean destinations that compete with each other, each country, on its own, cannot create a credible threat to solve the problem. But by joining together, they may be able to find a solution.[7]

Third, deterrence might *require cumulative sanctions* that can be more easily applied and enforced through an RJCA. Fourth, it is often difficult to *impose a penalty* on firms located elsewhere. Finally, the creation of a new authority – at the regional level – may be an efficient way to overcome deep-rooted limitations of existing authorities, including corruption, inefficiency and bureaucratic obstacles. Indeed, starting afresh might also reduce human resource constraints, as skilled individuals may have stronger incentives to join.

Such benefits of RJCAs may accrue whether or not there are cross-border effects within member states. Interestingly, some RJCAs provide solutions to enforcement resource and capability constraints even in cases with no cross-border effects. For example, COMESA is empowered to deal with national competition-law issues, if requested by a member state due to its limited capacity. Indeed, the EU has acted in a similar fashion with regard to small member states such as Luxembourg.

---

cooperation from other competition authorities. This results, *inter alia*, from the great importance of potash to the Indian agriculture industry, informational problems, and the fact that foreign governments in which some potash producers are located seem to endorse the cartel.

7 Stewart, T., 'Regional Integration in the Caribbean: The Role of Competition Policy', in this volume, Ch. 8. It should be noted, however, that such a solution might possibly need to use tools beyond competition law.

2.3 Reducing Public Choice Limitations

Political pressures from interest groups are especially significant for developing and for small jurisdictions, since economic power in such countries tends to be more concentrated in the hands of a few, whether private or state-owned, enterprises. Such interests might trump public welfare considerations.

A joint authority can alter some of the effects of well-organized pressure groups on decision-makers in adopting a competition law, since a push towards regionalization creates internal and external pressures for adopting a competition law. This is especially true if competition law is part of a wider agreement on trade. Also, once created, the aggregation of different incentives in a regional authority, which is one step removed from each member state, reduces the ability of a domestic group to exert pressure on the legislature or regulator to change the regulatory environment. Finally, once the framework is agreed upon, it is much more difficult to change than a domestic law, even if it harms the interests of strong groups in some member states. The RJCA might therefore work as a commitment mechanism which allows members to create binding commitments of compliance that will be enforced beyond the term of the government that signed the commitment.

2.4 Strengthening Competition Culture

An additional factor that often plays a role in the low enforcement levels of developing countries involves the weakness of their competition culture. Most consumers in WAEMU countries, for example, prefer similar prices for competing products, in order to make choices easier, over lower but different prices. An RJCA can create economies of scale in educational and in advocacy activities. Furthermore, the fact that the jurisdictions chose to include competition law on the regional agenda might, in itself, serve as a signal of its importance for the region.

2.5 Furthering the Goal of a Common, Integrated Market

RJCAs have the potential to further the goal of a common, integrated market. As the European experience demonstrates, joint competition-law enforcement can play an important role in supporting the creation of an integrated market. The reduction of entry barriers results in an increased ability of firms to operate in larger areas, thereby increasing their ability to enjoy economies of scale and scope, and increasing competition. This, in turn, might signal to the international community that the states in the region can work together towards common goals, thereby strengthening the standing of both the regional authorities and its member states in international circles.

2.6 Increasing Certainty and Compatibility

RJCAs might also increase certainty and compatibility of competition-law enforcement either by transferring enforcement powers to the regional authority (e.g. requests to merge firms that operate at the regional level are filed only with the regional authority), or by adopting tools to increase compatibility between national competition laws. This, in turn, may strengthen incentives to enter and expand in regional markets.

2.7 Overcoming Negative Externalities

If decision-makers ignore the impact of their decisions beyond their borders, their decisions might impose negative externalities on other jurisdictions. Externalities among member states can be overcome by an RJCA, which is based on joint welfare considerations. Cross-border mergers provide a useful example. In the region covered by COMESA, Lafarge took over all the cement companies and South African Breweries took over almost all the breweries in the area. This, of course, reduced competition significantly within the region. An integrated merger policy would have been able to limit the negative welfare effects of some of these mergers on the region.

Interestingly, a successful RJCA can also create positive externalities by itself. A positive cooperation experience may allow the agreement to extend to other areas in need of regional cooperation, such as environmental protection, water quality and dealing with region-wide natural disasters.

To sum up this part, RJCAs have a potential to supply a collective good that may significantly enhance the welfare of all jurisdictions involved.

3. OBSTACLES TO THE SUCCESSFUL REALIZATION OF RCA BENEFITS

Given the potential benefits RCAs can offer, it is not surprising that many regions have adopted RCAs. Yet as the experiences outlined throughout this book indicate, most RCAs have not realized their potential. Rather, most do not justify their costs of creation, and some even create negative welfare effects on their member states. The Senegalese experience provides an example. The Senegalese competition authority was operational. However, the WAEMU regional agreement, which Senegal joined, was interpreted by the Court of Justice of WAEMU as assigning the WAEMU Commission the sole responsibility of applying competition law, and assigning to national authorities the role of cooperating with the WAEMU Commission. This was understood as mandating that all competition law be centralized. Accordingly, the Senegalese authority ceased to operate several years ago, but WAEMU has not as yet created a viable alternative, although some cases have been brought at a regional level. As a result, Senegal lost its ability to deal with most of its domestic anti-competitive conduct.[8]

What, then, are the obstacles to the successful realization of an RCA's potential benefits and what can be learned from the experience of existing RCAs? This is the focus of this section. The first subsection focuses on some preconditions for a successful agreement and illustrates the effects of their inexistence on some agreements. The second subsection analyses possible obstacles to an RCA's efficient operation. The analysis thus differentiates between two interconnected but separate stages: reaching an agreement and enforcing it in practice.

Obstacles to the provision and operation of an RCA can arise on the supply side or on the demand side, or both. Supply-side obstacles relate to the ability to reach an agreement and to maintain its benefits over time, which are inter-connected: the ability to enforce the agreement, once created, will affect the incentives to commit to it in the first place. The fact that the agreement involves a long-term commitment in a changing environment rather than a one-shot game increases the difficulties, since commitment should be continuous.[9]

Demand-side obstacles relate to the ability of potential member states to overcome internal obstacles to committing to an RCA that can increase their social welfare, and to enforcing it. Such obstacles might be legal, political or economic. They might result from real threats to welfare (e.g. political economy constraints of interest groups), or from perceived threats (e.g. misconceptions of the effects of competition). They might be specific

---

[8] See, e.g., Weick, D.P. (2010), 'Competition law and policy in Senegal: A Cautionary Tale for Regional Integration?', *World Competition*, **33** (3), 521.

[9] Ostrom, E. (1990), *Governing the Commons: The Evolution of Institutions for Collective Action*, Cambridge: Cambridge University Press, p. 45.

to competition law, or general (e.g. a high hurdle on the ability to commit to any international or regional agreement).

3.1 Preconditions for Adoption of an RCA

3.1.1 The overarching precondition: Pareto-optimality for each member state

The overarching precondition to an RCA is that it creates a Pareto-superior situation for each and every member. Otherwise, why join? Benefits might differ from one jurisdiction to another, but all members must be better off with than without the agreement. This precondition determines, *inter alia*, the limits of how far members are willing to cede their sovereign powers in order to further other national interests.

More specifically, the greater the ability of a country to solve its anti-competitive issues on its own, the lower its incentive to cede sovereignty.[10] South Africa and the SADC agreement provide such an example. South Africa is unlikely to cede its sovereignty and join an RCA or provide information on infringements of its national firms in foreign markets, because that would not be Pareto-superior to the current situation. This is because currently South Africa can generally deal with anti-competitive externalities from other member states and its firms are likely to benefit from engaging in anti-competitive practices elsewhere, given their dominant position in many markets in the region. Accordingly, even if the other members of the SADC agreement are likely to benefit from increased information sharing and from joint enforcement, it is not likely that such an agreement could be reached, at least not under the current situation. Indeed, the SADC agreement mostly focuses on creating a competition culture in member states.

The boundaries of the RCA also depend on the relative situation in the different member states. In COMESA, for example, some member states are plagued by political and financial instability, a fact that reduces their realistic commitment levels. This, in turn, reduces the benefits that other members can gain from the RCA. Indeed, some members left COMESA to join smaller but more stable RCAs. Given that political and financial constraints are common to many developing countries, we might observe such switching in other regions in the future.

---

10 Guzman, A. (1998), 'Is International Antitrust Possible?', *N.Y.U.L. Rev.*, **73**, 1501.

The temporal element may also affect the analysis. Several RCA representatives, including those from CARICOM and ASEAN, have indicated that joining an agreement with countries with no competition law or competition culture might be more costly than strengthening one's competition law internally. Of course, the scales may tip in the other direction once others apply a competition law, or when the competition culture is strengthened so that fewer resources must be spent on its creation.

In short, there should be at least some degree of *commonality of interests*, which creates a *Pareto-superior situation for each and every member state*, to create the RCA. Such benefits should be analysed against the backdrop of current and alternative solutions to competition-law problems of member states. If the RCA is part of a wider agreement, the cost–benefit analysis may be calculated overall. Indeed, national trade interests often lead jurisdictions to adopt a competition law or to join an RCA, especially if these are a precondition for joining the trade agreement.[11]

Yet benefits need not always relate (only) to the competition-law sphere. Rather, if the RCA is part of a wider agreement such as a trade agreement, costs and benefits to each member state should be analysed overall. Similarly, joining an RCA may be part of the 'price' paid by a jurisdiction to international bodies that assist it in times of need. These facts, by themselves, do not necessarily imply that the RCA is not beneficial for the jurisdiction adopting it, but a more careful analysis is needed. In addition, such factors might reduce the motivation of the jurisdiction to invest efforts in making the RCA work, once adopted.

Given this Pareto-optimality precondition, we explore the costs involved in creating the RCA, both direct and indirect, that need to be balanced against the benefits explored above. It is noteworthy that while at least some of the costs are immediate and relatively easily quantified, most of the benefits are not, and they depend upon the successful operation of the RCA. This risk factor must also be taken into account when the balance is calculated.

---

[11] For example, the CARICOM trade agreements have led OECS countries to attempt to create an RJCA in order to meet the requirements agreed upon in the CARICOM agreement.

3.1.1.1 Costs of RCAs[12] Creating an RCA and especially setting up a joint authority involves the *direct costs* of building a new institution and resourcing its operation, including enforcement and monitoring compliance activities. Following Buchanan and Tullock, we can differentiate between up-front transformation costs and second-stage enforcement costs.[13]

Transformation costs are the costs involved in the process of considering and (possibly) changing a rule. Such costs are affected, *inter alia*, by the number of stakeholders making institutional choices, the heterogeneity of interests at stake and the mode of negotiations. Enforcement costs involve both monitoring and actual enforcement of laws. They are affected, *inter alia*, by the rules adopted, by the institutional arrangements made and by the legitimacy of the rule in the eye of the potential enforcer.[14] Such costs can be significant, especially where human and financial resources are scarce. If the RCA is inefficient, its costs may create an additional burden on already limited resources. Furthermore, an RCA might increase states' internal costs. For example, complying with a requirement to adopt a competition law and enforce it domestically can be very costly for some jurisdictions, due to their inadequate institutional and regulatory capacity or the small size of their markets relative to the costs of enforcement. Such a commitment can also make them vulnerable to sanctions imposed if they do not comply with such requirements, therefore further increasing their costs.[15] Even a relatively simple requirement of sharing information can impose high costs.

3.1.1.2 Indirect costs Indirect costs in an RJCA arise from the fact that some or all competition-law decisions are made by an external entity. This can be split into two main concerns: first, harm to sovereignty, and second, the decision of the joint entity might harm the domestic interests of the jurisdiction.

Joint enforcement *limits the sovereignty* of member states to decide all competition-law cases surfacing at their shores. Yet harm to sovereignty is

---

12 Based on Gal, *supra* n. 3.

13 Ostrom, *supra* n. 9, p. 198; Buchanan, J. and G. Tullock (1962), *The Calculus of Consent: Logical Foundations of Constitutional Democracy*, Michigan: University of Michigan Press.

14 Ostrom, *supra* n. 9, pp. 203–205.

15 Birdsall, N. and R.Z. Lawrence, 'Deep Integration and Trade Agreements: Good for Developing Countries?', in I. Kaul, I. Grunberg and M.A. Stern (eds) (1999), *Global Public Goods: International Cooperation in the 21st Century*, Oxford: Oxford University Press, at p. 141.

generally not prohibitive. First, entering into an RJCA is voluntary: each jurisdiction exercises its discretion and decision-making power in deciding whether and under which conditions to enter the agreement. Second, sovereignty – in its embodiment as unilateral enforcement – has proven to be a highly problematic tool, especially with regard to multinational issues.[16] It should thus be weighed against other tools which allow the jurisdiction to further its domestic policy of deterrence of anti-competitive conduct by overcoming its existing enforcement problems. Finally, an intermediate solution can be applied to reduce sovereignty concerns, in which member states are part of an advisory committee to the regional authority, like in the EU. This leads to the second concern.

As shown by Guzman, joint enforcement might not always lead to decisions that benefit all member states.[17] Assume, for example, that a merger or a joint venture benefits consumers in some states, since their markets are less concentrated, and harms consumers in others. Any joint standard set for review of such conduct will harm some states and benefit others. If it is based on total welfare-counting benefits and harms by their absolute size, then the outcome will generally be driven by the effects of the conduct on the larger jurisdictions. If it is based on a calculation of effects in each jurisdiction in relative terms, then the outcome might be driven by the effects on a small number of consumers in micro-states. Accordingly, setting such a standard is highly contentious. Thus, if the optimal policies for different members clash, regionalization will require that some measure of domestic welfare be sacrificed, at least in some cases. Such sacrifice might be especially costly for those potential members that can create a stronger credible threat to prevent anti-competitive conduct than others, and for those whose interests are most harmed by the common standard. The lack of substantive convergence in some areas of competition law, most notably monopolization, may further increase the problems involved in reaching a common standard.[18]

Such costs, while important, can be reduced in several ways. One solution is to jointly enforce only those cases that further the interests of all countries involved, such as the pursuit of regional or international cartels, and to leave others outside the scope of the agreement. Indeed, some RCAs limit their scope to such conduct. This case-by-case Pareto-optimality standard, however, reduces the benefits from the agreement for all involved.

---

16 Gal, *supra* n. 5.
17 Guzman, *supra* n. 10.
18 Sokol, *supra* n. 2.

A more effective although less simple way of tackling such issues is by ensuring that an overall balance of social welfare exists. While, for example, a merger might not be blocked if it benefits most jurisdictions, those jurisdictions that are harmed might be otherwise compensated, whether by transfer payments as Guzman suggested, or by giving their interests priority in other enforcement decisions.[19] While Pareto-optimality might not be reached in each case, it might be reached overall.

An additional tool involves the recognition of the special interests and special needs of member states in specific markets, such as strengthening an export joint venture in a currently weak industry that allows domestic firms to reach scale economies in marketing. One possible tool, which follows regional trade agreements, involves the inclusion of special-treatment provisions for specific industries in order to ensure their reasonable adjustment to the full impact of competition. This has been done in the ANDEAN Community and in ASEAN, for example, where exemptions are determined by each member state and are not subject to overall limiting principles as in the EU. Yet, since one member's export joint venture might be another's import cartel, such exemptions might significantly limit the RCA's ability to generate benefits, and should be severely limited. Otherwise, competition might be limited in many important regional markets. As long as exemptions are the exception rather than the rule, the overall benefits of the RCA can still be achieved.

The ability to reach such solutions might be reduced, however, by power dynamics: by the fact that negotiations might sometimes tilt towards the interests of jurisdictions with stronger power, due, for example, to their relative size or contribution to the agreement or the fact that the RCA's skilled officials might come mainly from them. Such jurisdictions might be able to alter the choices of other jurisdictions and coerce them to adopt a joint standard which serves such jurisdictions' domestic interests, in order to reduce the possible negative effects on their consumers.[20] The less homogeneous the member states, the higher such potential costs, *ceteris paribus*. While such costs are undoubtedly important, they should still be

---

19 Guzman, *supra* n. 10. Of course, attempts should be made, before reaching this stage, to limit the harm to all member states, either by structural or conduct remedies.

20 Simmons, B.A. (2001), 'The International Politics of Harmonization: The Case of Capital Market Regulation', *Int'l Org.*, **55,** 589 at 591; Vogel, D. (1995), *Trading Up: Consumer and Environmental Regulation in a Global Economy*, Cambridge, MA: Harvard University Press, at pp. 5–6.

checked against the existing situation. The most important question that each jurisdiction should ask is whether the standard likely to emerge has the potential to further its domestic interests relative to the existing situation. If the agreement makes the signatories better off, there is a rationale for committing to it. This issue is further explored below.

It should also be noted that enforcement at a regional level might also reduce the accessibility of the authority to small local firms.

Finally, an RCA might *reduce the comparative advantage* of some countries relative to their neighbours, given their different unilateral enforcement capabilities.[21] Once again, the loss of such an advantage must be balanced against benefits from a coordinated and stronger regional competition policy.

Let us now explore more subtle preconditions and their effect on the adoption and the scope of an RCA.

3.1.2 Equal distribution of benefits as a precondition?

An RCA might create real or perceived unequal distribution of benefits among member states, which might result from trade patterns, legal regimes or geographic, economic and cultural differences. The question arises whether such distributive effects would or should inhibit the creation of an RCA.

This issue is highly relevant, as most RCAs are composed of members with different conditions. Indeed, many are characterized by significant economic or legal superiority of one or more members (e.g. Singapore in ASEAN, South Africa in SADC, Trinidad and Tobago in CARICOM, Nigeria in ECOWAS, Brazil in MERCOSUR). This might lead to an unequal distribution of benefits from the agreement.

The distribution of costs and benefits depends on the model of cooperation adopted. For example, where the agreement is reliant on information sharing and unilateral enforcement, it will benefit those members who can actually apply their competition laws and create a credible threat of enforcement to firms operating within their borders. Alternatively, if the

---

[21] Each jurisdiction has incentives to improve its own position relative to other jurisdictions in order to create local comparative advantages that would enable it to benefit relative to others. For example, a country that can credibly commit to legal stability and enforcement will generally create a stronger motivation for investors to invest in it relative to other jurisdictions with a lower level of commitment, *ceteris paribus*. For such arguments in the federalism context, see, e.g., Rose-Ackerman, S. (1981), 'Does Federalism Matter? Political Choice in a Federal Republic', *J. Pol. Econ.*, **89**, 152.

model chosen is one of joint enforcement, the weakest states might be the greatest beneficiaries in a regional agreement, given that otherwise they might not be able to apply a competition law. At the same time, large members with a strong competition regime might be the biggest contributors (resource-wise and also due to the fact that their national firms might now be subject to more stringent limitations in the region), but not necessarily the biggest gainers. This can be exemplified by the CARICOM agreement, which will enable micro-states that could not have applied their competition laws on their own to benefit from joint enforcement, even against firms from Trinidad and Tobago, which dominate some of the regional markets.

Yet, interestingly, an unbalanced distribution of costs and benefits among member states does not necessarily create an obstacle to the creation of an RCA. Rather, in some situations it might be a necessary condition for its creation. This results from the first condition observed above, that the RCA be Pareto-optimal for all member states. If some members incur higher costs, or they can apply alternative solutions for solving their competition-law issues, it might be necessary for them to enjoy higher gains in order to join.

It should be noted, however, that fairness perceptions with regard to such unbalances might sometimes create obstacles to the adoption of RCAs. Indeed, fairness has a comparative element – studies have shown that often people prefer that their relevant group face similar conditions, even if at a higher price, over a situation in which all are better off but some members in their relevant group are much better off. These considerations should thus also enter into the Pareto-optimality analysis of joining the RCA.

3.1.3 Competition culture as a precondition?

An interesting question is whether a basic understanding and national application of competition law is a prerequisite for a successful RCA. The answer is negative. In most RCAs not all member states have a competition law and even when they have one, the competition culture is often not developed. For example, in CEMAC only Cameroon and Gabon have a competition law and in CARICOM only Jamaica and Barbados have such a law. Indeed, one of the most important goals of an RCA is the proliferation of a competition culture, as exemplified by both the experiences of SADC and the EU. A top-down approach can serve to limit political-economy obstacles to the adoption of domestic competition laws.[22] Moreover, such an approach can overcome obstacles to RCAs that result from demands to adopt domestic competition laws, which might instead create a backlash to regional efforts.

Yet a successful competition-law regime, at least in some member states, can act as a catalyst to the adoption of an RCA and its successful operation. For one, the positive experience of some member states can serve as a basis for competition-law advocacy. Absent such an experience, members might be reluctant to leave issues that affect their jurisdiction or their domestic firms to a regional body.[23] Second, the accumulated knowledge can be built upon in setting up and operating the RCA. In the CARICOM, for example, many of the Competition Commission's officials come from Jamaica, which has an operational competition law.

3.1.4 Differences in competition-law cultures

Differences in competition-law cultures can also create obstacles to an RCA In some situations an entrenched competition culture might create an obstacle to the setting up of the RCA, especially if it involves joint enforcement. This might occur when the national competition culture is quite different from the one the RCA attempts to create. For example, WAEMU member states use different definitions of dominance, a fact that made it more difficult to reach a consensus. The SADC agreement provides an additional example: members follow different competition-law models, mostly based on models in their donor countries or on their members' unique goals. South Africa, for example, includes a public interest goal of strengthening previously weakened groups of society. Such a goal is less relevant to other member states. Moreover, an existing competition law that is applied inefficiently can create a vicious circle. This is the situation in some ANDEAN countries: the fact that several countries have competition laws that have not brought benefits to consumers has created scepticism with regard to the benefits that an RCA can bring.

Yet such differences should not necessarily inhibit an RCA. For one thing, most competition laws are based on core principles common to all models. Prohibition of cartels that limit competition without the offsetting

---

22 On such obstacles see, e.g., Gal, M. (2004), 'The Ecology of Antitrust: Preconditions for Competition Law Enforcement in Developing Countries', in P. Brunsick et al. (eds), *Competition, Competitiveness and Development: Lessons from Developing Countries*, Geneva: UNCTAD, p. 22.

23 For a more sceptical view on this point see Dabbah, *supra* n. 2, p. 303.

benefits to society is but one example. Secondly, differences in goals or tools can affect the boundaries of the RCA, but do not necessarily prevent its operation. Rather, in the long run, convergence might be enhanced by mutual learning and sensitivity to differences.

3.1.5 Sufficient resources

Sufficient resources (both financial and human) are an important precondition for an operational RCA. Indeed, resource deficiency has plagued many RCAs. For example, although COMESA has a Competition Commission, it cannot make decisions because of insufficient funding to employ the necessary staff. Additional examples involve the SADC, in which only one official is designated to deal with competition-law issues, CEMAC, in which the number rises to two, and WAEMU, in which the number is three, despite the large number of member states. The effectiveness of the RCA thus depends on the commitment of all or at least most of its member states to provide sufficient resources for its operation.[24]

Insufficient resources often result from wider macro-economic conditions in RCA member states. Members of many RCAs are plagued by issues of deep poverty, regional conflicts or natural disasters. In such circumstances competition law often is not a priority. This fact strengthens the need to determine, from the outset, whether indeed it is in a country's or a region's interest to invest in an RCA. It might well be that setting up an RCA with insufficient resources for its successful operation is worse than no investment at all. This is because such investments are wasteful and they might also create long-term harm to competition-advocacy efforts as well as to the RCA. Yet, as studies have shown, there is often an economic justification for investing in competition-law enforcement in order to increase total welfare, and thus the question becomes one of sequencing and of governmental preferences of what to do first.[25]

---

[24] This can be partly solved by reputational effects and tit-for-tat retaliation strategies in a multi-period game. Trebilcock, M.J. and R. Howse (1999), *The Regulation of International Trade*, 2nd edn, New York: Routledge, at p. 130.

[25] See, e.g., Clarke and Evenett, who find that, taking into account the savings an authority can make by stopping anti-competitive practices, the benefits of having a competition authority are significant, and justify the initial set-up costs and regular maintenance charges. Clarke, J. and S. Evenett (2003), 'A Multilateral Framework for Competition Policy', in R.E. Baldwin and L.A. Winters (eds) (2004), *Challenges to Globalization: Analyzing the Economics (National Bureau of Economic Research Conference Report)*, Chicago: Chicago University Press, at p. 411.

3.1.6 The ability to cede powers to the RCA

An important precondition involves the ability – both legal and practical – to cede legislative and enforcement powers to an external body, especially if an RJCA is created. Uganda and Kenya exemplify this point. In both countries a political referendum to change their constitution is a precondition to committing to regional enforcement.

3.1.7 Differences in market underpinnings

A serious problem faced by many RCAs in developing countries is the fact that large sectors of their economies are informal or state controlled. As Bakhoum and Molestina observe, this leaves little room for competition law to apply[26] and reduces the benefits that other states can achieve from entering into an RCA with such jurisdictions.

In addition, it might be difficult to agree on a joint policy if significant differences exist in the role of the government in regulating markets. This is the case with ECOWAS, in which a complexity of market regulation patterns creates significant obstacles to reaching a consensus.

3.1.8 Political economy obstacles

Another important set of obstacles involves political economy influences, both from private parties and from regulators. While an RCA can be Pareto-optimal for a country, it might not necessarily be adopted. Private actors might use their influence in a potential member state in order to create obstacles to the adoption and enforcement of RCAs that would upset the status quo from which they benefit. Political economy obstacles can also arise from existing regulators unwilling to cede their powers to a regional authority. Indeed, where national competition authorities already exist, favouring their participation in the decision-making process at the central level may make an RCA more politically acceptable.[27] Tools for overcoming such influences are explored elsewhere.[28]

To conclude this part, significant obstacles exist to the adoption of RCAs. One may ask, however, whether the fact that RCAs have been erected all

---

[26] Bakhoum, M. and J. Molestina, 'Institutional Coherence and Effectiveness of a Regional Competition Policy: The Case of the West African Economic and Monetary Union (WAEMU)', in this volume, Ch. 5.

[27] Ibid.

[28] Gal, M.S. (2002) 'Reality Bites (or Bits): The Political Economy of Competition Policy in Small Economies', in B. Hawk (ed.), *International Antitrust Law and Policy*, Huntington, NY: Juris Publishing, p. 605.

over the world does not indicate that such obstacles are not high. The answer is negative. The mere fact that RCAs have been adopted, in itself, does not serve as such an indication. This is because what matters is not the creation of the RCA itself (which might simply be an indication of external pressures for its adoption). The right question to ask is thus what mode of cooperation was adopted and what institutional settings were agreed upon to allow its operation in practice (e.g. whether an RCA was adopted or not).

3.2 Obstacles to the Successful Operation of an RCA

Should the above preconditions be met, there is a stronger probability that the RCA can be adopted. Yet its effectiveness in practice is determined by its ability to deal effectively with practical obstacles. The main obstacles that arise from the case studies explored throughout this book are analysed in this subsection.[29]

Some of these obstacles can be understood as collective-action problems, which relate to the difficulty of getting individuals to pursue their joint welfare, even when such pursuit is Pareto-optimal for all involved. Indeed, creating a new collective legal regime is the equivalent of providing any other public good. The literature on collective action, first modelled by Mancur Olson[30] and further developed by many others, challenges the presumption that the possibility of joint benefit is sufficient to generate collective action to achieve that benefit. Olson's argument largely rests on a free-riding argument: if those who will ultimately enjoy the fruits of the collective action once the good is produced cannot be excluded, then each has little incentive to contribute voluntarily to the provision of that good. If all actors choose to free-ride, the collective good will not be produced. Alternatively, some will contribute and others will free-ride, often leading to a lower-than-optimal provision of the collective good. Importantly, these outcomes may be rational from the point of view of the individual actors, at least in the short run or when a presumption of action by others holds true.

Accordingly, when potential members have little trust in each other that they will be bound by their agreements, or have little capacity to create monitoring and enforcement mechanisms, collective-action problems will most likely lead to a sub-optimal outcome: either the jointly beneficial RCA will not be adopted, or it will not achieve its goals.

---

29 Some of these obstacles are also explored in Gal, *supra* n. 3.

30 Olson, M. (1965), *The Logic of Collective Action: Public Goods and the Theory of Goods*, Cambridge, MA: Harvard University Press.

Yet the collective-action problem can be significantly reduced. Internal or external pressures and sanctions may be used to coerce members into action.[31] But more importantly, ways can be found to enhance the capabilities and incentives of those involved to overcome their unilateral constraints in order to work towards Pareto-optimal joint outcomes. Such solutions are especially promising when a small number of players repeatedly communicate and interact with each other and have strong ties in several areas.[32] Such tools will be elaborated in this section, alongside the obstacles they seek to remedy, as well as in section 4 below.

3.2.1 Sequencing and monitoring

Committing to an RCA often creates a sequencing problem of supply of the goods promised (funding, changing one's laws, supplying information, enforcing, etc.). First-movers face considerable uncertainty in their investment and commitment, which might be eroded by other members if they do not meet their commitments. This, in turn, creates a significant risk at the formative stages of the RCA that might lead jurisdictions to be more reluctant to commit to an RCA. Accordingly, establishing trust that others will also follow and meet their commitments is an important element in setting up a successful RCA.

Several tools can be used to mitigate the commitment problem. Olson recognized that the number of actors involved and the noticeability of their actions may affect their incentives to contribute to the creation of a joint good.[33] This is especially true since the RCA is not a one-shot game, but rather involves a long-term repeated sequence of cases that may affect member states.

Another solution, elaborated below, involves monitoring and imposing sanctions on member states that do not comply. Such monitoring can be formal (e.g. through the RCA authorities) or informal (e.g. an informal application of one member state to another). Such sanctions might apply in the area of competition law, or in other areas connected to the regional agreement (such as trade).

A preferred solution, in our view, involves the strengthening of external and internal pressures to create incentives to comply. A general change in

---

[31] For coercive solutions to the collective-action problem see, e.g, Hardin, G. (1978), 'Political Requirements for Preserving our Common Heritage', in H.P. Bokaw (ed.), *Wildlife and America*, Council on Environmental Quality, at p. 314.

[32] Ostrom, *supra* n. 9, pp. 7 and 183–4.

[33] Olson, *supra* n. 30.

socio-economic ideologies towards more pro-market orientations and creating knowledge of the potential benefits of the RCA, as well as external pressures by international, regional or national bodies might motivate jurisdictions to overcome sequencing obstacles. By altering the structure of incentives member states perceive, members might have a stronger willingness to commit themselves to following rules and to monitor their own conformity to their agreements.[34]

3.2.2 Inefficient institutional design

Inefficient institutional design is one of the major problems that plagues RCAs. As this issue is elaborated elsewhere, it will not be explored here in detail.[35] Unfortunately, there is no shortage of examples of how institutional design can limit the effectiveness of cooperation. Almost every regional agreement can provide at least one such example. Interestingly, the examples vary tremendously between the regions. CARICOM provides one illuminating case in point regarding the geographic locus of the RCA. Good intentions to strengthen the weakest part of the region led to choosing Suriname as a basis for the joint commission. Yet this created significant difficulties in convincing professionals to move there in order to serve on the Commission. Funding issues, elaborated above, also create institutional limitations. In CEMAC institutional limitations arise, *inter alia*, from the fact that the competition council is a temporary rather than permanent body. This, in turn, creates instability and lack of confidence in the new regional institutions.

3.2.3 National–regional relationship[36]

A related issue involves the institutional relationship between national and regional competition authorities, which is also crucial for effective operation. As Heimler and Jenny argue, the goal should be to form synergies between the RCA and national competition authorities by creating an efficient and effective system of education, idea sharing and case allocation

---

[34] Ostrom, *supra* n. 9, p. 45.
[35] Gal, *supra* n. 22.
[36] Interestingly, in some areas regional–regional relationships might also require clear rules. This may be the case when a jurisdiction belongs to two or more RCAs.

and encouraging cooperation in the enforcement of competition law by all institutions concerned.[37]

Not all RCAs follow this principle, however. In CARICOM, for example, the Commission must first request the national competition authority to undertake a preliminary investigation of alleged anti-competitive conduct. Only if dissatisfied with the outcome may the Commission initiate its own investigation. Yet, should a dispute arise between a domestic authority and the Commission as to whether a particular conduct is anti-competitive, the Commission must refer the issue to the CARICOM Council for Trade and Economic Development.[38] Because the Council is a political body, this may create opportunities for politically based decision-making that might prevent prosecution of politically sensitive cases. Moreover, domestic competition authorities could significantly limit the practical ability of the Commission to deal with disputed practices.[39]

The MERCOSUR agreement provides another example. There, competition-law proceedings must first be initiated before the competition authority of each member state. The national authority can then submit the case to the MERCOSUR institutions if it affects regional trade. Since only Argentina and Brazil have adopted a competition law, they are the only ones who can currently initiate such proceedings. Were the regional institutions empowered to deal with regional competition-law issues on their own initiative, it could have created a regional competition culture and overcome some of the competition-law problems that plague countries in the region.

Finally, incentives should be created for efficient cooperation between potential enforcers. WAEMU is a good illustration. As noted above, the WAEMU Court of Justice has ruled that the only role of national competition-law authorities is to assist the WAEMU Commission. However, as Heimler and Jenny note, rarely will an institution act efficiently when it is only feeding into the decision-making process of another one. Indeed, domestic authorities have almost no role in the WAEMU Commission enforcement record.[40]

---

[37] Heimler, A. and F. Jenny (2011), 'Competition Law and Policy in Developing Countries: National and Regional Enforcement' (on file with the author).

[38] Article 176 of the Revised Treaty of Chaguaramas, 2001.

[39] See Smith-Hillman, A. (2006), 'First a Glimmer, Now a . . .? The Prospect of a Caribbean Competition Policy', *Journal of World Trade*, **40** (2), 405.

[40] Heimler and Jenny, *supra* n. 37.

In contrast, as Heimler and Jenny observe,[41] the EU system is based on a workable institutional design that can limit some of the problems noted above. The EU case-allocation principles are based on parallel enforcement of the law by national authorities, combined with the principle of supremacy of community law and institutions.[42] The EU system allows each national authority to bring cases that affect its national market, maintaining for each the incentive for action, thereby strengthening the competition culture and increasing enforcement. The principle of superiority ensures that all national decisions comply with EU competition-law principles and that the Commission can deal with those cases that have a strong regional dimension. Yet in exceptional circumstances the Commission may deal with national cases as well, for example, when the case addresses a new competition issue or when the Commission may ensure more effective enforcement. To limit overlaps, information exchange between national authorities is facilitated. Of course, the EU system cannot always be applied elsewhere. Especially where differences in national competition laws are significant, adopting one set of joint rules to be applied through a regional competition law might be problematic. Yet finding solutions to the obstacles created by case allocations and governing law are crucial for the effective application of an RCA. It is noteworthy that the COMESA agreement also grants supremacy to regional institutions and rules in dealing with issues with a cross-border dimension, and mandates member states not to undermine or jeopardize that supremacy, much like the EU model. Many other RCAs, however, choose not to grant the regional institutions supremacy. It will be interesting to analyse the respective success and stability of the two different models in the future.

3.2.4 Unclarity

Unclarity in the RCA can also create obstacles to its efficient application. Once again, the CARICOM agreement provides a useful example. The Treaty creates a dispute-resolution system that is applicable to disputes among member states. It is not clear whether a firm can appeal a decision by the CARICOM Competition Commission.

Another example involves the WAEMU agreement. Uncertainties exist with regard to the respective scope of community and national competition

---

[41] Ibid.

[42] European Commission (2004), 'Commission Notice on Cooperation within the Network of Competition Authorities' (2004/C 101/03).

laws. The WAEMU Commission has exclusive competence over anti-competitive practices (agreements, abuse of dominant positions and state aids) in the WAEMU territory. Member states are authorized to deal with individual restrictions of competition in the form of abuse of economic dependence. This creates uncertainty, since individual restriction of competition can also sometimes be analysed under the abuse-of-dominant-position prohibition, which is under the exclusive competence of the Commission.

4. TEN SUGGESTIONS FOR A SUCCESSFUL RCA

The experiences outlined throughout this book, as well as the analysis above, serve as a basis for the following set of recommendations to enable RCAs to unleash their potential, suggestions that are additional to those explored above. Many of the recommendations result from the fact that while RCAs create collective-action benefits, they also suffer from second-order collective-action problems, such as free-riding.[43] All the recommendations are relevant to new RCAs, but most are also applicable to existing ones, whether by way of reconstructing and strengthening their existing framework of operation or by way of adding to it.

First, member states must be *clear about the objectives* that they would like to achieve and their relative importance. For example, is the goal the economic development of RCA members by removal of barriers to trade and investment, or is it integration and the creation of a common market?[44] Is the focus on strengthening capacity building at the national level by sharing information and experience, or is it on capacity building at the regional level? Some goals can be pursued in parallel, but even so, priorities must be determined, as an RCA is not value-free. Goals should be set in relation to the conditions of countries in the region, the special competition-law issues facing them, and the tools at their disposal to deal with such issues. Interestingly, not all members must seek to achieve the same goal – it might be that some members will seek mainly to strengthen their own capacity, while others seek to strengthen regional capacity. This is possible, so long as these goals do not clash.

---

[43] Bates, R.H. (1988), 'Contra Contractarianism: Some Reflections on the New Institutionalism', *Politics and Society*, **16**, 387.

[44] For an interesting and thought-provoking analysis of such goals see Fox, E., 'Competition, Development and Regional Integration: In Search of a Competition Law Fit for Developing Countries', in this volume, Ch. 13.

Second, it is important *to acknowledge and resolve the difficulties of collective action*. Such difficulties might include, *inter alia*, lack of predictability, information and trust, and high levels of complexity and transactional difficulties.[45] In some cases such difficulties may lead to the conclusion that an RCA has better chances if it is part of a wider trade agreement or that external pressure might be needed for its creation and operation. In other cases, self-imposed enforcement mechanisms may be needed, as explored below. Some difficulties might be easier to deal with than others. For example, where potential members lack information regarding the potential benefits and costs of the RCA, their incentives to enter the RCA will be significantly reduced. This informational obstacle might be overcome by discussions that analyse the conditions and point to successful, relatively similar agreements elsewhere. International institutions such as UNCTAD, OECD and the World Bank can also play a role in providing such information and in suggesting ways to overcome perceived obstacles.

The above two considerations should determine the next three recommendations. The third involves *membership of the RCA*. It is not axiomatic that it is always preferable that all countries in a region become members of the respective RCAs. Rather, the degree of commonality of interests and the ability to take active steps to further joint objectives is a better yardstick for membership. Accordingly, in regions where there are significant differences in legal culture, economic development or political and economic stability, bridging such differences may not always be worthwhile. For example, where the majority of countries in a region would significantly benefit from an RCA, it might sometimes be better to not include those countries that do not agree to take part in the RCA.[46] Yet when doing so, member states must take account of the costs that such exclusion might create. An alternative solution may involve a two-tiered membership in the RCA: 'full membership' and an 'observer' status, which will be granted to states that are not yet able to comply with the RCA requirement of membership.

Fourth is determining the *mode of cooperation among agencies*. Cooperation can be set at different degrees – from a low level (information sharing, technical assistance) to a high one (RJCA). The level and mode of cooperation should be based on the question of which cases are better

---

45 Ostrom, *supra* n. 9, pp. 25–6.

46 A partial solution to this problem involves the creation of an RJCA in a sub-region of the RCA, as the OECS countries, which are part of the CARICOM agreement, seek to do.

tackled at a regional level, and by what means. Whatever the mode chosen, it is important to ensure Pareto-optimality for all member states. Importantly, the mode of cooperation should be determined with regard to the realistic capabilities of member states, including institutional weaknesses.

The fifth, related, issue involves the *kind of cases that should be put on the agenda of the regional agreement*: should the RCA deal with all competition-law matters or with only some of them (e.g. mergers are not dealt with in ANDEAN competition law or in CARICOM); should it deal with external firms only, or also with local ones; should the RCA deal with easy cases, in which all members agree on the outcome, or also with more difficult ones, where there is a clash of interests among different members. Possibly, RCAs might expand their case selection in stages: first deal with the easy cases and only when the benefits of the RCA are apparent, deal with more difficult ones.

The sixth issue concerns the *order of steps*. An important question to consider is whether national law must precede regional law, as some RCAs require. The answer depends, in part, on the mode of cooperation chosen. If the mode is based on joint enforcement, through an RJCA, then it is not necessary that all member states first adopt a competition law. Rather, the RJCA can serve at least as a partial cure to the domestic inability to set up an operational competition law, and as a catalyst to its adoption elsewhere. But even if the model chosen involves a much lower degree of cooperation, it can sometimes function without competition laws in all members. Information about cartel activity that is sought by another member, for example, can be gathered by other governmental bodies.

Seventh, following Ostrom, tools for *monitoring and enforcing compliance* with collective decisions should be created.[47] Committing to an RCA *ex ante* might be relatively easy, as the experience of many RCAs indicates. Such commitments may reduce internal or external pressures to join the RCA. Yet following such rules in practice is oftentimes much more difficult. Even in repeated games in which reputation for compliance is important, if deviations are not readily identifiable or if sanctions for non-compliance are not high, members will have incentives to deviate. For example, members might prefer not to spend resources on information sharing that may harm their domestic firms, even if they committed to it in the RCA. This is why monitoring and enforcing compliance are important. A causal circle can be identified here: the ability to perform such tasks rests, in part, on the existing competition culture and the perceived need for the RCA.

---

47 Ostrom, *supra* n. 9, pp. 92–6.

Monitoring and enforcing compliance are also important to solve the sequencing problem: if each member state is concerned that it will be the only one complying, its incentives to comply will be significantly reduced. Yet if assurances are created that others will comply as well, the sequencing problem is significantly reduced. To ensure that a fear of sanctions does not prevent members from entering into beneficial RCAs, it might be better to set stages of compliance. Only if all or most members comply with the current stage will the RCA advance to the next one. Such sequencing may also enable members to learn how to organize themselves, to develop shared norms and patterns of reciprocity, and to solve collective-action dilemmas.[48] Sequencing might also enable RCAs to build on social capital created in relatively non-controversial issues (e.g. an international cartel that affects all members negatively) in order to solve more complex problems and create more complex institutional arrangements.[49] Finally, enforcing the agreement through monitoring and compliance enforcement reduces the ex-ante risk involved in entering the RCA in the first place.

Eighth, also following Ostrom, low-cost and readily available *conflict-resolution mechanisms* should be created to mediate conflicts among members, and between the members and the regional authority.[50] If members are to abide by the RCA, there must be a mechanism to discuss and resolve disputed issues. It is worth considering whether the use of such a mechanism would be available to market players and not only to the member states themselves.

Ninth are *institutional design issues*. As elaborated above, creating bodies that have capabilities that fit agreed-upon functionalities is an extremely important condition for a successful RCA. Indeed, the inability to meet this condition has plagued many RCAs. Institutional design should include, *inter alia*, clear and detailed rules regarding the relationship between regional and national institutions, as well as the modus operandi and financing. An interesting idea in this regard that might serve at least as a short-term solution in very poor regions is setting a rotation system whereby competition authorities in member states will carry the responsibility of applying the RCA for a set period of time, and carrying out such

---

48 It should be noted, however, that such sequencing does not come without a cost. It might be that the creation of the RCA was a formative moment, in which political economy pressures and other elements created a window of opportunity to adopt the RCA. Such a window might not open again for some time.

49 Ostrom, *supra* n. 9, p. 190.

50 Ostrom, *supra* n. 9, p. 100.

responsibility will be funded by other member states. This suggestion carries, of course, its own limitations.

Tenth and last is a *mechanism to change the rules* of the RCA to incorporate hard-learnt lessons from experience about how to organize the agreement in order to gain benefits and avoid harm or to overcome obstacles not perceived beforehand. Designing such rules involves a basic tension. On the one hand, flexible rules introduce a level of uncertainty into the system. The possibility of change might also reintroduce a power struggle among member states, thereby upsetting the equilibrium reached. On the other hand, rigid rules would not be able to provide solutions to changing environments. A middle ground must therefore be found, depending, *inter alia*, on the specific conditions of the RCA and the type of rules to be changed. Changing an operational rule, for example, should be easier than changing a rule with regard to the parameters of the decisions to be taken.

5. CONCLUSION

Regional agreements hold an important potential to overcome the main obstacles that plague small and developing jurisdictions in the enforcement of their competition laws, thereby furthering the goal of economic development. They also hold promise for developed jurisdictions in strengthening their ability to deal effectively with anti-competitive issues, both domestic and regional. Whether developing or developed, by joining forces in an RCA member states can strengthen their voice and create credible threats to sanction anti-competitive conduct that harms their economies. RCAs can also strengthen members' voices in international settings.[51] It is thus not surprising that many RCAs have sprung up around the world.

Unfortunately, however, experience has shown that most RCAs so far have been unable to unleash their potential. This chapter has built upon the experiences analysed throughout this book to reach more general conclusions regarding the preconditions for a successful RCA and the common obstacles faced by many, and, finally, to suggest some guidelines to overcome such obstacles. As observed, some of the obstacles relate to the fact that the agreement involves competition law, especially in places where a competition culture does not exist. Others result from collective-action problems among member states.

---

[51] See Gal, *supra* n. 3, p. 251.

The analysis creates a basis for some optimism: if structured efficiently to overcome foreseen obstacles, including the lack of a competition culture, collective-action problems, legal obstacles and political-economy issues, RCAs may increase the welfare of their members. If hard-learnt lessons from existing RCAs, such as those elaborated throughout this book, as well as lessons from other agreements that face relatively similar problems, are acknowledged and applied to avoid similar obstacles, at least some RCAs may be able to develop rules and institutions that will enable their members to achieve some of the perceived benefits. It might be a long road ahead, one which involves high and hard-earned learning costs; it might require a careful, in-depth, ongoing analysis of conditions and solutions necessitating a high degree of artisanship and innovation to create institutions that are carefully calibrated to generate incentives for mutual commitment; it might not be applicable in every situation, given the existing conditions – but it may well promise significant benefits to those who succeed in overcoming the obstacles.

Index

MERCURY IN THE ECOSYSTEM

Its Dispersion and Pollution Today